QUEEN CONSORTS OF ENGLAND

THE POWER BEHIND THE THRONE

QUEEN CONSORTS OF ENGLAND

THE POWER BEHIND THE THRONE

PETRONELLE COOK

Facts On File

Queen Consorts of England: The Power Behind the Throne

Copyright © 1993 by Petronelle Cook

Facts On File, Inc.
460 Park Avenue South
New York NY 10016
USA

Library of Congress Cataloging-in-Publication Data
Arnold, Margot.
    Queen consorts of England: the power behind the throne
Petronelle Cook.
    p. cm.
    Includes bibliographical references and index.
    ISBN 0-8160-2900-8
    1. Great Britain—Queens—Biography. 2. Wives—Great Britain—
Biography. 3. Great Britain—History. I. Title.
DA28.2.A76 1993
941'.099—dc20   93-16463

A British CIP catalogue record for this book is available from the British Library.

Facts On File books are available at special discounts when purchased in bulk quantities for businesses, associations, institutions or sales promotions. Please contact our Special Sales Department in New York at 212/683-2244 (dial 800/322- 8755).

Text design by Grace M. Ferrara
Jacket design by Nora Wertz
Composition by Facts On File, Inc.
Manufactured by the Maple-Vail Book Manufacturing Group
Printed in the United States of America

10 9 8 7 6 5 4 3 2 1

This book is printed on acid-free paper.

To Mary Powell Fowler and Joan Pring,
❖   friends and classmates of   ❖
St. Anne's College, Oxford.

CONTENTS

INTRODUCTION

"GOD SAVE THE QUEEN!" say the English, without seeming to care that, since Harold Godwinson fell with an arrow in his eye in 1066, they have rarely had a queen (or king) with even a smidgen of English blood. There have been Normans, French, Germans, Danish, Dutch, Scots, but hardly ever a purely English rose.

History books usually start with 1066, the climactic date of the Battle of Hastings, when the offshore island became securely, if uneasily, linked with the continent of Europe. But in order to understand what happened later, we must take a quick look at what went before this memorable, if arbitrary, date.

The curtain rises in 54 B.C., when Julius Caesar led his legions on an unsuccessful foray into England and then was forced to march them out again. He found the country ruled by the Celts (with whom he'd already had trouble in Gaul), who had taken over the islands from the original inhabitants some 500 years earlier.

The might of Rome, however, was not to be denied, so less than a hundred years later, Claudius Caesar finished what Julius had started, and England became one of the farthest-flung Roman provinces. The Celts, after some initial resistance, found that their new status improved the quality of their lives. The Romans were responsible for a good road system, centrally heated houses (for those who could afford them), well-planned towns, and, most important of all, the Pax Romana, which kept their continental neighbors off their backs and the Celts from each other's throats. Anyone who did not like the new system could always emigrate to still-Celtic Ireland, which the Romans left severely alone.

So things stood for some 400 years, until mighty Rome itself fell on hard times and decided that the island Brittanica, whose climate had always been a sore trial to Roman governors and soldiers alike, was expendable. The Roman legions withdrew, leaving the Romanized Celts, who had become accustomed to the *dolce vita romana*.

The island was defenseless. Enter the invading barbarian Anglo-Saxons and Jutes, who lit fires on top of the beautiful mosaic pavements, let the fine road system disintegrate, burned the towns and liquidated as many of the indigenous inhabitants (called Britons) as possible. After the brief heroic period of Arthur (Ambrosius), and the battling Britons, the remaining British Celts gave up and retreated to the extremities of the island—Cornwall, Wales and Scotland—where they continued to nurse their grievances and nurture their legends.

For 600 years the Anglo-Saxons dominated the land. They left the Celts to their mountain fastnesses, which weren't much good for farming anyway, and concentrated on keeping out other barbarian hordes who tried to do as they had done. Their efforts were only partially successful, as recurrent invasions of Vikings and Danes proved. The battle for the upper hand between Dane and Saxon was still going on when a nearer, more deadly enemy hove into sight—the Normans.

The Normans, or Norsemen, were originally from Scandinavia like the Danes and Vikings, but, unlike them, had started their quest for a more temperate homeland on the continent itself. They had grabbed control of that part of France now known as Normandy, and had managed, by a combination of treachery and might, to put the fear of God into their neighbors on all sides. Unhappily for Anglo-Saxon England, at that particular time in history the Normans were ruled by a man who would have been a major force at *any* juncture of history, and who regarded England as a particularly luscious plum ripe for plucking. In 1066 he plucked it.

William the Conqueror had no legitimate claim to anything, not even legitimacy, being the bastard offspring of Robert (le Diable), Duke of Normandy, and a tanner's daughter, Harleve of Falaise. His one stroke of luck was that his father had no legitimate sons and convinced his feudal barons to accept William as his heir, before dying on a pilgrimage to Jerusalem. William's second stroke of luck was in marrying Matilda of Flanders, and it is here the story begins.

THE NORMANS

MATILDA OF FLANDERS
(ca. 1028–1083)

m. William I   1052

Children: *Robert, Richard,* WILLIAM, *Cecilia, Agatha, Adela, Gundrada,* HENRY, *and two other daughters who died unmarried*

BEFORE LAUNCHING INTO THE PERSONAL stories of some of history's most famous women, we need to take a brief look at the position of European women in general. Since the fall of the Roman Empire and the onset of the Dark Ages, the lot of women had generally been an unenviable one. Whether highborn or lowborn, they were chattels over whom their menfolk had complete power and control. Only two careers were open to them. They could be wives or they could be whores—although with the spread of Christianity through the barbarian world, a third career became available—they could become brides of Christ, or nuns.

Many women jumped eagerly onto this bandwagon; not only did it offer a head start on the delights of the next world, but in this world it protected them, at least in theory, from the persecution of oafish husbands, cruel fathers and ungrateful sons. But the monastic life was not to everyone's taste. It had drawbacks—the vow of chastity for one, the vow of poverty for another. It was a genuine and vital escape route for many, but for others it was an escape into a sterile prison. Certainly it was not to the taste of a woman like Matilda of Flanders.

History has seen its quota of reluctant brides, and Matilda was probably one of the most reluctant. Born into the powerful House of Baldwin, rulers of Flanders, her destiny and duty from birth was to make a powerful marriage. This responsibility she knew and accepted—but when young Duke William of Normandy came courting she was far from impressed. Her reluctance was understandable, on several counts. In the first place, she undoubtedly thought she could do better than this upstart bastard son of a tanner's daughter. His father had foisted him upon his feudal barons, and William had fought successfully to keep himself where accident had placed him, but he was still a bastard, and a half-peasant one at that. His position would last only as long as he could maintain the strength of his sword-arm and convince men that he was their superior. Besides, Matilda had her eye on someone else.

The "someone else" was an Englishman named Brihtrik (Meav) who had been sent by the gentle Saxon king Edward the Confessor to be English ambassador to Baldwin's court. He was rich, and probably too smooth a diplomat for his own good. He turned down the amorous advances of the young Matilda and returned discreetly to England. It took Matilda almost twenty years to get her revenge.

William had started his suit for her hand as a lad of 19. At that time he was still in the throes of fighting for his inheritance, and Baldwin, his prospective father-in-law, was understandably noncommittal, particularly in view of Matilda's marked reluctance—but William's position got steadily better and more secure. In 1051, after a visit to England, he returned to Normandy with the electrifying news that the childless Edward had promised him the English crown on his death. Now Baldwin looked on the match with a kindlier eye; but Matilda still said no.

Her reluctance was backed up by a Papal prohibition of the match, promulgated at the Council of Reims in 1049. The circumstances of this prohibition were somewhat suspect: The normal grounds for such an action by the Church was consanguinity, but, so far as is known, Matilda and William were, at most, very distantly related. She was descended on the distaff side from Alfred the Great of England. William could claim kinship to Edward the Confessor (also kin to Alfred) through his father Robert, making them very remote cousins. Possibly the Papal Council knew more about the doings of William's father (who had earned the sobriquet "*le Diable*" or "Devil") and Matilda's mother than history records; but more probably it was a political maneuver on the part of William's foes. They viewed the possible union of Normandy and Flanders, which would have constituted a powerful bloc in the Europe of the time, with understandable alarm. Whatever the real reason, the prohibition gave Matilda another excuse to go on saying no.

Then there occurred a fantastic event. According to the story as recorded in the Anglo-Saxon Chronicles, one evening at twilight, when Matilda was returning home from church vespers in Bruges, William, now seven years older and wiser than when he had started his courtship, suddenly rode up out of the dusk, leaped off his horse, gave Matilda a sound thrashing and threw her down into the gutter. He then remounted and rode away. After this, the chronicler goes on, the lady Matilda agreed to become his wife. The episode is so melodramatic, so unlikely a story for a monkish chronicler to make up, that it might just be true.

The fact is they suddenly *did* marry in the teeth of Papal opposition in 1053, and were immediately in trouble on all sides. Henry I of France, who had supported William in his youthful struggles with his rebellious barons, suddenly took fright at the powerful combination of Normandy and Flanders. He allied with Duke Geoffrey of Anjou and Maine, and they twice invaded Normandy. William beat them off each time and, when both Henry and Geoffrey conveniently died, enlarged his holdings by annexing Maine in 1062.

He and Matilda, who had begun producing children with rapidity and enthusiasm, had meanwhile patched things up with the Church, and in 1059 Pope Nicholas II granted a dispensation for their marriage. The permission did not come free: as part of their "penance" William and Matilda agreed to build two abbeys, to St. Stephen and to the Holy Trinity, at Caen, their capital. The resulting "Abbaye aux Hommes" and "Abbaye aux Dames" are two of the most magnificent accomplishments of Romanesque architecture, and the most lasting and fitting memorial that remains of two very remarkable people. An added dividend was the dedication of their eldest daughter Cecilia to the Church from birth; she later became an abbess. History is silent as to what she may have thought about her parents' decision.

Never one to commit herself half-heartedly, Matilda produced 10 children for William—four sons and six daughters. Some of them she loved, others she loathed. Robert, the future Duke of Normandy, was the apple of his mother's eye and a constant annoyance to his father. Richard, the shadowy second son, was the first, but not the last, of his family to meet a sorry end in the shady groves of the New Forest after the English conquest; and both William Rufus (his father's favorite even though he was homosexual) and Henry, the youngest (who was his mother's boy) were destined to become kings of England. Of the girls, besides Cecilia, the only one of note was Adela, who married Stephen, Count of Blois; in due time she produced a son of the same name who became one of England's weakest kings.

A remarkable aspect of the marriage of William and Matilda was the fact that he remained faithful to her. This was a feudal age, when a man of any importance was supposed—indeed expected—to have as many mistresses as he could collect, and to exercise the "droit de seigneur" wherever he went. Most feudal lords enthusiastically followed this custom, but not William. Whether this was because he was devoted to his remarkable wife or because he was afraid of her we don't know. We do know that he trusted her implicitly and beyond all others. When he sailed to conquer England, he left Matilda behind to keep his rambunctious barons in line. And keep them in order she did. The task certainly could not have been easy for her, with her small horde of children to cope with, but she had great success on both counts. In fact, nine of her children lived to maturity, in an age when the infant mortality rate was 75 percent because of the appalling hygienic conditions that prevailed.

The battle of Hastings was fought on October 14, 1066, and though it left the English king, Harold, dead on the battlefield and the English forces in full flight, there still remained months of bitter fighting ahead of William before he could be sure of his grip on the country. At Christmas his barons urged him to be crowned king so that he would have the powerful sanction of the Church behind him. William protested; he wanted to wait for Matilda so that they could share the greatest triumph of his life together. But conditions in England were still too unsettled for her to come over with safety, so, common sense and the barons prevailing, he was crowned king in the abbey of Westminster on Christmas Day, and the fight went on.

We owe Matilda another debt from this period. Even while coping with the barons and the children, she somehow managed to find time to initiate a project that has given us a unique pictorial view of the highlights of the Norman Conquest. She and her ladies in waiting were to start the amazing piece of needlework known as the Bayeux Tapestry—a 231-foot-long graphic record of the whole dramatic series of events. Other matters were soon to claim her attention and she was forced to leave the project in the hands of Odo, Bishop of Bayeux (William's half-brother), and the nuns of his diocese. But the initiative was undoubtedly hers.

By Easter of 1067 England was subdued enough to please William, so he sent for Matilda and she was crowned queen with great pomp on Whit Sunday. Her bastard, half-peasant husband had shown her what he could do—he had won her a kingdom. And to show her how he felt about it, he offered her an honor that had not been given to any woman before her. The wives of previous English kings had merely been called "Lady companion to the King"; she was anointed queen, coequal to himself, and he had a crown specially made to place on her long dark hair.

They undoubtedly were delighted to see one another again, and the fruit of their reunion appeared exactly nine months later in the form of their youngest son, Henry, born in 1068.

Meanwhile, Matilda had an old score to settle. The love of her youth, Brihtrik, Lord of Gloucester, had prospered. He had married, raised a family, and acquired large land holdings in Gloucester, Devon and Cornwall. Being a diplomat and a man of peace, he had played no very active part in the English opposition to William's conquest. In fact, he seems to have spent the time adding a chapel onto his manor house at Hanley. At the consecration of this chapel, presided over by Wulfstan, Bishop of Worcester, Matilda showed her power. A troop of Norman soldiers appeared, seized Brihtrik, and carted him off to a lightless, waterlogged underground cell in Worcester Castle, where he was kept until he died. His possessions were all confiscated, the city of Gloucester deprived of its charter and civil liberties, and his penniless family turned out as beggars.

In the Domesday Book, that great survey of England that tells us exactly who had what after the Conquest, all the possessions of the unfortunate Brihtrik appear under Matilda's name as personal property. After her death they reverted to the Crown.

This period, starting with the reunion of Matilda and William and her coronation, was the high point of both their lives and their marriage. From here on there would be trouble, and the trouble would come from a source from which marital troubles often arise—their children.

Throughout history, the relationship between a king and the son who is destined to step into his shoes has been the difficult one of old lion versus young lion. This particular situation was aggravated by Robert's being his mother's favorite and the potential object of his father's jealousy. Robert himself was rash, quick-tempered, extravagant, short on common sense and with a great belief in his own importance. As a youth he is recorded as having almost killed his younger brothers William and Henry just for playing a practical joke on him.

Equally, Matilda loathed and was jealous of William Rufus, whom his father favored—possibly as a counterbalance to the Matilda–Robert alliance, for there was little else to recommend him. He was small, bowlegged and ugly; he was also "gay" in an era when homosexuality was considered a major crime. His only probable claim to his father's love was that he, like William, was passionately addicted to the hunt, and could stay in the saddle for 10 hours at a stretch, while larger and stronger men fell from their saddles in sheer exhaustion. As the boys turned into men, trouble started.

The relationship was not much better between William and his youngest son, Henry, who had a special place in his mother's heart as the youngest and as the product of an especially happy time. The jealousy was not as overt or as passionate as in the case of Robert, but it showed up at William's deathbed, when he left his youngest son only 5,000 pounds of silver and no land at all, in an age when a man's importance in society rested solely on what lands he held and what titles he bore. Matilda had died by this time, but had she been alive she undoubtedly would have opposed William. She had, however, provided Henry with an advantage the others lacked and that was to prove very useful to him. She saw that he received an education.

In an age when lord and commoner alike were usually untutored and unlettered, Henry was taught to read and write. He became a master of the French language, could read (but not write) Latin, and could even speak a little English, the language of the conquered kingdom—the first of his family to do so. For his time he was considered a learned man. Although Matilda knew that the great lands were the prerogative of her beloved Robert, she hoped Henry would become a great cleric—possibly Archbishop of Canterbury in his brother's future kingdom.

As for the second son, Richard, he died in a hunting accident that took place in the New Forest while he was still in his teens.

Matilda's relationships with her six daughters are more shadowy. She was apparently fond of her fifth daughter, Gundrada, who was allowed to marry one of her father's Norman knights. William de Warenne had been one of William's staunchest supporters, but he was neither very powerful nor very rich. By the time Gundrada was of an age to marry she could have had the pick of European nobility, but she married him instead—a love match. She died young in childbed in 1085, in the castle her husband had built for her at Lewes in Sussex. Grief for Gundrada may have hastened Matilda's end the same year.

Matilda seems to have had no such tender feelings for her daughter Agatha, the second (or possibly third) of her daughters. As a child Agatha had been betrothed to the widowed King Harold of England (the breaking of this betrothal had been one of the many excuses her father had used for the invasion). But in 1074, when she was about 17, her parents offered her in marriage to King Alfonso of Castile, an ally of William's at the time. Agatha was dead set against the match, but unlike her mother she did not have the luxury of saying no. She was packed off to Spain for the wedding, but foxed them all by dying on the way. According to the chronicler Ordericus Vitalis, "It was the mercy of God releasing her from a fate that she hated"; being her parents' child it is more likely that she died of sheer suppressed rage.

Adele, the fourth daughter, made a "good" marriage in that her husband, Stephen, Count of Blois and Chartres, was an important and wealthy man with the added attraction of being extremely handsome. What her relationship with her mother was like we don't know, but in many ways the two women were strikingly similar. She was a forceful woman who often intervened in both political and church matters. She governed Blois and Chartres ably while her husband went off on the First Crusade, and when he died in Palestine she continued, just as ably, to be regent until her son Theobald was old enough to be Count. She then "retired" to a Cluniac priory, but remained very active behind the scenes, and was probably one of the motivating forces in pushing her equally handsome, if inept, second son Stephen onto the throne of England.

Of the other three girls we know nothing, except that Cecilia became a nun, in keeping with her parents' vows, and that all three were dead before their father died in 1087. Ultimately, however, they were of little importance, for it was around the boys that their parents' difficulties swirled, eventually growing to catastrophic proportions.

Trouble began in earnest when Robert came of age in 1076. Customarily, at this juncture he should have been given lands, a title, and money enough to live in a style befitting a king-to-be; but William provided for none of these things. While Matilda tried to reason with her stubborn husband, the short-tempered Robert left in a rage and started to intrigue with his father's enemies, who were legion on the Continent by this time. This action did not improve his father's temper.

Matilda became so desperate that she sent all the way to Germany for a hermit who was supposed to have the gift of prophecy, asking advice on how to reunite father and son. With more wisdom than tact, the hermit sent back a message to the effect that he could not see the remotest chance of William's giving up *anything* so long as he still breathed. However, in 1081 William relented enough to make Robert Count of Maine and to promise Matilda that Robert would indeed have Normandy. The concession was not enough for Robert, and, as a result of his intrigues, parts of the Vexin, which had been William's, fell into the hands of Philip of France.

All this time Matilda had been sending her spendthrift son large sums of money on the sly, since her husband had forbidden any contact with his ungrateful heir. Finally, one of her messengers was caught. Neither cowed nor contrite, she told her husband, "If Robert, my son, were buried seven feet under the ground and I could bring him to life by shedding my heart's blood, gladly would I give it." William solaced himself by having the messenger's eyes put out.

But continued strain was telling on Matilda, and in 1083, at the age of 50, she died. Although 50 was a goodly age in a time when most people did not live much beyond 40, it was widely stated that her death was caused by a broken heart from the continuing quarrel. Her death did have a terrible effect on William, who grieved inconsolably; his health and temper both began to suffer, and he grew immensely fat. It seemed that not only had he lost the one he loved, but with her had gone all his luck.

Robert remained at the French king's court, safe from his father's wrath, and William was kept busy keeping his kingdom in order and putting down subversive elements on all sides. In 1087, however, infuriated by the jibes of Philip of France, William invaded the Vexin and put the town of Mantes to fire and sword. His ill luck dogged him, however; his horse stepped on an ember from the burning town, stumbled, and threw him, and his great weight did the rest. He was carried back to Rouen, where he lingered on in great pain for six weeks. He knew he was dying, so he summoned his remaining sons to his bedside and made a verbal will. Even after all Robert had done, William could not bring himself to break his promise to Matilda; Normandy was left to Robert. As to the rich plum of England, which, as his father's favorite, William Rufus fondly expected to receive, even there William could not bring himself to cut off Robert. The dying king merely told William that he hoped England would be his, but that he would have to fight for it just as his father had done. To Henry, of course, he gave only the aforementioned 5,000 pounds of silver.

His disappointed sons wasted no time. Henry went at once to collect his money from the treasury and lock it safely away. William Rufus left immediately for England to get a head start on his own conquest. William lingered miserably on for another day or so: As soon as he was dead, the priests and attendants appropriated all they could of the king's property, even stripping off the bed coverings, leaving the body of the Conqueror naked and neglected on the floor.

William's burial at the Abbaye aux Hommes was in marked contrast to the magnificent funeral he had given Matilda at the Abbaye aux Dames four years earlier. No one took charge of the arrangements, and the body was loaded on an ordinary wagon to be taken back to Caen. Along the way a fire broke out on the roadside and the cortege was disrupted. When the procession finally arrived at St. Stephen's, a man named Asselin stepped out of the crowd and claimed that the land on which St. Stephen was built had been taken from him unjustly and without payment by the Conqueror, and he demanded just recompense. Before the interment could take place the clergy had to promise to pay him a fair price. Then the grave was found to be too narrow for the coffin, so the corpse had to be removed from its coffin and squeezed into the narrow hole. In a belated gesture of filial piety, William Rufus built an elaborate monument embellished with gold and silver over this makeshift grave, but even that gesture did not mark the end of the luckless Conqueror's troubles. Both 17th-century Huguenot rioters and French Revolutionaries wreaked havoc on William's grave; his bones were thrown to the winds. Matilda's remains rested undisturbed in the Abbaye aux Dames.

History sometimes has a way of adding a postscript that makes the remarkable even more so. Until recently we had very little idea what Matilda actually looked like. Contemporary chroniclers did say she was beautiful, and made particular mention of her long, lustrous dark hair. Because of her formidable personality, imagination through the centuries had pictured her as a large, majestic woman, almost as big as her husband—a Norman Brunhilde. The stiff effigy on her tomb gave little clue to her beauty, but did nothing to dispel this image of commanding majesty. In 1967 it was decided to open the tomb to see whether the grave was indeed undisturbed, for the same Huguenot rioters who had destroyed William's tomb had torn down the magnificent memorial studded with gems and gold that William had placed over her. They found the tomb intact, but decided to take a look at the body itself. They opened the sealed coffin and gazed in amazement at the remains of the mighty Matilda: she was tiny.

She stood only four feet two inches in height and had a slight build to match—she was the size of an average nine-year-old American child. Somehow the fact of her minute size seems to make Matilda's achievements seem all the more remarkable: to bear and rear nine children, to manage not only a mighty husband but his obstreperous barons as well—and still to keep a hold on all their hearts.

MATILDA (EDYTHA) OF SCOTLAND (1080–1118)

m. Henry I   1100

Children: *William, Ethelric* [Matilda], *Richard, Euphemia*

Born to the Scottish king Malcolm Canmore and Queen Margaret, who was an acknowledged saint in her lifetime, Edytha of Scotland was one of a family of two daughters and six brothers born since Malcolm and Margaret's marriage in 1070. Her deeply religious mother not only had brought the Scottish church in line with the rest of the Catholic fold, but also had succeeded in bringing civilized Anglo-Norman manners to the rough Scottish court. She brought up her eight children in similar fashion, and for the first 13 years of Edytha's life all went very pleasantly and peaceably.

But in 1093 her father and eldest brother were treacherously slain at Alnwick by the English; her brother Edgar escaped the massacre and hurried to Edinburgh Castle, where his mother Margaret lay sick, to break the news. It was too much for her—the royal marriage had been a true love match—and four days later she also died. The crown was seized by Malcolm Canmore's illegitimate brother Donald Bane, and the half-grown orphan family had to be rescued from his clutches by Edgar Atheling, Edytha's late mother's brother, who had long lived as an exile in England. He took Edytha and her sister to the nunnery of Rumsey, where their mother's sister, Christina, was abbess. Christina was determined that both her nieces should join her order, and so in the six tranquil years Edytha spent there she functioned as a nun.

Then in 1099 her brother Edgar succeeded to the Scottish throne and Edytha's fortunes changed again, for her hand in marriage was suddenly being sought by Prince Henry of England. Since her brother was indebted to King William Rufus, Henry's older brother, who had helped the new King of Scotland to his throne, he looked with a very kindly eye on the proposed match.

Prince Henry, soon to be King Henry I, never did anything on a whim, and his suit was part of an ongoing and well-thought-out plan. He needed to marry Edytha, because through her mother, Margaret, she was a direct descendant of the ancient Anglo-Saxon kings, being the great-granddaughter of Edmund Ironside and a great-niece of Edward the Confessor. This in addition to his own "English" birth—for Henry had been born in 1068 in England after that rapturous reunion of William and Matilda after the Conquest—would give Henry a solid foothold with his Anglo-Saxon subjects. And it was a foothold he badly needed, for of all the Conqueror's sons he was the only one who, until then, had no land to call his own. The date 1099 when Henry began his courtship has an additional significance. William Rufus had ruled England with a heavy hand since his father's death, but as a homosexual he had never married and so had no heir: On his death, by primogeniture (in which the eldest son has the exclusive right of inheritance), his most logical successor would be his brother Robert, Duke of Normandy—not Henry.

But history had given both William Rufus and Henry an unexpected opportunity when, in 1095, the First Crusade had begun. Robert, Duke of Normandy, along with so many of his European peers, had heeded the call and gone off to fight for the Holy Land. The First Crusade—unlike all subsequent crusades—was a success; by 1099 Jerusalem had been captured from Islam and the Holy Land again firmly Christianized. For the younger sons of the Conqueror, however, the news was bad, for it meant their elder brother would be coming home.

Henry had to act quickly—but his suit was not without its obstacles. Aunt Christina claimed Edytha was a "veiled nun" and so it would be sacrilege to move her from the convent. Henry lost no time. He recalled the exiled Archbishop Anselm; a Church Council was convened at Lambeth, and Edytha was summoned to appear before it. Henry's cause was supported by his Anglo-Saxon subjects, who thought that a queen of the royal Anglo-Saxon house might help to lighten their repression. His Norman subjects were not so enthusiastic, but Edytha's golden-haired, blue-eyed good looks softened even their hearts, and she neatly cut the ground from beneath her Aunt Christina's feet by claiming that she had been *forced* to act as a nun. Edytha clearly was not averse to the match. The council, after much deliberation, decided she was free to marry Henry.

The year 1100, when their marriage was solemnized on November 11th at Westminster, also had seen, in the month of July, the death of William Rufus while hunting in the New Forest. Whether it was accident or murder, has never been resolved, but the speed with which Henry seized the reins of power, not to mention the English treasury, has led to speculation.

By the time Robert had returned to his own duchy of Normandy, Henry and his Scottish queen of the English blood royal had been happily crowned and acknowledged by his English subjects. In a rather remarkable gesture, Edytha changed her name to Matilda at her marriage. The reason is unclear.

Perhaps she hoped to please her Norman subjects by giving up her Anglo-Saxon name; perhaps she hoped to please her new husband by taking the name of his formidable mother, and to influence him as her mother had indeed influenced her kingly husband.

The new Matilda did everything that was expected of her. In rapid succession she produced four children—two boys and two girls. William, Henry's much-needed legitimate heir (about half his 35 illegitimate children were boys), came first; then Alice Ethelric (later also to change her name to Matilda), Richard, and Euphemia, who died young. The fate of Richard is the topic of much learned confusion, but in all probability he too died young. But this was as far as Edytha's queenly role took her: There is no evidence that she ever had the slightest influence over her husband or, for that matter, over her children as they grew up. Still deeply religious, she continued circumspectly and discreetly in her queenly role, and if Henry did not treat her well at least he did not treat her badly. He was himself a good-looking man with a fine, commanding voice, and was markedly attached to his children, both legitimate and illegitimate. She did try to help her Anglo-Saxon subjects as much as she could, and they in turn loved her for it—dubbing her "Good Queen Mold" ("Mold" being the usual nickname for Matilda). Her Norman subjects were less impressed. A measure of her helplessness to influence her husband is seen by his crackdown on married priests in the English church, whom he ordered to abandon their wives and children. The hundred or so Anglo-Saxon priests lined the sides of the road as the royal couple rode into London, weeping and begging the king not to force them to abandon their families. An angry Henry rode on, but Edytha lingered behind and began to weep with them. "God have mercy on you!" she sobbed, "I can't help you, I can't help you."

In the seigneurial way of his time, Henry was a notable philanderer both before and after marriage. He is credited with at least 20 *acknowledged* bastard children. One of his long-term mistresses, Sybil Corbet, began bearing him children ten years before his marriage and continued for at least seven years after it. Even with his bastards, Henry had a plan, and most of them made extremely influential marriages. A typical, and surprising, example of this was Sybil Corbet's eldest daughter Sybil, who married Edytha's brother, Alexander, then king of Scotland, in 1107.

In 1106 Henry took off for the continent to confront Robert. He defeated his feckless brother, whom he then kept imprisoned in Cardiff Castle in Wales, where he died of starvation in 1134 at the age of 80. In the teeth of much opposition, Henry then annexed the Duchy of Normandy to England—a mixed blessing, as it turned out. After 1106 Henry was out of England much of the time looking after his newly conquered realm of Normandy, but even when he did return, he fathered no further children with Edytha (although his bastards continued to be born at a steady rate).

In 1109 there began a series of events that were bittersweet to Edytha. Her seven-year-old daughter Ethelric was sought in marriage by the Holy Roman Emperor Henry V of Germany, a 45-year-old widower. It was a brilliant match. The child was married by proxy to the emperor and, like her mother, changed her name to Matilda at that time. Five years later she was shipped off to Germany, where the wedding was promptly performed, and then enthroned empress in the Cathedral of Mainz. Her father was delighted, but Edytha knew she would never see her daughter again.

Both in looks and in character, her dark-haired, high-spirited daughter was far more like her redoubtable paternal grandmother, whose name she had taken, than like her mother. Although Henry was markedly indulgent to all his children, his disobedient daughter tried his patience to such an extent that on one occasion he had her tied and dragged through the stinking moat of the castle until she apologized,

Edytha still had her eldest child and heir to the throne—William, who was growing into an able and high-spirited lad. Watching him grow and dividing her time between the royal residences of Winchester, the Tower of London and her own favorite, Windsor Castle, where Henry had built a home especially to please her, she led a quiet existence, with Henry away most of the time and England mercifully at peace.

On May 1, at the age of 41, she died quietly in London of unknown causes. She was buried in Westminster Abbey by the side of her kinsman, Edward the Confessor. Her Anglo-Saxon subjects were desolated, since for them her death foretold grimmer times to come. Her Anglo-Saxon ladies-in-waiting were so grief-stricken that three of them immediately became nuns. If Henry did not share in the widespread grief, at least he did not immediately seek another wife. He was too busy planning his next important step to a land-grab: the marriage of his son William to the heiress of Maine, which took place in 1119.

By dying, Edytha was spared the great grief that was to befall Henry, and which would bring all his carefully laid plans tumbling into ruin. In 1120, Henry's son William, returning to England after campaigning with his father against William Clito, the son and heir of the unfortunate Robert of Normandy, embarked on "The White Ship" along with his closest friend and bastard half-brother Richard (son of Ansfride) and his favorite bastard half-sister Maud (daughter of Henry's mistress Edith). During a storm in the English Channel, the ship foundered, and the story goes that William did manage to escape in a small boat but then turned back to the wreck when he heard Maud screaming for help. It was a vain effort, for they all perished, a butcher from Rouen being the only one who survived to tell the tale. The news of this loss so crushed Henry that he reportedly was never seen to smile again in the remaining 15 years of his life.

On his deathbed in 1135, Henry tried, in the teeth of opposition from his Norman nobles, to leave his English kingdom to Matilda, his half-Anglo-Saxon daughter. The country immediately erupted into civil war, and to the embattled Matilda's aid marched David, king of Scotland, Edytha's youngest brother, who was considered by the Scots to be as much of a saint as his mother Margaret had been. But in spite of his efforts, nothing could save Matilda's cause, although, when the long-drawn-out civil war finally faltered to a close, at least there was a guarantee that Matilda's son and Edytha's grandchild, Henry Plantagenet, would one day rule in England.

Considering all the years of peace in England in Edytha's lifetime and all the misery that followed her death, it is small wonder that she was perpetuated in English memories as "Good Queen Mold." It would be centuries before the English would have a queen of their own stock again.

ADELICIA (ADELE) OF LOUVAIN (1103–1151)

m. Henry I   1121

No issue

IT TOOK CONSTANT URGING AND MUCH PRESSURE from his barons and illegitimate sons to bring Henry I out of the daze of grief the loss of his son, William, had brought about. They advised him to marry again, to produce another legitimate male heir as quickly as possible, for William Clito, the son of Robert of Normandy, still lived, and by right of blood stood as the next legitimate and logical heir to England's throne and to Henry's hard-won French possessions.

Even in his sorrow, Henry continued with his strategic plans: His choice for a bride was Adelicia of Louvain, daughter of William, Count of Louvain and, more importantly, of Alice, daughter of the powerful Fulk, Count of Anjou, an area directly adjacent to Normandy and a man with whom Henry needed to be on good terms. It would help to detach Fulk from his former support of William Clito.

Adelicia (or Adele) was, besides, a type he evidently favored, being both in coloring and nature very similar to "Good Queen Mold." She had golden hair, blue eyes, was considered beautiful of features, and had a gentle and understanding nature—she was called "the Fair Maid of Brabant." Although she was not Norman, she was French-speaking and so was more acceptable to the Normans than her Anglo-Saxon predecessor had been.

She was married to Henry in 1121 and crowned queen. He was 53 years old, she was 18—in fact slightly younger than Henry's last remaining child, the Empress Matilda. Henry was now a melancholy old man who snored terribly and was subject to such terrible nightmares that he would leap out of bed and slash with a sword at his mind's demons, roaring at the top of his voice; but she accepted her lot with good grace and played the part of the devoted wife. In one vital aspect she failed him completely, however, for no child was born of the marriage, although in her second marriage she bore at least seven children. After a lifetime of begetting all those children upon at least 16 different women (including his late wife), Henry was spent.

Almost immediately after the marriage, he was again embroiled in a war with William Clito, who was now supported by Louis VI ("The Fat") of France and a growing number of the barons of Normandy. Henry squelched his rebellious Norman barons and persuaded his son-in-law, Holy Roman Emperor Henry V of Germany, to invade France, which brought Louis into line in 1124. This campaign, at the Emperor's now-advanced age, also hastened his end, for he died the next year, and for the first time Henry saw some hope on the horizon—his daughter Matilda was now a widow. She could be married off again and could produce the male children he needed but could no longer produce himself.

The Empress Matilda returned to England, and a truly regal, tall, dark-haired and dark-eyed imperial creature she was, a startling contrast to the gentle, golden-haired Adele, her stepmother. Amazingly, there is ample evidence to show that the two women, of similar age but such dissimilar natures, became firm friends and remained so through all the troubles that followed.

The year after Matilda's return, Henry forced his Norman barons to recognize her as heiress to his throne; but then he proceeded to take a step that infuriated both her and his barons. He arranged a marriage between the 25-year-old Matilda and the 15- year-old Geoffrey of Anjou, heir to the powerful Count Fulk. Henry had become so single-minded in his dream of dominion that he had lost all perspective—his Normans *hated* their territorial neighbors the Angevins. More importantly, he was demanding that the proud Matilda, who had been premier queen of Europe for 11 years, now marry a humble count, an adolescent boy 10 years her junior.

In her fury she withdrew from the public eye into the household of Queen Adele in Westminster and continued her battles with her father out of the public eye. The situation was complicated by her having fallen in love with Stephen of Blois, a grandson of William the Conqueror through his mother Adele—a happily married man with several children and a darling of the English court. The gentle Adele tried to do what she could in this difficult situation, attempting to interest the restless and rebellious Matilda in her own exquisite needlecraft and, more importantly, keeping the headstrong ex-empress away from the charismatic and impressionable Stephen.

Matilda held out against the marriage to Geoffrey of Anjou for two years, and how the wily old Henry managed to change her mind is not known. Possibly, the argument that she had to help herself if she was to be queen of England, and that Stephen, who was of royal blood and had just added another son to his family, would be her greatest threat in that regard, may finally have persuaded her. Sullenly she emerged from the shelter of Adele's apartments and went with Henry to Normandy, where she was married to the now-17-year-old Geoffrey Plantagenet in August of 1127.

The marriage was a disaster. Three times over the next three years Matilda left her husband and returned to England, only to be persuaded by Henry to return and try again. His own hopes had been strengthened in the meantime by the death of William Clito after the latter had been wounded at the Battle of Alost. Now Henry's chief concern was the fact that the marriage of Geoffrey and Matilda had so far yielded no children.

When Matilda returned again after five years of this childless union, with a quite genuine list of grievances against her arrogant and uncaring husband, Henry was more lenient and let her stay.

The minute she was back she started to pursue Stephen again, scandalizing the court. Surprisingly, when after almost a year Henry suggested it was time to return to her husband and scotch this growing scandal, Matilda did not put up a fight. Perhaps she had at last realized that nothing would ever part Stephen from his wife. Fond as she was of Matilda, Adele, who had a marked dislike of scandal, was relieved.

In the very next year, 1133, all Henry's plans appeared to have paid off, and Adele's own childlessness became unimportant when Henry Plantagenet was born to Matilda. The king was markedly showing his age now; he was physically unsteady and had a crotchety temper, neither of which could have made Adele's lot easy as she accompanied him on the endless trips he took around his kingdom. In 1135 he summoned enough energy to go over to the Continent to see his one and only legitimate grandchild and to have a stern word with his son-in-law, Geoffrey, who had been stirring up his disaffected barons in Normandy. The king took with him Robert of Gloucester, his eldest and ablest bastard son—and Stephen of Blois.

As soon as he arrived he went for a long day's hunting in Rouen. He returned hungry to Lyons Castle, ate hugely of a tainted dish of his favorite lampreys, and immediately became violently ill. He lingered for several days and then died at midnight on December 1, 1135. With his dying breath he urged Robert of Gloucester to ensure that Matilda received his bequest to her of all his dominions. But Stephen of Blois, who was also at his bedside, had other ideas.

Adele received her husband back, embalmed with salt and wrapped in a bull's hide, and buried him, according to his wishes, at Reading, where she endowed land to keep a lamp burning before his tomb in perpetuity. In the meantime, Stephen of Blois had returned to London and declared himself king, to the acclamation of his faithful Londoners and many of the Norman barons, who wanted no woman to rule over them.

And yet for Adele, who had done her duty nobly in a thankless marriage for 15 years, virtue was its own reward, and she was free to marry whom she chose at last. The Dowager Queen did marry for love, her choice falling upon William d'Aubigny, a handsome, brave and honorable knight. They settled in Arundel Castle in Sussex (now the seat of the Dukes of Norfolk), which had been given to her by Henry I. There she produced seven d'Aubigny children— four boys, William, Reyner, Henry and Godfrey, and three girls, Alice, Olivia and Agatha. And with the years, by all accounts, and in her own happiness, she grew even lovelier to look upon.

Until 1139, Matilda, who had produced another son, Geoffrey, did not attempt to take back her annexed kingdom, although her husband, along with Robert of Gloucester, had gradually been winning Normandy back. But in 1139 she and Robert decided the time was right to make her move on England, even though the invasion by her uncle, David of Scotland, on her behalf had met with little success. Matilda and Robert landed at Portsmouth with only 150 followers, expecting the country to rise immediately to her aid. They were disappointed, and rode quickly to Arundel Castle to Adele for shelter.

The request put Adele in a terrible position, for she had stayed quietly apart from the hurly-burly since her remarriage. But her genuine friendship for the waspish and worn Matilda won out, and she received them warmly. Robert immediately left for Bristol to raise his army, leaving Matilda with her stepmother.

For once Stephen acted quickly. He appeared before the castle with his forces, demanding Matilda's surrender. Arundel was a strong castle, but inside there were few men capable of fighting. The future of Adele's family was at stake, for defiance to a crowned king—as Stephen was—constituted high treason, punishable by death and disinheritance. Nonetheless, Adele, with much inner agony but true to her principles, sent out word to Stephen that she and her supporters were prepared to protect her stepdaughter to the death.

This gallant gesture had the desired effect, for Stephen quixotically (and stupidly) reacted by sending in a safe-conduct for Matilda to join Robert of Gloucester at Bristol, and even appointed his brother Henry, Bishop of Winchester, to accompany her. He waved gaily to Adele and Matilda, who were on the battlements, and rode away with his troops. Adele and the d'Aubigny family were saved, but the move was an incredibly foolish one on Stephen's part. By taking Matilda then he could immediately have stopped the threat to his throne, instead of plunging England into 14 disastrous years of a dreadful civil war.

In the maelstrom that followed, Adele disappears from view, and all that is known is that she died at Arundel in 1151 at the age of 48, leaving her husband and family disconsolate with grief. Her husband William appears once more, and in a crucial role. In 1153, Stephen was again facing battle—this time with the now-grown son of Matilda, Henry Plantagenet, at Wallingford—and William d'Aubigny intervened. Stephen also was grieving, for not only had he lost *his* devoted wife in 1151, but his son and heir Eustace had died of a fever just a few months previously. William begged him to bring the terrible war to a close by agreeing to let Henry Plantagenet rule after him; Stephen agreed, and so the Treaty of Wallingford was signed, whereby Stephen was to retain the throne for his lifetime, and Henry, son of Matilda, would succeed him.

One cannot help but wonder if, aware of the horror that her simple gesture of friendship in 1139 had unleashed, Adele did not repent of her hospitality many times during those long years at Arundel. Henry I's first queen remained long in the minds of the English; his second queen, so similar to her predecessor in so many ways, they quickly forgot—and, in the circumstances, who can blame them?

MATILDA OF BOULOGNE
(ca. 1103–1151)

m. Stephen of Blois 1125

Children: Baldwin, Matilda, Eustace, William

MATILDA OF BOULOGNE WAS BORN to the rich Count Eustace of Boulogne and his wife, the Princess Mary, younger daughter of Malcolm Canmore and Margaret of Scotland, who had shared with her sister Edytha the dubious comforts of the Abbey of Rumsey under "Aunt" Christina, its abbess. Her father was of a famous crusading family; his two brothers, Godfrey and Baldwin, had both been kings of the newly established Christian realm in the Holy Land. Eustace himself had even been considered for the honor. He was a rarity in those rough times, a fine and "gentle" man, and when it came time for his daughter to marry she was allowed to marry the man of her choice—and her choice, then and forever, was Stephen of Blois: a true love match.

On the face of it, the marriage was not a brilliant one for such a rich heiress, as Stephen was the younger son of the Count of Blois and thus not even in line for his father's lands; they were to go to the elder son, Theobald. His impressive lineage came only through his mother, Adele, daughter of William the Conqueror and as strong-minded as her own mother, Matilda of Flanders. There is no doubt that, like the other strong-minded women who followed in Stephen's life, his mother doted on him above everyone—and she was quick to point out to her brother, Henry of England, what an advantageous marriage her younger son was making.

Neither of them was surprised at the match, because Stephen was credited as being the handsomest man in Europe—tall, fair, and with great vivacity and charm that won over even the most cynical men and women. Henry was so delighted by this marriage of his favorite nephew that he persuaded the young couple to come and live in the English court after their marriage in 1125. Tight as he was with money, he built a residence for them in London, the Tower Royal, almost equal in magnificence to the Tower of London itself and much more comfortable.

Here the couple settled down to become the darlings of the English court, and here Matilda quickly bore Baldwin, a sickly boy, and a daughter, Matilda, both of whom were treated from the start with all the pomp of royal children. Half the women in the court fell in love with Stephen, but he obviously doted on his diminutive, fair wife just as much as she doted on him. But then the newly widowed Empress Matilda returned to her father's court in England. The Empress looked at her cousin Stephen, liked what she saw, and started a determined pursuit of the handsome man.

It is clear from what transpired years later between these two very disparate Matildas that Matilda of Boulogne was aware of what was in the Empress's mind, but at the time she gave no sign of it. She pitted her own quiet strength and devotion to her husband against the magnetic attractions of her rival, who did evidently fascinate Stephen. And in the long run Matilda of Boulogne won out.

The production of another son, Eustace, to replace the sickly Baldwin, who had died, may have signaled to the Empress that, despite her machinations, she had not been able to drive a wedge between the royal couple, and caused her finally to return to Normandy to obey her father's wishes and marry Geoffrey of Anjou.

The departure was a great relief to Matilda of Boulogne—but it was a relief that was short-lived, for the Empress kept returning, and with each return the old trouble would begin again. Yet Stephen is credited with only one "affair"—with a Norman woman called Dameta, who produced three sons by him, one of whom, Gervois, Stephen subsequently made Abbot of Westminster. But this liaison happened long before his marriage and there is no subsequent evidence of his straying from Matilda's side.

The Empress eventually went back to the arms of Geoffrey Plantagenet and bore him a son, Henry.

The speed with which Stephen acted to seize the crown after Henry's death on December 1, 1135 raises questions as to whether he had not had this strategy in mind all along. He was crowned king on the Christmas Day following Henry's death, his adoring queen and son Eustace by his side at the magnificent ceremony in Westminster Abbey.

Stephen would soon prove himself one of the weakest kings ever to sit on the throne of England. Stephen loved to be loved, and so would make promises to everyone he wanted to win over—his barons, the Church, the citizens of London; promises he could not possibly keep. His Norman barons soon realized this weakness and began to exploit the situation to its fullest, building hundreds of unlicensed strongholds and castles from which they proceeded to tyrannize the helpless Anglo-Saxon peasantry and ravage the land.

Even in 1139, when the Empress Matilda returned to claim her kingdom, it was this same fatal desire to please that led Stephen to allow her out of his clutches to join with Robert of Gloucester and raise her standard in the west. His exploitive barons now had a double-edged sword to use against both of them—for by switching sides, or even threatening to do so during the long civil war that followed, they constantly augmented their own power. In no time the careful legal system that Henry I had so painstakingly built to heal the division of his Anglo-Saxon/Norman kingdom, and that had earned him the title "Lion of Justice," had been swept aside. Terrorism and anarchy were abroad in the land.

Though personally brave and a good fighter, Stephen was no more of a general than he was a statesman, and so towards the end of 1139 his wife Matilda took their young son Eustace to France, hoping to negotiate with the young King Louis VII for a marriage between Eustace and Louis's even younger sister Constance. Louis proved agreeable to the match, for Eustace was at least heir to his mother's dower of rich Boulogne and, at most, if Stephen's cause succeeded, heir to the realm of England and Normandy. So the betrothal was arranged, with Matilda hoping to keep the Empress's husband, Geoffrey of Anjou, in check as he moved on Stephen's Norman and French possessions.

Well satisfied with her mission, she returned to England in 1140, only to find disaster: Stephen had been captured by the Empress's forces.

England had become polarized by the two royal rivals: the west supported the Empress; London and the eastern counties backed Stephen. As long as he stayed among his loyal Londoners Stephen was safe, but in his wife's absence he had taken a trip to Lincoln to reinforce its loyalty, and there the able Robert of Gloucester had made a lightning raid and had captured him. He had been taken to the west, to Gloucester, where the Empress Matilda was, and there imprisoned in a dank dungeon. From the woman he had rejected he could expect no such gallant treatment as he had accorded her the year before. He attempted to escape, and this further whetted her appetite for vengeance. Loaded down with chains and tethered to his saddle, he was then transported as a public spectacle to Bristol, where he was entrusted to the care of Amabel of Glamorgan, the formidable wife of Robert of Gloucester.

Stephen's wife Matilda was distraught; her one overpowering thought was to get her beloved Stephen free, no matter what the cost. She sought and was granted an audience with the Empress, and there completely humbled herself. She promised that if the Empress would only let him go free Stephen would give up his claim to the throne and leave England forever, and that she, herself, *would never see him again* but would retire to a nunnery—showing quite clearly that she had understood all along the sexual jealousy that motivated the

Empress. The only stipulation she made was that her son Eustace was to retain the earldom of Boulogne (which was hers by dower right) and the county of Mortagne, which had been a personal gift of Henry I to Stephen.

Like her grandmother, Matilda of Flanders, who had waited 20 years to get revenge on the Anglo-Saxon noble who had spurned her, the Empress had not the slightest intention of letting the hapless Stephen out of her clutches. She scornfully spurned Matilda's offer and would grant no further discussion.

This put steel into Matilda's backbone. Returning to the eastern counties and securing the help of William of Ypres, a faithful baron, she rallied Stephen's scattered forces and began to fight back. She accompanied the army wherever it went.

She would probably not have made much progress except for the Empress's arrogance. Londoners, deeming Stephen's cause lost and tired of the long struggle that had nearly ruined their rich trade, were prepared to give the daughter of "Good Queen Mold" the benefit of the doubt and recognize her as their rightful sovereign. But when she entered London, instead of placating the people, as the wise Robert of Gloucester counseled, the Empress treated them like bond-slaves and demanded enormous taxes and penalties as punishment for their former support of Stephen. Londoners rose against her as one, sending her and her party fleeing from the city to the safer haven of Oxford, and proceeded to join forces with the small army of Matilda of Boulogne, now strong enough to lay siege to the royal stronghold of Winchester.

The army of the Empress was forced to retreat, and Matilda of Boulogne had her first stroke of luck when, fighting a rearguard action to cover the retreat, Robert of Gloucester, the Empress's chief general, was captured.

Robert was a rich prize, and Matilda immediately tried to exchange him for Stephen; the Empress still refused. So Matilda decided to go directly to another formidable woman—Stephen's custodian, Amabel, wife of the imprisoned Robert of Gloucester. She bluntly told Amabel that if she did not release Stephen, Robert would be sent to rot in the Keep of Boulogne and that she would never see her husband again. Amabel, without even consulting the Empress, agreed to the exchange. Stephen rode a free man into captured Winchester to be reunited with Matilda, and was subsequently crowned a second time in Lincoln, the site of his capture.

But his two-year imprisonment had taught Stephen nothing, and all her devotion could give him neither boldness nor the ability he so obviously lacked. The war dragged on, year after year. Stephen again had a chance to capture the Empress when he captured Oxford Castle; but he dilly-dallied so long that she managed to escape through the snow with a handful of her followers.

When peace came at last, it was not as a result of his efforts. On October 31, 1147, Robert of Gloucester, who had so faithfully carried out his father's wishes and strongly supported his half-sister, died. Without him the Empress knew she could no longer carry on, and so she retreated with her teenage son Henry to Anjou. Nothing had been settled.

In gratitude for the peace—however uneasy—Matilda and Stephen founded the Abbey of Faversham in their loyal county of Kent, where they often stayed. But all the anxiety and stress of war had been too much for the frail Matilda. Completely worn out, on May 3, 1151 she died at Heningham Castle in Kent and was buried in the newly founded abbey. Stephen was lost without her, but by dying when she did she was spared the grief of losing her son Eustace, who died in 1153, and of knowing that her children had been disinherited from the throne by the Treaty of Wallingford, which, after Stephen's death, gave the throne to Henry, the son of her detested rival. His will to live gone, Stephen survived this treaty only a year, and in 1154, at the age of 52, he died and was buried beside his Matilda at Faversham.

All traces of their tombs have disappeared, covered over by Henry II—and small wonder, for what Stephen did to England could be neither forgotten nor forgiven. During his 19 years on the throne an estimated third of the population died, not so much from the casualties of war but from starvation and privation caused by the terrorism of his barons.

THE
PLANTAGENETS

ELEANOR OF AQUITAINE
(1122–1204)

m. (1) Louis VII of France   1137
m. (2) Henry II   1152

Children: *William, Henry, RICHARD, Geoffrey, Eleanor, Matilda, Joan, JOHN (& three daughters by Louis VII)*

IF A PRIZE WERE TO BE GIVEN FOR ENGLAND'S liveliest queen, Eleanor of Aquitaine would undoubtedly win. From the moment she kicked her way into the world in 1122 she was a ball of fire that never stopped rolling.

Her father, William, was a devout man and heir to the rich Duke of Aquitaine, another William who had spent a long and successful life in pursuit of *l'amour* throughout the length and breadth of his huge domains. In fact, by the time Eleanor was born, Aquitaine had become the world center of the "Courts of Love."

Such notoriety was not at all to her father's taste. He had spent a long time on the Crusades, but managed to stay home long enough to father two daughters, Eleanor and her sister Petronille. The old Duke was disappointed that his son had produced only girls, but was delighted when they showed from an early age that they took after him rather than their father.

By the time she was 15, Eleanor was beautiful—black-haired, black-eyed, with creamy skin; lively, amusing, a fashionable dresser, and already recognized as queen in the Courts of Love. In that year her father died and her grandfather decided it was high time to find a legal husband for his very lively heiress. Eleanor, apart from her personal attractions, was a rich prize, for with her fair hand came the even fairer land of Aquitaine. The King of France got an edge on the rush that followed, and proceeded to marry her off quickly to his son and heir, Louis.

Louis was none too bright, and had pious inclinations much like Eleanor's father. Eleanor apparently bedazzled him with her unusual clothing and striking manners, and certainly did not object to being Queen of France, the most important country in Europe. On August 1, 1137 they were married.

The match did not work out well. Louis was not particularly virile, and Eleanor was very passionate. She bore him two daughters in quick succession, but by then he had succeeded his father as King of France, and French law ordained that no female could succeed to the throne. He lacked an heir.

Eleanor also inadvertently put a burden of guilt on him that he never managed to shake off. Her sister Petronille, as passionate as Eleanor, became involved with a married man, the Count of Vermandois, who divorced his wife to marry her. The divorced wife's family was a powerful one, so it went to war with the newlyweds. Eleanor convinced Louis to join the fight against his feuding vassal during which 1,000 innocent people burned to death while praying in a church. Louis felt he had incurred the wrath of God and became more melancholy, while Eleanor grew correspondingly more restless.

To save both his soul and his marriage, Louis determined to do what all good men did at that time—go on a Crusade. The only snag was that Eleanor insisted on coming along too; she also insisted on bringing along her own troop of female crusaders, all highborn ladies who did not know a longbow from a crossbow.

They designed their own uniforms (white tunics embroidered with red crowns and slit at the sides to show scarlet tights and long red leather boots). They attracted a great deal of attention, but their presence was a catastrophe for the Crusade. They insisted on taking so much baggage that the marches crawled at a snail's pace; the young knights accompanying them were utterly distracted, and on one occasion 7,000 Frenchmen lost their lives because Eleanor and her ladies insisted on camping in a valley that turned out to be a Saracen trap.

Finally they did reach the Holy Land, and the situation improved, at least for Eleanor. Her uncle, Raymond of Poitiers, the younger son of old Duke William and very like him in character, was the ruler of Antioch, and Louis left her in his care while he went off to fight the infidels. This uncle was handsome, not too much older than his niece, and much better company than the melancholy Louis. The results were predictable, and the news eventually got back to Louis. Nor was this all: Rumor had it that a certain Saracen sheik was so smitten with her charms that he used a variety of disguises to sneak into the French camp, and subsequently into Eleanor's tent. The scandal was growing.

As for the Crusade, Louis had been making no headway at all; Eleanor's female Crusaders were fed up with soldiering; and Eleanor herself was becoming alarmed at rumors that her uncle planned to divorce her from Louis and marry her off to the Sultan of Iconium. The French contingent hurriedly drew together and headed home.

But the key word now was divorce. Both Eleanor and Louis had it in their minds by this time—but a divorce was difficult to obtain, even for people in their exalted positions. If Louis used the grounds of adultery, neither of them could ever remarry, and he still lacked that all-important male heir. So they made another effort to save the marriage, and another child was born of the reunion—another girl.

Eleanor was in a quandary. She openly despised Louis by this time, but liked being Queen of France, and didn't see another good prospect in sight. Then Henry Plantagenet appeared.

Henry II was made of the same stern mettle as his great-grandfather, William the Conqueror, and was as virile and as much of a ladies' man as his grandfather, Henry I. And he was himself about to be crowned King of England.

It did not matter to Eleanor that Henry was 11 years her junior. He was just what she had been looking for: a man as passionate and as strong-willed as she was, and a king into the bargain. Henry saw in her an attractive and lively woman who could give him something he needed to bolster his own power—a substantial foothold in France to add to his own possessions of Anjou, Maine and Normandy. It is evident from what followed that they were also extremely attracted to each other.

Eleanor's marriage to Louis was dissolved on March 18, 1152, after 13 years, on the very lame grounds of consanguinity. Louis, shortsighted and gentlemanly as usual, gave her back all her lands without any restrictions, so that Aquitaine and all its vassal domains were back under her control. No sooner was that very important point settled than a disguised Henry crossed to France and married her in Bordeaux on the first day of May. That they had anticipated the honeymoon somewhat became clear on August 17th of that year, when Eleanor gave birth in Rouen to their son William. Poor Louis fussed and fumed, but as usual took no action, and the newlyweds crossed the Channel to take possession of their kingdom in peace. Eleanor proceeded to produce four more sons, in addition to three more daughters, and with the exception of the first-born William, who died at the age of three, raised them all to adulthood.

Her relationship with Henry was to be of a very different caliber from that of the doting and weak-willed Louis. She was 30 years old to Henry's 19 when they married—and for those times 30 was already middle-aged—and by the time she was finished bearing his eight children she was 45 (John the youngest, was born about 1167). There is no whisper that she was ever unfaithful to him; even if she had had the inclination, he kept her too busy; but there is plenty of evidence that he was frequently, and often flagrantly, unfaithful to *her*. His behavior was in no way unusual; like kings before and after him, it was expected of him. Even a woman as high-spirited as Eleanor expected and accepted this double standard up to a point. But she did not like it, and on more than one occasion she unleashed her fury with telling effect.

Legend has it that the "fair" (English) Rosamund Clifford, mistress of Henry II, was poisoned by the wicked Queen Eleanor. The only part of the story that is true is that Rosamund shared Henry's bed both before and after his marriage. She bore him one son, William Longsword, even before he became king. After he returned to claim his kingdom with Eleanor at his side, Rosamund bore him another, Geoffrey. For a time he kept her near his palace at Woodstock in Oxfordshire, but after his and Eleanor's coronation, Rosamund quietly returned to the nearby convent of Godstow, where she lived for another 20 years. Henry saw to it that she never lacked for anything and gave preferential treatment to the two boys, particularly Geoffrey, whom he preferred to most of his legitimate sons, and whom he had reared and educated with them at court. It was this last fact that bothered Eleanor; she was always a protective, dedicated and loving mother (and, in the cases of her sons, this affection was freely returned). There is no evidence that Eleanor was much concerned about Fair Rosamund herself, or about any of her successors in Henry's bed. What *did* upset her was Henry's relationship with "Fair Alice," the daughter of her ex-husband Louis by his third marriage. Louis had finally been fortunate this time: not only had he had more daughters, he had finally begotten the long-hoped-for male heir, Philip-Augustus. Personal feelings could not be allowed to interfere with matters of state, and at the age of five, Princess Alice of France was betrothed to Richard of England, Eleanor's third son, and sent off to the English court to be raised as an English lady.

The trouble began in earnest when the princess reached the age of 15, at which point the wedding to Richard should have taken place. Henry started to find multiple reasons to postpone it, and to spend more and more time with his prospective daughter-in-law. Here was a situation to which Eleanor could not turn a blind eye. It was one thing to ignore his previous dalliances, quite another to ignore an affair with a king's daughter, particularly considering that the king was her ex-husband. To let the affair go on would make her the laughingstock of Europe.

Even during her busy childbearing years she had been very active, both managing the turbulent English during Henry's many absences overseas, and in shouldering the administrative cares of her own domains in France, a full-time job in itself. She had even found time to be a patroness of the arts: her court at Poitiers had become a center for troubadors and a model for courtly life and manners. She was an important and respected figure in civilized Europe and, as such, could not bear the snickers and whispers that would follow her if this affair continued. She was well over 50 now, and already considered "old." Henry was in his early forties, and Alice was in the full flower of her late teens. But Eleanor had a weapon—her loving sons, particularly Richard, Alice's fiancé, who, though there is no evidence he ever cared about Alice, was nevertheless the other injured party. These weapons she brought into action. Richard demanded that the marriage take place; Henry continued to delay and to dote on Alice.

In 1173, with Eleanor's assistance, Richard and his brothers revolted against their father. The revolt, however, backfired, as the young cubs were no match for the wily father-wolf when it came to fighting. Eleanor was captured and imprisoned by her husband in Winchester Castle, where she was to spend a miserable (but not inactive) 16 years, while her sons continued a futile struggle against Henry.

With Eleanor out of the way, Henry no longer kept up a front: He and Alice began openly living together. King Louis at last became sufficiently upset to insist that Henry let the wedding with Richard take place. Henry continued to refuse, and after Louis died in 1180, his son, Philip-Augustus, took up the cause. Henry tried to obtain a divorce, but he was turned down by the Pope. He nevertheless resisted the temptation to have Eleanor done away with, an assassination he could easily have had accomplished in prison.

Philip-Augustus, quicker off the mark than his father, soon started to lend a helping hand to Henry's sons, for he saw fair pickings for himself and France from Henry's domains. Henry was 56 by now and had been fighting for his Fair Alice for 17 years. He was worn out, and, after a defeat at the hands of his rebel sons and the French, he died in 1189. At his deathbed was the only son who had remained faithful to him, the one he had always favored over his legitimate sons—Geoffrey, son of the Fair Rosamund. All the rest were in arms against him in the enemy camp.

As Henry's sun went into final eclipse, Eleanor's burst forth anew in splendor. Richard, the new king (his older brother Henry had died), sent to England to have her let out of prison. She was nearly 70 when she was released, but just starting to get her second wind. But she had also mellowed with age. Richard, for instance, wanted to punish her jailer, Ranulf de Glanvil—but sensible Eleanor would have none of it. She had lived long with the knowledge that Ranulf could have killed her at any hour of the day or night in those 17 years and no one would have been the wiser. Instead, while he had carried out his duties strictly enough, he had treated her with every consideration; for that she was duly thankful. She was not, however, without her own brand of malice. Fair Alice, now 32 and fading fast, was imprisoned in Eleanor's place at Winchester.

Eleanor now went into an absolute whirlwind of activity to make up for lost time. First, she had to marry off Richard, at 32 still a bachelor (and still technically engaged to Alice). He disappointed his mother when he insisted on marrying Berengaria of Navarre, the daughter of a minor king. Eleanor had had a far more brilliant match in mind for him, but was so fond of him that she went along with his wishes, and even traveled herself to the capital of Navarre, Pampeluna, to make the wedding arrangements.

She was less tender about the personal feelings of her daughters, for she saw to it that they all made brilliant marriages which she had planned for them. Her namesake, Eleanor, was married off to the King of Castile, Alfonso VIII; Matilda, named for Henry's mother, was married to the Duke of Saxony and Bavaria; and Joan married the King of Sicily, William II (after his death she married for love to Raymond of Toulouse). All produced children; one of the many sobriquets Eleanor earned is "royal grandmother of Europe."

There is no doubt that she played favorites in the family. She does not seem to have cared much for her son Henry, his father's favorite, but Richard she truly loved, even if he was a bit of an oaf. Geoffrey, Duke of Brittany, her fourth son, did not seem to matter much to her either. He was the family troublemaker and had married early, in 1171, the heiress of Brittany, Constance (through whom he had become the Duke), who was a strong-willed woman herself and would allow no interference from her mother- in-law or from any of the other members of his family. Beyond question, though, Eleanor's favorite child was her youngest, the child of her middle age, the sneaky and cowardly John. He was her blind spot, for she could find no fault in him even when it became obvious that he was arrogant, cruel and selfish. His father thought so little of him that he left him no land—hence the nickname that followed him all his life, John "Lackland"—and, as it proved, with very good reason. When John later took possession of Normandy he immediately lost it to the French king. Even in his marriages, Eleanor does not seem to have been able to act with her usual wisdom. True, his betrothal to the heiress of Maurienne had been broken off by the family fight between Henry and Eleanor over Fair Alice, but when he did marry it was to an English girl, Avisa, who was a first cousin once removed, causing much trouble with the Church because of the close kinship. John must have gone ahead with that marriage because he *wanted* to; his mother did nothing to stop him.

Similarly, after he had become King of England—largely through his mother's efforts—he rejected her good advice to make a royal progress through all his new domains, and fell in love with the young daughter of the Count of Angoulême (a minor vassal of Eleanor's in Aquitaine), divorced his first wife and married Isabelle of Angoulême (she was 15 at the time and he 32). Again, though Eleanor was not against the divorce from his first wife, who had always been beneath him in station, she was certainly not in favor of his marriage to Isabelle, who was hardly his equal. Still, blindly, she went on letting him have his way.

But Eleanor had already shown how able a woman she was. During her seventies she ruled England in all but name. Richard, no sooner than he had been crowned king in England, was eager to be off again on a Crusade. Eleanor had had her fill of Crusades, but she helped raise money and sent him off with a heavy heart, for he left her in charge of a troubled and neglected kingdom.

The Crusade was a failure as usual, and to make matters worse, Richard, on his way back home, fell into the hands of his enemy, the Duke of Austria, who conveyed Richard to the Emperor, who in turn demanded a huge ransom for his release. John, in the meantime, had been intriguing with the barons remaining in England against his brother. Eleanor had to find out where Richard was imprisoned and try to have him freed, yet she dared not take her eyes off John or leave England. Her terrible anxiety can be seen in the letters she sent at the time—to the Pope, to the Emperor of Germany and to many others, all demanding Richard's release, all signed "Eleanor, by the wrath of God, Queen of England." She knew her true enemy was her old nemesis, Philip-Augustus of France, who had never forgiven Richard for turning down his sister Alice, or for owning most of France, or for showing him up as a poor fighter on the Crusade. It was Louis's son she had to beat, and he was a formidable opponent.

Doggedly she persevered, somehow managing to scrape together a ransom of 150,000 gold marks with the help of Hubert Walter, Archbishop of Canterbury and a true friend of Richard's. But there was still the problem of getting it safely to Germany, and then of getting Richard safely home again. Although she was now 73, Eleanor decided to go herself—fortunately, as it turned out. The Emperor was too intimidated by her not to deliver Richard once the money was paid—but she knew Philip-Augustus was lurking in the wings somewhere, urging the Emperor to go back on his word. So she rushed the whole party across Europe to Antwerp, where she had a boat waiting under full sail to take them all to England—and in the nick of time, for, just as she had feared, the Emperor did change his mind, and sent orders for them to be stopped and Richard brought back. Thanks to Eleanor's foresight, however, by the time the Emperor's troops reached Antwerp the boat had already sailed.

Philip-Augustus was enraged at being outmaneuvered, particularly since John in England had (unsuccessfully) attempted to assume the crown on the French king's guarantee that Richard would never return. Philip-Augustus did have the decency to warn John that his brother was on his way, and, never one to make a fight of it, John through his mother's intercession, was reconciled with his brother.

Personally valiant Richard undoubtedly was, but as a king he was weak. His marriage to Berengaria, though a love match, turned sour, just as Eleanor had feared. When Richard had himself crowned again to underline his being back in command, he never even offered to have Berengaria crowned beside him. For him there was only one Queen of England—his mother. Berengaria was also infertile (Richard had produced several bastards), so there was no heir of either sex.

Eleanor failed to keep Richard at home to put his mismanaged and plundered kingdom to rights. He was disgruntled by the results of his Crusade—blaming its failure on Philip-Augustus—and by the humiliations he had undergone during his captivity. His one thought was to take revenge on the King of France. He frittered away his time on the Continent, baiting and sparring with his French rival, going so far as to erect his famous castle of Chateau-Gaillard in the Vexin, right on the edge of Philip- Augustus's territory. On one of these pointless forays he was wounded. Gangrene set in and he died in 1199, leaving behind a legacy of trouble.

Despite her grief at both his childless marriage and his death, Eleanor was still the doting mother: Her fair Richard was dead, but her fairer John would be king. Of course, Geoffrey of Brittany was the next oldest son after Richard and should have succeeded his brother, but his mother liked neither him nor his wife, and so she threw her all-important support to John.

First she knew she had to mend fences with the King of France to have any chance in this highly illegal enterprise. Although she was 80 years old, she went to Castile to collect her granddaughter Blanche from her daughter Eleanor, and took her back to France to marry Philip-Augustus's son and heir, Louis. Just to be on the safe side, she had the marriage performed by proxy in Spain, having previously appeased Philip-Augustus by personally doing homage to him for Aquitaine. She had patched up the quarrel between France and the House of Plantagenet. It was perhaps her greatest diplomatic triumph.

It is interesting that the granddaughter Eleanor picked out for this was the one most physically like herself as a young girl; she must have hoped the girl was of the same mettle, too. She was not mistaken. Much later, Blanche would urge her French husband to claim England in *her* name. Eleanor did not quite make it to the court of France to see this spirited granddaughter wedded and bedded to Louis; her strength gave out on the way and she had to spend some time recovering in her native Aquitaine. But she still was not finished.

Geoffrey of Brittany had conveniently died, but had left a son, Arthur, whose claim to the English throne was stronger than John's. The boy was still young, but Constance of Brittany, his mother, who had always hated the Plantagenets, took up arms on his behalf; she was joined by a host of John's many enemies. John, predictably, was not up to the task of fighting them: Eleanor had to do it, defending both Anjou and her own Aquitaine against invaders, and thus saving her son's French possessions.

In 1202, still engaged in this struggle with Arthur and his mother, she was besieged in the castle of Mirabeau, a stronghold that was neither well fortified nor stocked for a siege. The garrison had only one advantage: It had Eleanor. Hobbling around on a cane, she put starch in the defenders. The news that she was in danger so electrified John—who knew he could not do without her—that in a most unusual show of alacrity he force-marched his troops 82 miles in two days not only saving the town and Eleanor but capturing Arthur of Brittany as well.

Eleanor, who may have had guilt feelings about depriving her grandson Arthur of his rightful inheritance, made John swear a solemn oath that he would never lay a violent hand on the boy. John agreed, as he always did with his mother. Naturally, he did not keep his promise, and the boy was subsequently murdered. The enraged people of Brittany flared into revolt again, just as Eleanor was looking forward to a bit of peace and quiet. She was 82 years old, and John's only victories were those she had won for him. Now she was too tired; John would have to take over. The rebellious Bretons swept over Normandy. Chateau Gaillard, Richard's great stronghold, was taken; Rouen, which had held out for a month in the hope the John would relieve it, finally fell, because he had ignored the problem and had returned to England. Normandy was gone, finally and irretrievably lost.

Eleanor died shortly after the capitulation of Rouen. She was almost 83, an enormous age for the period, and she had fought a magnificent fight. Her great riches went to her unworthy son; her huge store of jewels went to his parvenu wife. At least at the end Eleanor had some compensation: She was buried in the Abbey of Fontevrauld, between the husband of her choosing, of her grief and her delight, Henry, and her beloved and valiant son, Richard— even in death she held center stage between the men who had loved her. History has largely disapproved of Eleanor, but her record stands solid and complete: a very remarkable woman.

BERENGARIA OF NAVARRE
(1165–1230)
m. Richard I   1191

No issue

Any QUEEN FOLLOWING ELEANOR OF AQUITAINE would probably be overshadowed, and in the case of Berengaria her obscurity is especially poignant. She has the distinction of being the only queen consort who never set foot in England during her lifetime. She was never even crowned.

The mystery of Berengaria begins with Richard's reasons for marrying her. His father, Henry II, had found England and the French possessions in a shambles after the debacle of Stephen's reign, but by the time he died he had turned things around to such an extent that Richard inherited the richest and fastest-growing kingdom in Europe. He could have had his pick of European princesses, and yet his choice—and it *was* his choice—fell upon Berengaria of Navarre, daughter of Sancho the Wise, king of the obscure if picturesque little country on the Spanish side of the Pyrenees.

Richard had seen her only once. As a young prince being raised in his mother's Aquitaine, he had attended a tournament in Pampeluna as a guest of his bosom friend Sancho the Strong, heir of Sancho the Wise and the brother of Berengaria. Obviously he was smitten by the small, dark-haired girl, who loved poetry and music—as he did—and was a shy, ethereal creature. But at that time there could have been no thought of marriage, since he was already betrothed to Princess Alice of France, sister of Philip-Augustus and daughter of Louis VII, his mother's first husband.

On Berengaria's part it is easy to see why she was smitten. Richard was by far the handsomest of Eleanor's children—tall, fair, virile, and with a beautiful baritone voice like his great-grandfather Henry I, and who deserved his nickname "the Lion-hearted." He was the greatest "catch" in Europe.

In 1189 Richard ascended the throne at the age of 32, and was finally in a position to do something about his own marriage and to provide the heir who would save his throne from his grasping brothers. He certainly had no intention of marrying his betrothed, Alice of France, who had been his father's mistress and the cause of his mother's long imprisonment. Instead, he had "Fair Alice" imprisoned in Winchester Castle, from which Eleanor of Aquitaine had so recently been liberated, and sent his mother off to Navarre to ask for

Berengaria's hand in marriage and to bring her back as soon as possible. He was too busy to go himself, because he was preparing to go off on the Third Crusade in yet another attempt to liberate the Holy Land.

An unenthusiastic Eleanor did what had to be done, and waited while a trousseau was prepared for the delighted Berengaria. By this time Richard had already set sail from England, so they made plans to meet him at Marseilles. When the wedding party arrived in the French port it was only to find that the English fleet had already sailed for Naples. There was no alternative but to trek the bride-to-be overland to southern Italy.

The long journey had at least one good effect: Eleanor grew quite fond of her unobtrusive and undynamic daughter-in-law. She probably saw that this quiet little woman would present no threat to her own paramount hold over her son, and we can well imagine that the shy Berengaria was suitably terrified of her redoubtable mother-in-law.

Berengaria then had one of her infrequent strokes of luck in life. When they got to Naples, again Richard had already departed, but they were met by Eleanor's daughter Joan, the recently widowed queen of the Norman king of Sicily, who had been thrown out by his successor. Joanna was the only gentle member of Eleanor's family. The two young women retired to Brindisi on the Adriatic coast and spent the rest of the winter and part of the next spring there, becoming fast friends. Berengaria was to be in sore need of this firm friendship, for Richard had started to dither about the marriage.

He was at Messina in Sicily quarreling with his fellow-crusader Philip-Augustus of France about the fate of the "ruined" Alice. Philip had no intention of giving in on the former betrothal, and was insisting that his sister's marriage go on. It was a terribly trying time for Berengaria, for if Richard did not go through with *their* marriage she would be obliged to spend the rest of her life in a nunnery.

The question was finally resolved by Eleanor, who lost her patience. She told her daughter Joanna, "Take this damsel for me to the King, your brother, and tell him to espouse her speedily," and without further ado stumped angrily back to England. Richard never listened to any other woman in his life, but did obey his mother, so as Philip-Augustus set off to the Holy Land in a fury, Richard finally met the woman he had been in such a hurry to wed.

And still he dithered. Whether he found the 25-year-old Berengaria—an advanced age for an unmarried princess—not the attractive teenager he remembered, or whether he was so bound up with his desire to get to the fighting, we do not know—but it is certain he was not devoured by ardent passion at the sight of her. Though not at all religious, he decided to postpone the wedding until after the Lenten season of 1190.

Off he went again with his fleet of 200 ships, Joanna and Berengaria sadly trailing after him in another ship. Only when he arrived in Cyprus did he at last decide, and on May 12, 1190, with great pomp and circumstance, Richard and Berengaria were married in Limasol by the Bishop of Bayonne. The chroniclers tell us in great detail what the handsome Richard wore; no mention is made of the bride. The wedding feast lasted three days and then Richard was off again in his flagship, Berengaria and Joanna trailing behind, as before, in another ship.

Philip-Augustus, who had been having bad luck in the fighting, was so relieved to see Richard and the English forces that he decided Alice was a dead issue. He even went so far as to meet Berengaria's boat and carry the bride ashore in his arms, although quietly continuing to hate Richard.

After Richard's capture of Acre and the resultant infamous massacre, Joanna and Berengaria were lodged in one of the city's great palaces while he went off to fight. Without doubt he fought brilliantly against great odds, but at the crucial moment, when he had reached Bethany and Jerusalem was in sight, Philip-Augustus abruptly withdrew the French forces. Richard did not have the forces to go on alone; so the Third Crusade ended, and in October a thoroughly despondent Richard sailed from the Holy Land. As usual, Berengaria did not go with him; by his orders, she embarked on a different ship, along with Joanna, and it was evident to everyone by this time that he did not care at all about his bride.

In all the adventures that followed, Berengaria played no part: Richard's shipwreck on the way back; his capture by Leopold of Austria; his conveyance to his enemy the German emperor, who slapped him in prison and demanded a huge ransom for him. Again it was Eleanor who was the heroine, raising the ransom, taking it to Germany, outwitting the Emperor, and arranging Richard's escape back to England before Philip-Augustus could intervene. Berengaria, neglected and ignored, sat out her exile in Anjou.

Richard arrived back in England in March, and was acclaimed a hero by his mistreated and long-suffering English subjects.

His second coronation in Westminster Abbey would have been the perfect opportunity to bring Berengaria over, introduce her to her English subjects, and have her crowned queen—but she was not invited.

Richard was soon off to the Continent to take up his quarrel once more with Philip-Augustus; he never returned to England. And not until Richard fell ill in France did Berengaria again appear on the scene.

While he was very sick, his priests had been urging him to ponder his many sins, not the least of which was his treatment of his wife. Also, undoubtedly, his mother had been prodding him about his lack of an heir. Having seen what John—beloved though he was—had done to England, she knew full well what his ultimate succession would mean to the empire her husband had so painfully acquired. Richard sent for Berengaria, and she came to nurse him back to health.

When he had recovered, they went together to Eleanor's Aquitaine and spent the Christmas of 1198 there—possibly the only "close" time in their whole marriage. But as soon as the holiday season was over Richard was off again, hoping for a final confrontation with Philip-Augustus.

He did allow Berengaria to accompany him, keeping her stashed away in various manor houses behind the lines while he was in the field with his troops. But she was with him at the final—and to him fatal—siege of the Castle of Chaluz in Limousin. He was wounded in the shoulder by an arrow, and the surgeon who extracted it bungled the job. Gangrene set in and began to spread. Berengaria stayed with him as the poison gradually sapped his great body and he faded away, dying in 1199 at the age of 42.

Further grief was soon heaped upon her. Her greatest friend Joanna, who had remarried for love to one of Richard's fellow crusaders, Raymond of Toulouse, had come to beg her brother for help for her husband. She arrived just as Richard died, and the shock brought on a miscarriage and the subsequent death of Joanna herself. Shortly thereafter, Berengaria's only sister, Blanche, died. Berengaria sadly buried her dead—Richard beside his father, Henry II, in the Abbey of Fontevraud, where his mother would eventually also lie. Berengaria retired to the city of Le Mans, where she was to live out the remainder of her lonely life.

She was as neglected and ignored as Dowager Queen as she had been as queen consort. As Richard's widow and under his will she was entitled to a substantial state pension—but extracting it from the parsimonious John was none too easy. She was soon in such desperate financial straits that she had to appeal to her mother-in-law, who immediately saw to it that son John paid up, and that he continued to do so as long as Eleanor lived. But after her death in 1204 John again stopped payment. He never even relinquished what the old queen had bequeathed to Berengaria. This time she had to appeal to the Pope, who forced the grudging John to pay up under pain of excommunication. Even so, at his death in 1216, she was owed thousands of pounds, which the guardians of the young king Henry III promptly paid and continued to pay thereafter. She used the money to found the Abbey of L'Espan (now L'Epau). When she died at the age of 65 in 1230, she was buried in the abbey she had founded. Even in death she did not lie beside her husband.

Berengaria never had a child, although Richard is known to have fathered at least one acknowledged illegitimate son, Philippe de Cognac. The rumor that Richard, like William Rufus before him, was homosexual, is probably incorrect. But why, when the production of legitimate children to succeed him was of such paramount importance, he so neglected his wife is a mystery.

Berengaria was the first unlucky Spanish-born English queen, but she was not to be the last.

ISABELLA OF ANGOULÊME
(1186–1246)

m. (1) John   1200
m. (2) Hugh de Lusignan   1217

Children: HENRY, *Richard, Joan, Isabella, Eleanor (& 8 more*
children by Hugh de Lusignan)

No GREATER CONTRAST WITH THE MEEK and undemanding Queen Berengaria could be found than her successor, Isabella of Angoulême. Although she has always been pictured as a villainess, her failings pale beside those of her first husband, John. No English king has had a worse reputation in his own time than John: He was thought to be mean, cruel, unscrupulous, immoral, cowardly, self-centered, and utterly lacking in the wisdom and statesmanship so important to kingly virtue. And historical fact bears the chroniclers out—Eleanor's beloved youngest son was every bit as bad as reputed, and maybe even worse.

Yet his strong-minded mother doted on him, and his long-suffering brother Richard forgave him again and again. He did have great charm—the only one of Eleanor's sons with that gift. He was witty, and also the most sophisticated member of the family. In that troubled age, someone with John's powers to amuse could be forgiven much. It is, however, doubtful whether Isabella saw him in that light.

She was his second wife. His first was the beautiful Hawisa (Isabella) of Gloucester, granddaughter of Robert of Gloucester and his Amabel and therefore John's second cousin. The marriage had lasted 10 years and had produced no children, although during this same period John had produced at least seven acknowledged bastards by an assortment of mistresses. This first marriage had been against everyone's wishes, for Henry II, having failed to make John king of Ireland, had arranged for him to marry the heiress of Maurienne, hoping to ensure for his youngest son a feudal landholding of his own. Henry's older sons were in line to inherit everything else, with nothing left for John. When his father died John ignored this betrothal and went ahead with his own desires, reluctantly condoned by his mother. But by 1199 Hawisa's charms had long ceased to enthrall him, and as soon as he had ensconced himself on the dead Richard's throne, he divorced his wife on the grounds of consanguinity and looked around for a more suitable royal mate.

Hawisa he quickly married off again to Geoffrey de Mandeville—at a stiff price.

When he chose again, he chose disastrously. His lecherous eye had fallen upon the 15-year-old Isabella of Angoulême, daughter of Count Adhemar, a vassal of the powerful Count of Marche. But the beautiful Isabella was already engaged to Hugh de Lusignan, son of the influential Count of Marche, the very man with whom John was trying to cement an alliance. Lechery won out. John hastened back to England, divorced Hawisa, and arranged for Hugh de Lusignan and his brother to set off on an expedition against the rebellious Welsh, conveniently removing them from the scene.

The Angoulême family had their eye on the main chance, and obviously the King of England was a far better catch than a knight, however young and handsome. No doubt the teenage Isabella, a materialist if ever one existed, was bedazzled at the thought of the riches in store for a queen. With Hugh out of the way, the wedding plans proceeded apace, and John and Isabella were married in the Cathedral of Bordeaux by its bishop in 1200.

Hugh was not killed in the campaign as John had hoped, and returned to France to challenge John to mortal combat. John, always a coward, refused, thereby ensuring endless trouble from his French vassals. He hastily left for England, where Isabella was crowned queen in Westminster Abbey on October 9th. Now she had her first glimpse of her husband's meanness: He skimped on her clothing for the ceremony and did not give her any of the customary jewelry for the occasion, even though he himself was decked in gems.

Still, he was clearly besotted with Isabella, and, to the scandal of his court, he would lie abed with her until noon every day, completely neglecting his kingly duties.

Her English subjects appreciated her great beauty, but did not like the way John had taken her from another man, nor the way the English Hawisa had been set aside for yet another French queen. It was the beginning of Isabella's unpopularity. But the aged Queen Eleanor seems to have accepted her as an improvement over Hawisa, and that, for the moment, was enough.

But the Lusignans had neither forgotten nor forgiven, and for two years they had been stirring up rebellion in John's French territories. To their aid came John's greatest threat, his 15-year-old nephew Arthur, son of Eleanor's third son Geoffrey, who by right of primogeniture had a stronger claim to the English throne than John. Arthur's widowed mother, Constance of Brittany, and Eleanor despised each other, and Arthur, schooled by his mother to hate Eleanor, laid siege to the town of Mirabeau, where Eleanor was installed. Spurring the townspeople to fight, she sent a message to John for help.

He appeared with such amazing and uncharacteristic speed that Arthur of Brittany and Hugh de Lusignan were caught off guard, the town was liberated, and they were all captured.

The 22 captured knights in Mirabeau were sent to England, most of them to Corfe Castle, where John had them starved to death (although he had promised Eleanor literally not to lay a finger on them). Hugh was sent to Bristol, where, on the intercession of Isabella he was spared and finally released unharmed. When Arthur's first jailer, Hubert de Burgh, failed to carry out his orders to do away with the boy, John moved him from Falaise to Rouen, where his second jailer, William de Braose, lord of Bramber, did the job.

Apart from securing Hugh de Lusignan's release, none of those developments seem to have concerned Isabella. She continued her hold on the king's passions, particularly after his mother died in 1204 and no one else was left to urge him to act like a king. In spite of his constant attentions, after seven years of marriage Isabella, like her predecessor Hawisa, still remained childless. It was not until 1207, when she was 22 and the increasingly debauched John was 40, that she became pregnant, and on October 12, 1207 delivered the long-awaited male heir, Henry. Then, as if to make up for lost time, she quickly had four more children—Richard, destined to become king of the Romans and the richest man in the world; and three daughters, the eldest of whom, Joan, was promptly betrothed to Isabella's jilted lover Hugh de Lusignan.

Although Isabella's beauty continued to grow with the years, in 1205 John began to take mistresses again, although they received little for their efforts judging by the "expense" accounts that mirror John's various conquests from 1205 to 1214 that indicate at least eight mistresses. But if his eye had started to rove, so had Isabella's, and she began to have love affairs, at some danger to herself and at considerable peril to her lovers. One ended up hanging at the end of her bed, strangled by John's orders with the cords of the bed curtains. This violent warning did not stop her, so for a time she was placed in prison, just as her mother-in-law had once been.

While John dealt with his wife's infidelities, the French king won Normandy back and proceeded to make further inroads on John's French possessions. At home, Norman and Anglo-Saxon alike joined to make common cause against his terrible misrule. Their discontent culminated at Runnymede in 1215 with John's grudging assent to Magna Carta, which in essence returned to England the Anglo-Saxon concept of justice and began a workable system of democratic government. His terrible record as king had at least this one beneficial result.

John of course had no intention of honoring this charter of rights. He was gearing up to strike back at his rebellious subjects when, in October of 1216, after losing all the crown jewels and the much-needed gold to pay his mercenary troops which fell into the water in an attempt to cross the flooding Wash, he fell ill—partly from sheer vexation and partly from overeating—and died shortly thereafter, bequeathing his kingdom and all its problems to his nine-year-old heir Henry. Isabella was free of her unsatisfactory husband at long last, and free of all the restraints that had been placed on her.

She returned to her native Angoulême in July of 1217, where her seven-year-old daughter Joan was being brought up by her maternal grandparents and where, more importantly, Hugh de Lusignan was. At 31 she was still quite lovely, and Hugh forgave and forgot all. His betrothal to daughter Joan was immediately called off, and he finally married her mother. Unfortunately, they married without consulting her son's Regency Council in England, who confiscated all her lands and stopped her pension as dowager queen.

But Isabella had been well-schooled in deviousness by John. She announced that she would not return the now-highly-eligible seven-year-old Joan to England, unless the Council returned everything. The Council was already negotiating to marry the child off to King Alexander of Scotland to ensure peace with the Scots and Alexander would accept no substitutes. So, reluctantly, they returned most of Isabella's possessions, much to Hugh de Lusignan's delight.

Isabella settled down happily in Poitou with the man of her choice and produced eight more children—for a total of 13. Family happiness, however, was not enough for her. She had been a queen too long, and over the years her dissatisfaction with her now-humbler lot grew, bringing tragedy and disaster in its wake. She could not forget that she had been the wife of a king and mother of another, and so she started to complain to Hugh about the treatment she was receiving at the hands of the French aristocracy.

Matters came to a head in 1241 when the young King Louis IX, grandson of Philip-Augustus, decided that his younger brother Alphonse was to rule over Poitou and took him there to receive the feudal homage of his nobles. Knowing how she felt, Hugh reluctantly took Isabella to pay homage, and their tempers did not improve when they were obliged to wait three days before being summoned to the king's presence.

At that meeting Isabella found herself face to face not only with Louis but with her long-time rival, his mother Blanche of Castile, widow of Louis VIII and Dowager Queen of France. Here indeed was irony, for Blanche of Castile was the granddaughter of Eleanor of Aquitaine cast in the same fiery mold as her grandmother. She was responsible for encouraging her husband Louis to pursue not only French lands but the throne of England as well. Of all this Isabella was well aware, so her fury was doubled when King Louis and his mother ignored and humiliated her at the audience.

Boiling with rage, Isabella left, and so upset was Hugh that the following Christmas he threw down the gauntlet of defiance to the king by publicly disputing Alphonse's right to Poitou, escaping from the court before he and Isabella could be arrested. He conspired with other disaffected nobles in the south and west, including Raymond of Toulouse, widower of Joanna of England, to rebel against the French king. They needed the help of England, and thus Henry, Isabella's son by John, was drawn into their conspiracy.

Well aware that his quarrel with France had been provoked by Isabella, his English barons refused to support him, but Henry went ahead anyway, and landed in France with his own small army, mainly consisting of mercenaries. The attempt was a fiasco, for when he arrived he was faced with the considerable might of the whole French army, and his French allies were suing for peace: Raymond of Toulouse had already submitted to the French king, and Hugh de Lusignan was negotiating with him for favorable terms. Henry was forced to retreat, and as a result lost more of his French possessions as well as 40,000 pounds.

Although Isabella was pragmatic enough to forgive Hugh de Lusignan for his double dealing—since that was the only way he could retain his lands and titles—she realized she could not count on him, nor could she count on son Henry again coming to her aid. And she could not put these facts out of her mind; she decided she would act on her own when the time was right.

By the year 1243 she was 57 years old and had become fixated on her hatred. Two years later, in 1245, the French court was stunned when two royal cooks were caught trying to poison King Louis, and under torture confessed that they had been in the pay of Isabella. Louis, although he had thus far been forgiving to the rebellious Lusignans, could not overlook this, and ordered their arrest. A conspiracy does seem to have been afloat, since Isabella was warned and took flight. Hugh and his eldest son were not so lucky; they were arrested and thrown in prison, accused of complicity in the plot.

Isabella fled for sanctuary to the Abbey of Fontevraud, where her mother-in-law Eleanor was buried between her warrior husband and crusading son. A prayer at their tombs was her last recorded public act before being escorted by the abbess to a hidden, lightless room deep in the bowels of the abbey. She was safe, but at a terrible price.

Hugh and his son were finally released, since the guilty cooks were long since dead and no evidence supported the charges of complicity. They were, however, shunned by their peers, and most of Hugh's lands were confiscated. Significantly, no further effort was made to find Isabella; Louis knew that if he did find her and she were brought to trial it would mean another war with England.

The following year, 1246, Isabella died in her dark sanctuary. When she was carried out of it she was unrecognizable, her beautiful body wasted to skin and bones, her face wizened, her hair perfectly white. A sad and unnecessary end for the beauty who had been dubbed "the Helen of Europe"—and one she had brought on herself by her own folly. At first she was buried secretly, but subsequently, at the urging of Henry III, she was given a final burial beside her Plantagenet in-laws.

Behind her she had left ruin for the man she loved and for her second family, and countless continuing problems for her first family. Greedy, vain and devious she may have been, but her five children by John all did very well. Henry III, although a disastrous king for England, was within his private circle a pleasant, loving and generous man. Richard, her second son, was both clever and pleasant, and ended up as Holy Roman Emperor and the world's richest man. Little Joan "Makepeace," whom her mother had so craftily used as a pawn, was adored by her husband, Alexander II of Scotland, and greatly mourned by her Scottish subjects when she died at the early age of 28. Isabella's second daughter, another Isabella, married the powerful Emperor Frederick II of Germany, and her youngest, Eleanor, married first William Marshall, Earl of Pembroke, one of England's greatest and most able men, and then, amazingly, her brother's nemesis, Simon de Montfort, Earl of Leicester, in 1239.

Isabella's second Lusignan family were of lesser social standing, but of these—and thanks mainly to Henry III's unstinting generosity—five did well in England. Alice married John de Warenne, Earl of Surrey; William was married off to a great heiress and became Earl of Pembroke; Aymer became Bishop of Winchester—a great disaster for Winchester—and Guy and Geoffrey became rich as two of Henry's notorious "King's men." Hugh, her eldest Lusignan child, eventually inherited his father's lands in France. Of her 13 children, 11 survived and prospered, and perhaps that, in itself, is a fitting memorial.

ELEANOR OF PROVENCE
(1222–1291)

m. Henry III   1236

Children: Henry, John, EDWARD, Margaret, William, Beatrice, Edmund, Richard, Katherine

AFTER THE DEATH OF JOHN IN 1216, the English were granted some breathing space. During the long minority of the boy-king, Henry, England was ruled by able and wise regents like William Marshall, Earl of Pembroke, and Hubert de Burgh, who tried to right the wrongs done by John and cement the gains made by Magna Carta for the populace as a whole and for the barons in particular. Even when young Henry did come of age, this happy state of affairs continued for a while. Unlike his father, Henry was no womanizer, and appeared in no hurry to marry. It was not until 1235, when he was 28, that the marriage of his next-to-youngest sister, Isabella, to the Emperor Frederick II of Germany seems to have spurred him to look for a wife and provide the necessary heir to the throne.

After a flirtation with the idea of marrying Joanne of Ponthier, a Norman, his choice finally fell upon Eleanor of Provence, daughter of Raimund Berenger, Count of Provence, and of Beatrice, daughter of Thomas I of Savoy. That their queen was to be another Frenchwoman could not have come as a surprise to the English, but the idea did not please them, since so much English blood had by now been spilt in France in the continuing struggle over the king's French possessions. To Norman and Anglo-Saxon alike, any French influence was highly suspect. English subjects who thought that such a young French queen could have little impact on affairs of state were quickly disillusioned when the 14-year-old landed in Dover in January of 1236 with a huge entourage of impecunious relatives, as well as countless servants and grasping hangers-on.

Henry and Eleanor were married immediately in Canterbury Cathedral by the archbishop, and she was crowned queen a few days later in Westminster Abbey. From the very beginning, she and Henry, despite the difference in their ages, got on remarkably well. To her subjects, however, she was to become a hated queen.

Yet Queen Eleanor had a remarkable background. Tiny Provence, over which her father ruled, was a cradle of European sophistication and culture, where minstrels and troubadours held sway and where everyone devoted time to music, poetry and merrymaking. Both her father and mother were composers of note and encouraged the cultured atmosphere at court, even though they were chronically short of funds and moved constantly from one of their chateaux to another just to keep eating. They had only two tangible assets— four beautiful and cultured daughters, and an officer of the court, aptly named Romeo, who was wily enough to marry off these dowerless daughters to their tremendous advantage. All four married kings. In order of birth: Marguerite was married to King Louis IX of France; Eleanor, to Henry of England; Sanchia (as his second wife), to Richard, Earl of Cornwall, who became King of the Romans; and Beatrice to Charles, Count of Anjou, who became King of Sicily. Their father did not expend so much as a penny on any of them by way of dowry; quite the opposite—he extracted all he could from his various sons-in-law.

Eleanor's lifelong single-minded rapaciousness and greed may be due in part to this deprived childhood, during which she wore her mother's and sisters' old clothes and was besieged by financial worries and uncertainties about the future. If she had restricted her greed to her own needs, all might yet have been well, but it extended as well to all her kin, for whom she went to extraordinary lengths to ensure wealth and preferment—at the expense of her English subjects.

Her cause was helped by the tremendous power she had over the naturally generous Henry. Eleanor soon saw to it that their courtiers consisted only of her French and Italian relatives, among whom she was comfortable and well-liked, and that the English and Norman elements all but disappeared save for the immediate members of Henry's own family and a few Englishmen who toadied to the king's wishes. She despised the "uncultured" English—a feeling that was to be returned a hundredfold.

She and the devoted Henry settled down and proceeded to produce a large family: two sons, Henry and John, both of whom died as infants; then Edward, born in 1239, who was destined to balance his father's miserable rule by becoming one of England's strongest kings. After Edward came Margaret, born in 1240, who married Alexander III of Scotland; another son, William, who died in infancy; and Beatrice, born in 1242, who married John, Count of Brittany. Another son, Edmund "Crouchback," born in 1245, became his father's favorite child and was elected King of Sicily in 1254, although he never ruled there. Yet another son, Richard, died as an infant. The last child was Katherine, born in 1253. In their domestic life they were a happy and united family, as the later devotion of the children to their parents and to each other attests. Eleanor and Henry were adoring parents, as revealed in their attitude toward their youngest. Born deaf and dumb, Katherine rapidly became the family favorite. When she died in childhood, both Eleanor and Henry were physically ill with grief, and Henry ordered the tiny tomb in Westminster crowned with a life-size figure of her in solid silver.

Eleanor also encouraged her husband along the lines of his own interests, two of these being architecture and construction. By the end of his long reign, England had soaring and glorious new cathedrals, like Salisbury, and most of the old cathedrals, including Westminster Abbey, had been renovated. Similarly, he carried out vast building schemes and refurbishings on royal residences like the Tower of London, the Palace of Westminster, and Windsor Castle.

Although some of Eleanor's machinations initially had a horrendous effect, they sometimes later turned out to be to the country's good. An example is her campaign to get her favorite maternal uncle, Boniface of Bellay, elected to the Archbishopric of Canterbury. Since he did not speak a word of English and was only interested in lining his pockets with the rich revenues that went with the position, hers was a highly unpopular move, especially since he was stepping into the shoes of an Englishman, the pious Edmund Rich (shortly to be St. Edmund). But she and her uncle won their battle and were, as a result, indebted to the Pope, who immediately flooded England with his own Italian clergy. In their wake came the two orders of friars, the Franciscans and the Dominicans, who through their teaching and medical foundations raised English standards of education and health care.

Eleanor and Henry were so attached to each other that when his mother asked him to support his stepfather's rebellion against the French crown, Eleanor followed him on the disastrous campaign. Typically, instead of mending fences with their disgruntled subjects after the campaign's failure, they concentrated their efforts on the lavish wedding of Eleanor's younger sister, Sanchia, to the widowed Richard, Earl of Cornwall. Their mother Beatrice came to England for the lavish ceremony and to solicit Henry for a loan to rescue her husband Raimund from his current financial difficulties. It is recorded that the wedding guests sat down to a dinner of 30,000 dishes—paid for by exactions from the Jewish community in England, which Henry had been bleeding unmercifully for years.

Worse was to follow: After his mother's ill-advised attempt to poison the French king and the ensuing ruin of the Lusignan family, five of Henry's half-brothers and half-sisters sought refuge at the English court. Henry was delighted, Eleanor markedly less so. He proceeded to load them with honors and riches, and for the first time, lively spats developed within the royal family over the division of the spoils. On one side were the "queen's men," on the opposite the "king's men," and in the middle, the king's full brother and sisters. This inner circle had been augmented by a highly significant new member. In 1239 Henry's youngest sister, the widowed Eleanor, was married—for love—to Simon de Montfort, Earl of Leicester. Simon was from Normandy, and he allied himself strongly with the English nobles eager to curb Henry's insatiable appetites and to institute constitutional reforms. Initially, he and Henry were on amiable enough terms; Simon was one of Edmund Crouchback's godfathers at his baptism in 1245. But after the arrival of the "king's men," who were so strongly *against* de Montfort, Henry also turned against him, and to remove him from court sent him off as overlord of Gascony for a time. He proved to be a good, if rigorous ruler there, but when Henry became suspicious of his activities he decided to make a visit to Gascony with Prince Edward, and compounded the error by leaving Eleanor in charge of affairs at home.

Eleanor was so hated by this time that on one occasion when she was being ferried from the Tower to the Palace of Westminster, angry citizens lined London Bridge, pelting her with rotten eggs and vegetables, shouting "Drown the witch!" and trying to sink the royal barge with paving-stones. She was forced to seek temporary sanctuary in old St. Paul's until she could be rescued.

In 1252 Simon de Montfort resigned his overlordship of Gascony in anger and returned to England, where he took his place at the head of the baronial opposition—but still nothing came of their repeated demands for reform, largely because of the continuing support Henry received from his strong and able brother Richard, Earl of Cornwall.

Richard was a remarkable man, head and shoulders above his older brother in intelligence, ability and character. He also has a unique status among the English as a royal business tycoon. Everything he touched turned to gold. He even made money for his brother Henry. But by the 1250s his immense riches and his succession of handsome wives were no longer enough to satisfy him, and he looked around for a kingdom of his own. That kingdom lay in Germany, so he departed to become King of the Romans—having bribed his way in—with an eye to becoming the Holy Roman Emperor, and leaving Henry without his much-needed support.

In Richard's absence, Henry tried to continue his money-making schemes, but failed miserably, and the royal family was soon in desperate financial straits. Henry and Eleanor decided to economize in ways that to us seem farcical. They never cut their own standard of living or the number of their hangers-on. Instead, they cut their servants' wages and, reverting to the pattern of Eleanor's youth, flitted from castle to castle to eat at the expense of the neighboring nobility, demanding expensive presents for the honor of their company. Their nobles grew even more irritated.

In 1254 they launched into another madcap enterprise. The kingdom of Sicily, which was under the control of the Pope, was up for sale. Having tried to sell it to several other candidates (including Richard of Cornwall) with no success, the Pope, well knowing Henry's character, offered it to Edmund Crouchback, Henry's nine-year-old son, and his father's favorite. (His fiery and intelligent older son, Edward, intimidated Henry.) Henry was delighted, and surreptitiously made all sorts of promises to the Pope, offering to provide 135,000 gold marks—which he did not have—and to go himself to Sicily with an English army to fight for his son's throne.

This was the last straw so far as his barons were concerned. In 1257, after a hard winter, crop failures and famine, their resources were exhausted. They denied his requests for money, and the struggle was on. At a council that met at Oxford in June of 1258, the barons pushed through the Provisions of Oxford, which proposed a limited monarchy, with the king dependent on an advisory council and the important proviso that all aliens should be expelled.

Eleanor was furious, but Henry was forced to agree to the terms. Her Italian relatives went peaceably enough; the Provençals and the Lusignans had to be driven out by force of arms. For some barons, headed by the Earl of Gloucester, this was enough—they were rid of the hated "foreigners." But for Simon de Montfort and those in favor of reform, it was time to strike while the iron was hot, and they continued to press for more rights for the towns and for the lesser nobles. While they bickered among themselves, Henry quietly went to his old friend the Pope, who obligingly issued a bull in June of 1261 absolving Henry from the oath he had taken at Oxford. Henry then smugly announced that he had resumed his full royal powers.

A disillusioned de Montfort retreated to the Continent, and Henry, bent on revenge, followed him. Louis of France tried to reconcile them, to no avail. But illness eventually drove Henry home, where he reverted to his old patterns of rule.

By 1263 the barons realized that civil war was inevitable. They summoned de Montfort back to lead them, while Henry received some much-needed backing from Richard, who had finally decided he was never going to be accepted by his German subjects. Eleanor was sent off to the Continent with one of Henry's English toadies, John Mansel, to hire mercenary troops for the upcoming war, leaving Henry, Prince Edward and Richard to confront the opposition. Before Eleanor could return with her army, the disastrous Battle of Lewes was fought, and all three of them were captured.

It was a terrible blow for Eleanor, but she pressed on with her hiring of mercenaries, even though Henry wrote to beg her not to, because the barons had threatened to kill Prince Edward if foreign troops landed on English soil. Perhaps Eleanor had more confidence in her son's powers of survival than Henry did. There were delays due to diplomatic bickering, during which some of the mercenaries drifted away to seek more profitable fights, but eventually her fleet set out. A warrior queen she was not: Her fleet was wrecked at Sluis in Flanders during a Channel storm and she had to retreat to France.

In the meantime, Edward, in the heroic mold in which he was to continue to grow, had escaped his captors, rallied the royalists, and defeated and killed Simon de Montfort at the Battle of Evesham. The balance had tipped again. Even though de Montfort's son, Simon, escaped, his attempts to rally his father's forces were in vain, and in 1267 he too had to submit. By the Statute of Marlborough, which reaffirmed the Charters and Provisions of Oxford, the dreary civil war was at an end.

Eleanor returned from France to be reunited with her family under the firm delusion that all would be as before. But, though Simon de Montfort had lost the proverbial battle, he had won the war, and the principles of English parliamentary government had been established forever, with Magna Carta as their cornerstone.

The exhausted country become so peaceful that in 1270 Eleanor's two sons Edward and Edmund were confident enough to go on the Seventh Crusade—leaving the running of the country to Henry. Eleanor's children were all gone now: Margaret in Scotland—although, to the fury of her Scottish subjects, she came home as often as she could; Beatrice in Brittany; and the boys in the Holy Land. The court grew subdued, because the aging Henry had begun to fail in health. In February of 1271 he wrote to Edward to hurry home, because the royal physicians had given him small hope of living much longer. He spent his last days in London, where he and especially Eleanor were most hated, and died in the Tower on November 16, 1272 while the citizens of London rioted outside.

Surprisingly, as soon as Edward was back in England and crowned king, Eleanor retired to a convent in Amesbury, Wiltshire, where she took the veil and lived out the rest of life in cloistered seclusion. Her reasons are more than a little obscure because, unlike Henry, she was not overly pious. Edward certainly did not insist. Maybe, because she had been queen for so long, she could not tolerate the thought of being outshone by Edward's beloved consort, Eleanor of Castile; maybe she was just tired of the unrelenting hatred of the English people.

She outlived her daughters, both of whom died in 1275, and her daughter-in-law, who died in 1290. Eleanor of Provence died the following year, in June, and was buried beside Henry in Westminster Abbey, which he had so beautified. Her deeds as queen have overshadowed her domestic achievements—for she was one of the few who raised a loving family and remained close to her husband.

ELEANOR OF CASTILE
(1244–1290)

m. Edward I   1254

Children: *Eleanor, John, Henry, Joane, Margaret, Berengaria, Alice, Blanche, Beatrice, Alfonso, Mary, Elizabeth, Katherine, EDWARD. Only five survived childhood.*

THE WEDDING OF 10-YEAR-OLD Infanta Eleanor of Castile to the 15-year-old Edward, heir to the English throne, in October, 1254, at the monastery of Las Huelgas, was the beginning of one of the great royal romances, a *Romeo and Juliet* with a happy ending. Yet at the beginning it was simply a marriage of state, a marriage of national convenience, and it is doubtful that either of them had set eyes on the other before their wedding day.

The marriage resulted from Henry III's worry that his son's fief of Gascony was being threatened with invasion by Alfonso, King of Castile—Eleanor's older half-brother—who claimed legal title to it. Henry thought an alliance between their two houses might dissuade him. Alfonso, who had truly gained his nickname "the Wise," thought little of Henry, but was taken by the tall, handsome and lively teenager Edward. And so the marriage was arranged by the two kings, the children, as was customary, not even being consulted.

Eleanor was the daughter of King Ferdinand II of Castile, who had died in 1252, and Joanne of Ponthieu, his second wife, whom Henry III had been about to marry before his brother Richard had drawn his attention to the beautiful Eleanor of Provence. Eleanor of Castile came from a different background from her mother-in-law; she was a royal princess, daughter of a strong king, and had a hefty dowry to boot, not the least of which was that her half-brother gave up all his claims to Gascony. Not as beautiful as her predecessors, like Isabella of Angoulême, nor as cultured and educated as Eleanor of Provence, she was, nonetheless, not only to become her husband's beloved partner but England's most popular queen-consort.

She was simply good: compassionate, kind, loving, with quiet common sense. Her future influence over her dynamic husband was all for the good during their 36 years of marriage. This happy outcome was not immediately apparent, however, for no sooner was the marriage ceremony over than the bride was whisked off by her royal in-laws, to remain apart from Edward until she was mature enough for the marriage to be consummated, leaving Edward behind to look after his fief of Gascony. She was not to see him again for at least three years.

One reason for keeping Edward out of England was that Henry was already finding him an intimidating presence, being so much brighter, stronger and more forceful than his father. Initially Henry trailed the young Eleanor up to the French court to meet Louis IX and Eleanor of Provence's sister Queen Marguerite, and then, after that lengthy state visit, returned with her to England.

At first she was looked on with deep suspicion by the English. She arrived with a large coterie of Spanish attendants, but the English were reassured when they realized that these people, coming from rich Castile, were not looking for English money, but were only helping the young princess. But the whole royal family was so unpopular by this time that her advent witnessed none of the praise or demonstrations of affection that she was to earn later. Since even the chroniclers were then "shunning" the royal family, we are not even sure when the marriage was consummated—whether when Edward returned to aid his father in the Civil War of 1258, or perhaps even later. As soon as the war began, she accompanied her mother-in-law to France for safety's sake, and there remained until the successful outcome—an outcome largely resulting from her young husband's efforts.

The man she married was totally unlike his parents, to whom he was devoted. He was moral like the earlier Plantagenets. Like Henry II and his grandfather, John, he had a fiery temper and ungovernable arrogance; in his love of war and striking good looks—being very tall, handsome and well-built— he strongly resembled his great-uncle Richard I, the Lion-hearted. From whom he inherited his fine mind and strong moral principles is not obvious—certainly not from his parents or grandparents. All he seems to have inherited from his feckless father was a drooping left eyelid, which everyone said gave Henry a "sly look." Nobody dared say that about Edward.

When Eleanor married Edward, his reputation in England was not the best. He and his coterie of young nobles were notorious for their arrogance and for their oftentimes cruel hell-raising. Like most young aristocrats, he also had had his share of love affairs—again very unlike his own father. He is credited with at least one bastard son, Sir John Botecourt, later a knight of the royal household and especially favored by Edward. Similarly, even after his marriage (but possibly before its consummation) he was said to have had a brief affair with the wife of the Earl of Gloucester, and another with his cousin, Alice of Angoulême.

But once Eleanor was old enough to stand by his side, all this stopped. His recklessness disappeared, his temper moderated, his judgment became sounder. They were so much in love that she had only to utter a word of reproof and he heeded it. They could not bear to be separated, and so began the pattern that was to make up the rest of her life, as she trailed him from place to place, war to war, producing child after child in far-flung places.

If this life was hard on her, it was even harder on her children. Some historians put the number at 17, others at 15; some, dying at birth, were either never named or their names have been lost. But of the 14 we do know of, only five survived to adulthood—four girls and one boy. Eleanor's own priorities were clear, as is demonstrated by her pronouncement in 1270, when Edward was about to embark on the Seventh Crusade with his brother Edmund. By this time she had already had three children, the eldest a girl, Eleanor, and two boys, John and Henry, both sickly children, and she was again pregnant. Everyone, except Edward, was against her going with him, but she was adamant. "Nothing ought to part those whom God hath joined together. The way to heaven is as near, if not nearer, from Syria as it is from England or my native Spain." Her priority then, and always, was Edward, no matter at what cost to her or to her children.

When she arrived in the Holy Land and delivered the child, it died. But she became pregnant again almost immediately, and was again about to deliver when disaster struck. An attempt was made to kill Edward in Acre, where they were based, by a member of a fanatical sect of Assassins. He was wounded in the shoulder, and the wound rapidly became gangrenous. Eleanor would not leave his side, and when the surgeon decreed that the flesh around the wound would have to be cut away if he was to be saved, she had to be dragged sobbing and struggling from the room before the operation could be performed.

Edward survived this ordeal and she nursed him back to health, delivering another daughter, Joanne of Acre, shortly thereafter. The Crusade was nearing its end when Edward received an urgent message from his dying father to return home as quickly as possible. So they left the Holy Land with the baby. On the long trek homeward, word reached them in Sicily of the deaths of Henry III, Richard of Cornwall, and their eldest son John. That Edward's priorities were much the same as Eleanor's is evidenced from an exchange between him and the King of Sicily (who was married to Edward's maternal aunt Beatrice). King Charles was frankly amazed that Edward's grief for his old and feeble father was so much greater than that for his own first-born son. "The Lord who gave me these can give me other children" Edward replied, "but a father can never be restored."

With Henry dead they took their time returning home. Eleanor left the baby Joanne in Castile to be raised by her maternal grandmother and namesake, the Dowager Queen Joanne of Ponthieu. They spent some time in Gascony and did not arrive in England until August 2, 1274, when they were met with a delighted and tumultous welcome—as much for the now-popular Eleanor as for Edward. They were reunited with their surviving children, whom they had not seen for over four years: Eleanor (her father's favorite) and the heir to the throne, Henry.

Shortly afterwards, Edward was crowned at Westminster Abbey, where he set another precedent by having Eleanor crowned with equal honor right beside him.

While Edward labored to manage his new kingdom, Eleanor tried to settle down with her family. She liked neither the Tower nor Westminster, so their primary residence became the King's House of Henry I at Windsor, which Edward had renovated for her. Their son Henry was gravely ill. Extreme measures—some medical, some spiritual—were taken to save him, but nothing worked, and the following year he died at Merton. Eleanor was again pregnant, with daughter Margaret, born in 1275. She continued to travel with Edward, and at Kennington in 1276 had her seventh child, named after the other Spanish queen of England, Berengaria; but she lived only a year and was buried beside her two brothers at Westminster. Other daughters followed—Alice, Blanche, Beatrice—none of whom survived infancy, and then finally and to their relief, another boy, Alfonso, named for Eleanor's half-brother, the King of Castile. Having supplied another heir to the throne, Eleanor resumed producing daughters: Mary, born in 1280, Elizabeth, in 1282—both of whom lived—then Katherine, who did not. And finally, another boy, Edward, born in 1284 at Caernarvon, while his father was fighting his second war to subdue the Welsh. Four months later Alfonso died and the infant Edward became heir to the throne. In 1301 the king gave his son the title Prince of Wales, establishing the pattern for every heir to the throne since that time.

By 1285 the Celtic Welsh had been subdued, and Edward turned his attention to subduing the Celtic Scots, in-between dashing over to the Continent to defend his French possessions. On all these campaigns Eleanor went with him, leaving the infant Edward in Wales to be cared for by a Welsh nurse. In 1284 she had shipped off the four-year-old Mary to the same convent where her mother-in-law Eleanor of Provence had become a nun. Mary was destined to do the same.

Although more trouble with the Scots was brewing, 1290 started out to be an eventful year, with the family circle augmented by the arrival in England of the Spanish-raised Joanne of Acre, who looked like her mother but had her father's fiery Plantagenet temper. At five years old she had been betrothed to the son of the King of the Romans, but he had drowned in an accident, and at the age of 18 she was coming home at last to be married to England's most powerful noble, Gilbert de Clare, Earl of Gloucester, who was her father's age. The ceremony took place in London with great pomp in April of 1290. This marriage is of particular interest to many Americans, because a descendant of this union, Thomas Dudley, was an early settler and governor of Massachusetts. Through him and his children many Americans are linked to this royal line.

With the Royal marriage accomplished, Edward once more set out with Eleanor to get on with his Scottish war. On the way north he summoned a meeting of his Parliament at Clipstone in Nottinghamshire, and while he was about this business of state Eleanor remained behind at the residence of a courtier in Harby, a small village nearby. There, however, she became feverish. At first the royal physician thought little of her condition, but she rapidly grew worse and the king was hurriedly summoned to her bedside. By the time he arrived she was dying—all those births, all those travels had worn her down and she had not enough strength in her frail frame to subdue the fever. On November 28th, at the age of 46, she died in Edward's arms.

He was shattered, staying by her for two days and letting no one approach him. A note he sent at that time has survived and it says simply, "We cannot cease to love our consort now that she is dead, whom we loved so dearly when alive." He never recovered from his loss.

All thoughts of the Scottish war banished, he turned homeward to accompany her embalmed body back to London. Wherever the coffin rested for the night he decreed that a stone cross emblazoned with her likeness be built—11 in all, the last at the village of Charing in London, where a replica of the cross still stands outside Charing Cross Station. She was entombed in Westminster Abbey, where her likeness in bronze was immediately executed by the English sculptor William Torell, and placed upon the tomb. Even in death, the qualities that had so endeared her, not only to Edward but to the people of England, were apparent, for in her will she remembered everyone, down to the most menial of her servants, dowering her ladies-in-waiting, even remembering the doctors who had attended her so unsuccessfully as she made her will while she lay dying.

A chronicler of the time said of her, "To our nation she was a loving mother, the column and pillar of the whole nation"—an epitaph that brings up an interesting point. The nation may have considered her a mother, but she was not much of a mother to her own children—in contrast to that most-hated queen, Eleanor of Provence.

Eleanor of Castile was devoted to Edward, but had little love for her offspring. She could give over her baby daughter Joanne of Acre to her own mother's care without a backward glance; she could send her daughter Mary off at the age of four to be a nun. She could leave her only surviving son Edward to be brought up by a Welsh nurse. While plenty of anecdotes support Edward as a fond father to his daughters—all of whom he allowed to marry men of their choice—none show that Eleanor had any such fondness.

The daughters apparently did not suffer to much from their mother's neglect. Three had happy marriages: Eleanor married the French Duke of Bar-le-Duc; Joanne (after the death of Gilbert de Clare when she was 23) secretly married the untitled Ralph de Monthemer, but was so happy her father forgave her; Elizabeth, the youngest, married her cousin, John, Count of Holland. Only Margaret, who also married the man of her choice, John of Brabant, was miserable—her handsome, dashing husband turned out to be a hopeless womanizer.

The one on whom parental neglect left its heaviest mark was her son Edward—and for that Eleanor has to shoulder at least part of the blame for what happened later.

MARGUERITE OF FRANCE
(1282–1318)

m. Edward I   1299

Children: Thomas, Edmund, Eleanor

MARGUERITE OF FRANCE was not only obliged to follow in the footsteps of England's beloved Queen Eleanor; she was not even the French princess that the aging Edward had wanted or intended to marry—she was a last-minute substitute. She faced this impossible situation with a grace and dignity that were a tribute to her character.

She was the younger daughter of Philip the Bold and Mary of Brabant, born three years before her father's death in 1285. She was also the "ugly duckling" of an extraordinarily handsome family. Her brother, King Philip IV, aptly called "the Fair," was strikingly good-looking, as were his brothers; her older sister, Blanche, was a dazzling beauty. Marguerite was not ugly; she just paled in comparison with the rest of her family.

Edward of England had mourned his Eleanor for nine long years, and their long and happy marriage had made him dissatisfied with taking casual mistresses. He was also far from pleased with his now-teenage heir Edward, and may have been hoping for a more suitable successor. So he started looking for another wife and, as his father had done before him, for a way to keep his French possessions from being absorbed by his enemies, premier among whom was Philip the Fair, who not only had designs on them but on England itself, and who was building an invasion fleet.

His brother Edmund Crouchback had been dispatched to France as part of a diplomatic negotiating team to arrange a peace, after Edward and a Flemish force had been defeated in 1297. Edmund sent back such glowing accounts of the wit and beauty of Philip's sister Blanche that Edward, in his eagerness for this marriage, actually gave Gascony up to Philip in return for two French princesses: Blanche for himself, and Philip the Fair's young daughter Isabella, another spectacular beauty, for his son, Prince Edward.

Philip was agreeable and the treaty was drawn up. But Blanche, the spoiled darling of the French court, flatly refused to marry Edward, who was old enough to be her grandfather. She had her eye on younger and bigger game, Rudolph of Austria, who was in line to be Holy Roman Emperor—or so she thought.

Philip was in a quandary, for he was being threatened on several fronts and wanted peace with England; Edmund Crouchback was in a panic because Gascony had already been given up to Philip. As a shamefaced compromise on both sides, Blanche's name was crossed out of the treaty and Marguerite's inserted. The obviously embarrassed Philip also provided Marguerite with a huge dowry. This was a welcome bonus to Edward, whose endless wars had exhausted his funds, and with no other options open he accepted the offer.

So the 17-year-old Marguerite was shipped off to England, and on September 8, 1299 was married in Canterbury Cathedral to the 60-year-old, white-haired Edward: her dowry was delivered on the church steps.

Surprisingly, this May–November marriage turned out well for husband and wife. Edward became very fond of his young bride and she, equally devoted to him. One chronicler goes so far as to say he "doted" on her.

A week after the wedding Edward headed north to his Scottish war, leaving her behind in the Tower of London. She was already pregnant. Perhaps, by the time he returned Marguerite had learned more about his relationship with Eleanor, for on his next campaign she insisted on going along with him to Scotland.

When her time drew near though, she had the sense to retreat from the rigors of Scotland to Yorkshire, and there gave birth in 1300 to a sturdy son, Thomas of Brotherton (the progenitor of the later and powerful noble Howard family). The following year, at Woodstock Palace in Oxfordshire, she produced another healthy son, who was named after his father's brother Edmund. He was destined to be the maternal grandfather of a king of England even though he ended up on the block himself. Finally, in 1306, Marguerite produced a daughter called Eleanor, after Edward's dead queen and the favorite daughter who had died in 1298. This Eleanor outlived her father, but died in 1311 at the age of five.

As for Marguerite's headstrong sister Blanche, her husband of choice, Rudolph, had become only King of Bohemia, a minor realm, and she herself died young in 1305. Two years earlier an embattled Philip had returned Gascony to Edward. So with Marguerite, Edward had gained a large dowry and had lost no territory after all.

Although the royal pair got along well together, Marguerite could do nothing to influence him on a national scale. In the nine years between Eleanor's death and her own marriage to Edward, he had become an embittered man, and many of the less attractive traits of his youth had resurfaced. His temper had become ungovernable and he quarreled with everyone: his Church officials, his nobles, his son Edward. His bigotry had reappeared. His mother, Eleanor of Provence, had been violently anti-Semitic, and she had apparently influenced her son. In 1290 he expelled the Jews from England and confiscated all their property. His arrogance returned along with some latent cruelty—to contradict him was alone enough to bring a savage reprisal. Only on a small, personal scale could Marguerite help the poor unfortunates who fell under Edward's wrath, and there is evidence in the records of her intervention—entries such as "We pardon him at the request of our dearest consort."

Part of Edward's bad temper and frustration stemmed from his failure to unify England, Wales and Scotland. Although he had won many victories in Scotland, he had made no substantial progress. He had killed the great Scots leader William Wallace, but then was faced with the even greater Robert Bruce. In fact, his dream of a united kingdom would not come to pass for some 300 years, with the accession of a Scottish king to the English throne.

Edward was too stubborn, however, to give up, so in 1307 at the age of 68 he started off for Scotland at the head of yet another army. Marguerite, who now had the three children to consider, stayed behind with them at Northampton. But, as he marched north, Edward became weaker and weaker, and by the time the army reached Burgh-on-Sands on the border, he was dying. Marguerite, with her baby daughter, hurried to him, but before she could reach him, on July 7th, he died. Even in dying he could think only of war; his final words were, "Wrap my bones in a hammock, and have them carried before the army, so I may still lead the way to victory."

Marguerite's own feelings were summed up in a letter home to France: "When Edward died, all men died for me." As Dowager, she lived out the remaining 11 years of her life very quietly, while her niece, Isabella, became queen consort to her stepson Edward II, and the battles of Edward's and Isabella's mutual hatred began. She died at the age of 36 in 1318, and so was spared the grief of her sons' relatively early deaths: Thomas in 1338, and Edmund, murdered by her own niece Isabella, in 1330. For Marguerite there was no national grief, as there had been for Eleanor, but compared to her successor she would be remembered by her subjects as an angel of light.

ISABELLA OF FRANCE
(1292–1358)

m. Edward II   1308

Children: EDWARD, *John, Eleanor, Joan*

"THE SHE-WOLF OF FRANCE," she was called during her lifetime: She brought about her husband's murder and the ruin and death of her French sisters-in-law, for which she had no apparent motive. Ultimately, she was to cause the deaths of thousands of innocent victims in the hundred years that followed. But if one queen consort has to be singled out as having the most influence on future events, it would have to be Isabella of France.

She was one of four children born to the well-named Philip the Fair and his plump, plain, intelligent wife Joan of Navarre. In looks she took after her father and was to develop into a spectacular beauty. Born in 1292, she was at the age of seven betrothed to the 16-year-old Prince Edward, heir to the English throne, under the same treaty that sent her aunt Marguerite to England as Edward I's second queen. She was too young to leave home, so she remained at the French court, and after the marriage of both her young aunts was the only royal princess left at court. That, plus her alluring beauty, ensured that she would be fawned upon and spoiled.

Her husband-to-be succeeded to the throne in 1307. The wedding was arranged for the following year and was celebrated in the Cathedral of Boulogne in February 1308, before a very distinguished audience that included her royal father, Philip, and the Dowager Queen Marguerite, her aunt. The beautiful bride was 13, her tall and handsomely attired groom 28. Even as she sat at the wedding feast, noting his strange behavior, she must have wondered about him—for scandalous tales about him had been current even before his father's death. When on February 7th they landed at Dover, they were met by Edward's great friend Piers Gaveston, on whom Edward immediately pressed most of the jewels he had been given as a wedding present by her father. She must have realized then that all that she had heard was indeed true.

It was a disaster both to her and to England that, just as his father had resembled the strong Plantagenets, Edward II resembled the *weak* Plantagenets. In many respects he was very like his grandfather, Henry III: vain, weak, vacillating, prodigal, and susceptible to flattery, but without Henry's loving heart or religious bent. Henry had liked to build things; Edward liked to make things with his hands; neither was warlike or had the least aptitude for warfare. Like his great-grandfather John, Edward had a cruel streak and was given to practical jokes and horseplay—often at the worst possible moments. Needless to say, he did not endear himself to the people of England, and his barons were already beginning to take advantage of his weakness.

But whereas Henry III had had wise mentors in his youth and later a wife and family who loved and supported him, Edward had none of these advantages. He was a neglected child. The only mother figure he had known was the Welsh nurse who raised him, and he was terrified of his father, who in his rages would drag the boy around the room by the hair and beat him. The king had also introduced the young, impoverished and charismatic Gascon squire, Piers Gaveston, into his son's household, where the strong-minded squire established a complete physical and psychological ascendancy over the young Edward, to the scandal of the English court. Edward I at last realized his mistake and exiled Gaveston to his native Gascony, but Edward II on his accession, immediately brought him back.

This then was the situation that faced Isabella when she arrived in England. Initially the problem was solved for her by Edward's leading nobles, headed by his cousin, Thomas of Lancaster, Edmund Crouchback's son. These barons were so shocked by his conduct that they threatened to boycott the joint coronation unless Gaveston was sent away. Edward hastily agreed. But just like his great-grandfather John, he was a master at the art of deception, and not only did Gaveston attend the coronation after all; he bore the king's crown to boot.

Still, Isabella kept a smile on her face and acted with great charm and grace, becoming very popular with the English people, who thought the queen far superior to their king and who acclaimed her everywhere she went. She nevertheless wrote home to France, "I am the most miserable of wives," enumerating her woes with Gaveston.

The barons put such continual pressure on Edward that Gaveston was sent into exile four times in the next three years—returning each time. After the fourth exile he turned up unexpectedly at Windsor Castle, where they were celebrating Christmas. When Isabella protested, he treated her with open contempt. The country sided with the queen, but Edward clung to Gaveston and, although Isabella was heavily pregnant, insisted she come north with them to escape the wrath of Thomas of Lancaster and the barons. She reluctantly agreed. Edward subsequently abandoned her at Tynemouth Castle—a highly vulnerable stronghold on the Scottish border—while he went to Scarborough in Yorkshire with Gaveston to establish him in the castle there. He then set off to rally royalists to his cause. In the meantime a band of nobles raided the castle, took Gaveston, and after holding a "kangaroo court," executed him on the spot.

Edward was beside himself with grief and rage. He buried his favorite with royal honors in King's Langley, but the arbitrariness of the barons' action rebounded in his favor, and a sudden reversal of feeling was strengthened when, on the 12th of November, 1312, Isabella had her first child—a sturdy boy and the future Edward III. The country was delighted, the king was delighted and so was she. For a while it looked as if the marriage would work after all—particularly when in 1316 she produced another healthy son, John, to reinforce the line of succession. Edward was treating her with more respect and was evidently fond of his children, and she was playing her part as dutiful wife.

But this king could not stay popular for long. In 1314 he had reluctantly led yet another English army against Robert Bruce and the Scots, and had been soundly trounced at Bannockburn: His father's dream was over and Robert Bruce became King of Scotland. On top of this, conditions in England had become very bad, and Thomas of Lancaster and his supporters took advantage of circumstances to gain control over the king. Isabella was secretly pleased for not only was she fond of Thomas (her cousin through his mother), she knew he had been the chief instrument in ridding her of Gaveston. Unfortunately for England, he was just as incompetent as his cousin Edward.

She bore two more children, both girls: Eleanor at Woodstock in 1318, and Joan at the Tower of London in 1321. But by the time her last child was born trouble had renewed itself, for Edward had fallen under the spell of two new favorites, a father-and-son team of grasping nobles, the Despensers, the younger of whom became Edward's new lover. Backed by them, Edward took action against his enemies: Lancaster was brought down and executed on a charge of treason, and Edward took revenge on all the nobles who had opposed him and his favorites.

The Despensers were the last straw for Isabella. But there was a new development in her life in the shape of Roger Mortimer. In Edward's purge of the barons, Mortimer had been imprisoned in the Tower—where Isabella was still in residence after Joan's birth. She fell passionately in love with him. Mortimer escaped from the Tower—most likely with Isabella's help, since this has never been an easy feat. He went straight to the French court.

The royal couple by this time had settled into mutual hatred. As the Bishop of Winchester said at his later trial, "The king carried a knife in his hose to kill the queen, and had said that if he had no other weapon he would crush her with his teeth." The next year Isabella left for Paris, ostensibly to arrange peace with her brother Charles IV, the last surviving member of her family, who had lately succeeded to the throne and was demanding that Edward do homage for his French possessions on pain of forfeiture. Edward was glad to see her go, but did not realize that she had no intention of coming back.

Once in Paris she issued a statement. "I feel that marriage is a joining together of man and woman maintaining the undivided habit of life, and that someone has come between my husband and myself trying to break this bond. I protest that I will not return until this intruder is removed, but, discarding my marriage garment, shall assume the robes of widowhood and mourning until I can be avenged on this Pharisee." This was only half of the truth, because as soon as she and Mortimer were reunited they became lovers; circumspectly at first, but then openly.

Her brother Charles supported her. "The queen has come of her own will and may freely return when she so wishes. But if she prefers to remain in these parts, she is my sister and I refuse to expel her." His assertion is surprising in view of the havoc she had already wrought in the French royal family by an action she had taken several years before, while her father was still alive. During that time her three brothers were hale and hearty and were all married to women of junior branches of their own Capetian dynasty: Louis to Margaret of Burgundy, Philip to Joan of Burgundy, and Charles to her younger sister, Blanche of Burgundy. Why Isabella chose to act as she did is unclear—perhaps it was a response to her own misery in the early years of her marriage, or perhaps her sisters-in-law had made unkind remarks about her and her plight. But it is certain that in 1310 she wrote to her father accusing all three wives of adultery—and she named names. Philip the Fair was a proud, cruel man, and he reacted violently. He arrested and tortured the lovers and imprisoned all three royal wives. When their lovers confessed, Margaret and Blanche admitted their guilt. Both were imprisoned in Richard I's Chateau Gaillard, where Margaret died of starvation and ill-treatment. The incorrigible Blanche had a child by her jailer, and was ultimately sent to close confinement as a nun for the rest of her life. Both marriages were annulled. As for Joan, against whom nothing had been proved, she was taken back by husband Philip. Needless to say, both avowed lovers suffered singularly gruesome deaths.

But there was an added complication: Margaret had already produced a daughter, Joan, for her husband Louis, heir to the throne, and the child's true paternity was now in doubt. In order to ensure that no bastard blood should ever taint the Capetian line, and in the highly unlikely event that Joan should stand to inherit the throne, Philip invoked a long-obsolete and forgotten French law, the "Salic law," which stated that no female should inherit the throne of France. No one at the time could have foreseen or had any idea what catastrophic results this was to have for France and England.

Then a blight struck the family. Philip the Fair died in a hunting accident in 1314 at the age of 46. His son Louis, who had remarried, succeeded him, but also died untimely of pneumonia in 1316. His pregnant queen produced a son, John, after his death, but the child too died. His brother Philip the Tall, invoking the Salic law and putting aside Louis's daughter Joan, ascended the throne, but he was suffering from tuberculosis and he died of it in 1322, leaving behind only daughters. His youngest brother Charles succeeded him, and at the time Isabella moved back to the French court all *he* had was a daughter. Of all her family *she* was the only one who had a sturdy and almost-grown son, Edward. Why should he not reign in both England and France? If Charles died without producing a son, the next in line would be their cousin, Philip of Valois, but he was not a Capetian; she was—and through her she thought, Edward had a valid claim. But first she had to bring him to France.

Somehow she inveigled Edward II, who was understandably loath to come himself, into letting the young prince come alone to to make homage to her brother for his father's French possessions. She bedazzled the young prince with all the glory of the French court: undoubtedly, in private she must have broached her grander idea to him. She pointed out that first they would have to establish him firmly on the throne of England.

Edward, of similar intelligence and ambition to his strong grandfather, Edward I, was well aware of his father's many failings, and at this juncture turned a blind eye to his mother's. He went along with her plans to invade England. She knew the English would never tolerate a French army, so her brother could only give her covert financial help: She had to hire an army of mercenaries. Off she set with Mortimer and Edward to the Low Countries, where, with the help of John of Hainaut (Edward was then betrothed to his niece Philippa), she raised forces from all parts of the Low Countries and Germany, who were joined by all the English refugee nobles in France. It was probably the high point of her life; for in the execution of her plan she was dynamic, charming—and successful.

On September 24, 1326, she landed with her army in Suffolk, and the English flocked to her banner, headed by her Aunt Marguerite's sons, the king's half-brothers, Thomas of Brotherton and Edmund of Woodstock. The king did not stand a chance. On November 16th he was captured in Wales with the small band of people who had remained faithful to him, and first imprisoned in Llantrissant Castle, later to be removed to Kenilworth, and finally to Berkeley Castle. The two Despensers were quickly dispatched, the elder by hanging, the younger by castration and burning. Isabella was in control, the king was deposed, and her 15-year-old son was crowned king on January 29, 1327 at Westminster Abbey, with Isabella as unofficial regent and her lover Mortimer at her side as chief minister.

But as long as her husband lived she knew he would be a constant potential threat to all her plans, so she conspired with Mortimer to have him murdered. The murder had to be "perfect"—indeed it set the pattern for all later royal assassinations, in that the body would show no marks of violence and death would appear to have been natural. The murderers first tried imprisoning Edward over a charnel house, hoping that the stench of decomposing bodies would kill him; it didn't. They then proceeded to more awful and direct means. On the night of September 21, 1327, a band of assassins entered his cell with a red hot poker which was inserted through a horn into his anus, burning out his entrails. There was not a mark on the body when the Abbot of Glastonbury arrived to accompany it for burial in Gloucester. Too many people in the castle and neighboring village had heard the agonized screams of the dying king, however; the whole country soon knew it was murder, and although there was an initial revulsion of feeling, the late king was only really mourned by the Welsh, whose first prince he had been.

Whether Edward III knew anything of the assassination plot is a moot point; the 15-year-old was in no position to oppose his mother. She in turn was somewhat concerned about his possible reaction, and deliberately kept him busy. First she sent him to fight the Scots—a humiliating experience for him since he was soundly beaten and obliged to retreat to York. Isabella had also sent for Philippa of Hainaut, and on January 24, 1328 Edward was married in York Minster to the 14-year-old Philippa, who had only been in the country a month but whom the people of English were already acclaiming with enthusiasm.

Mortimer, who was every bit as grasping and arrogant as the two Despensers had been, was becoming a problem to Edward. He was treating the young king as an equal, and acting more and more like a king himself. The besotted Isabella did not see the danger signals. What was of more concern to her was that her brother Charles had died on February 1, 1328 without male issue, so that his cousin Philip of Valois had come to the throne. The time was too soon for her to advance her son's claims—Mortimer had drained her of resources and perhaps slowed the drive to continue with her grand design, which would have to be accomplished with force of arms.

At the same time Edward had become convinced that something drastic had to be done about Mortimer and his assumption of power. In March of 1328 Mortimer had had the harmless Edmund of Woodstock, Earl of Kent, arrested and executed in particularly inhumane conditions. Edmund, although he had initially supported his cousin Isabella's invasion, had his half-brother Edward's fate very much on his conscience, and at this late date had agitated for a search to find out the truth of the matter. This was his only crime, and though he was not a popular figure, the country was horrified by Mortimer's cruel high-handedness.

The birth of his own first son Edward on June 15th—a child ironically destined to marry the daughter of the unfortunate Edmund—strengthened Edward's resolve to act. He was now 18, and a very mature 18 at that, and was more than ready to take over the reins of power. As throughout his long life, he did nothing precipitately but laid his plans with great care.

It was arranged that on the night of October 19, 1330, a small band of his knights led by his friend William of Montacute, using a secret passage, would enter Nottingham Castle, where he himself was being kept almost in isolation by his apprehensive mother and Mortimer. Edward joined the party but stayed outside when they entered his mother's chamber to drag the naked Mortimer from her bed and place him under arrest. Isabella knew that no one but her son would have dared make this move in a castle full of Mortimer's men, and she cried, "Fair son, have pity on gentle Mortimer!"

Mortimer may have been gentle with Isabella but he had been far from gentle with the rest of her kingdom, and her frantic appeal went unheeded. He was promptly shipped to London, imprisoned in the Tower, and swiftly tried and condemned for a long list of misdeeds. He was hanged, drawn and quartered at Tyburn like any common criminal. Through all the proceedings Edward had been very careful to keep his mother's name out of the discussion.

With the death of Mortimer, all the heart and spirit went out of Isabella. When Edward decreed that her royal residence should be the isolated Castle Rising in East Anglia, and that she be removed from affairs of state and the royal court, she made no protest. There her son lavished her with every luxury, insisted that she be treated with royal honors, and would visit her two or three times a year by himself, even occasionally allowing her to attend private gatherings of his fast-growing family at Windsor.

These visits bring up an interesting point: What was the bond that kept Edward coming to see her? Was it love, duty, compassion (a quality for which he was not noted), or guilt, because he was partly to blame for her crimes? The records are curiously blank on this mother–son relationship.

Certainly Isabella does not seem to have been much concerned about her other children: John, who died a bachelor at the age of 20; little Joan, who was shipped off to the Scottish court at the age of seven, after Edward's ignominious defeat, to be brought up there as the bride of five-year-old David Bruce, destined to be its king; and Eleanor, whose unhappy childhood left permanent scars and who was miserable in her marriage to Raynald, Duke of Gueldres. But Edward was a special case. She was fiercely ambitious for him, concentrated her attention on him, saw that he had a fine education and that he married the woman of his choice—but whether this was done out of love or was merely an adjunct to her own ambition it is now impossible to say.

During the long years she spent at Castle Rising, she saw the opening rounds of the terrible war with France that her ambition had planted so firmly in her son's mind. Edward, fighting brilliantly, winning battle after battle for England—Sluys in 1340, Crécy 1346, the defeat of France's allies the Scots at Neville's Cross in 1346, the capture of Calais in 1347, and Poitiers in 1356—but never having the men or the resources to follow up these victories and gain the object of his single-minded quest: the crown of France.

Towards the end of her long life she gave up her isolated royal splendor and joined the order of the Poor Clares, an offshoot of the Franciscans, and when she died on August 28, 1358 at the age of 66, her last request was to be buried in her nun's habit in the church of the Greyfriars at Newgate in London. This was a church built by her Aunt Marguerite, who also had been buried there. Thus she eschewed the right to be buried in the Abbey, where her husband Edward lay beside his beloved Eleanor.

Isabella made another astounding request—that the heart of Edward II, her murdered husband, be buried with her. There has been much speculation, much of it hostile, about this request, but perhaps there is a very simple explanation. In life, despite all her beauty and charm, she had never succeeded in capturing Edward's wayward heart; in death she would have it forever.

To her posterity and to her adopted and native countries she left the most terrible bequest possible: the Hundred Years' War.

PHILIPPA OF HAINAUT
(1314–1369)

m. Edward III   1328

Children: *Edward, William, Isabella, Joanna, Blanche, Lionel, John, Edmund, Mary, Margaret, Thomas*

At the outset of her marriage, England's first Flemish queen had much cause for self-congratulation, since, of the four flaxen-haired, blue-eyed, rosy-cheeked daughters of Count William of Hainaut, she was the choice of young Prince Edward of England. He had been obliged to choose one of them, for his mother desperately needed the help of Count William in raising her mercenary army of invasion to help dethrone her unsatisfactory husband and put her teenage son on the throne. It turned out to be a good choice, both for him and for England.

After a brief courtship and betrothal—Philippa was then 12—Edward and his mother Isabella returned to England, leaving her behind. Their cause was successful: the 14-year-old Edward was crowned in January of 1327, and Philippa thus became the future queen. She was not summoned to England, however, until the end of that year, when Isabella, anxious to take her son's mind off his father's murder, was suddenly eager to see him wed. Philippa and her train of Flemish knights and ladies-in-waiting were a welcome sight to the English after the enormous (and often greedy) retinues of former queens. They warmed to her even more when most of the rich Flemings, having seen the young bride well received, went back home again.

Philippa had to trek all the way to York to meet her husband-to-be, who was still smarting from his recent humiliating defeat at the hands of the Scots. They were married in York Minster on January 24, 1328. From the first, the young couple appeared to get along extremely well. Philippa immediately settled down to the most important task of any queen consort, the provision of heirs; she was to eventually produce a total of six sons and five daughters, only two of whom, her second son and third daughter, died in infancy—a remarkable record for the age.

The birth of their first son and heir, Edward, on June 15, 1330 was one of the spurs that the now-18-year-old Edward needed to make his move against his mother Isabella and her lover Mortimer. In October he carried out his plan, and by the end of that year Mortimer was dead and Isabella forever removed from court circles and affairs of state. Now Philippa came into her own and was truly the queen.

To her subjects she may have seemed somewhat colorless, after the beautiful and strong-willed Isabella, but she had a good mind allied with considerable personal courage and good sense. Like so many of her queenly predecessors, she trailed behind her husband on his endless military campaigns. This turned out to be another almost full-time job, particularly after 1338, when Edward, at last realizing his mother's and his own dream, made his bid for the French throne and began the long agony of the Hundred Years' War. Already Philippa had accompanied him on his Scottish campaigns of 1332 and 1333, where he had avenged himself on the Scots. By the age of 22 he had accomplished more than his grandfather Edward I ever had. During these campaigns she produced William, who died; Isabella in 1332; Joanna in 1333; and another girl, Blanche, who also died.

Philippa was with Edward on his first unsuccessful foray into France in 1338, when she gave birth in Antwerp to her third son, Lionel—destined to be her favorite child and the "gentle giant" of an otherwise combative family—he grew to be almost seven feet tall. She was with Edward again when the tide swung in England's favor, and gave birth in 1340 at Gaunt (Ghent) to her fourth son, John, the most ambitious and devious of her children and the one most like his father in looks and character. The following year, having returned to England to keep an eye on the households of her five young children, whom she could scarcely take along with her, she gave birth at King's Langley to her fifth son, Edmund.

Then, after all his martial successes, Edward ran out of money to follow up on his French conquest—a recurring theme in this endless war—and had to return to England. Daughter Mary was born during this time of peace, in 1344, but by the following year they were back on the Continent with new allies. At Crécy in August of 1346, Edward, accompanied by his 16-year-old heir Edward, the Black Prince, soundly trounced the French and began his lengthy siege of the port of Calais, which, being the closest French port to England, was of vital importance to him. Philippa, again pregnant, had stayed in England, but suddenly was called upon to take a martial role herself.

King David of Scotland, who had allied himself with the French, invaded England to help the beleaguered French king, hoping to draw Edward back home to meet this new threat. The plan failed for Edward had enough confidence in his wife to have her lead his army. Off she set with an army of 30,000 men headed by the northern barons and the Archbishop of York to Newcastle, and was there at Neville's Cross near Durham when the two armies joined battle. The Scots were defeated and David captured by a humble squire, Sir John Copeland. But when she demanded that the royal captive (who, after all, was married to Edward's younger sister Joan) be treated gently and handed over to her, the reply was "I will not give up my prisoner save to my lord, the king. The queen may depend on me to take good care of him."

Philippa sent posthaste to Edward (still besieging Calais). Copeland, who had imprisoned David in Bamborough Castle, was sent for by Edward, congratulated, rewarded and ordered to "return to England and take the King of Scots to my honored wife"—a duty Copeland carried out with profuse apologies. She did see that David was sent to the Tower of London, but it was a very lenient imprisonment, for he was joined by his wife Joan, and during 11 years they spent there they even participated in court functions in London.

Her battle won, Philippa set off again to be with Edward, and arrived just in time to take part in another dramatic incident—one which is, perhaps, the most famous example of her influence over her husband. Edward had finally managed to take Calais, but at great cost, and he was in a towering Plantagenet rage at its leading citizens, the six chief burghers of whom he was determined to execute. Philippa could see no sense in such an action, so, heavily pregnant though she was, she fell on her knees before him, weeping, and said, "Gentle sir, since I have crossed the sea with great danger to see you I have never asked you one favor. Now I most humbly ask as a gift to the Son of the Blessed Mary and for your love of me that you will be merciful to these six men."

The king just looked at her in silence for a while and then said with a sigh, "Ah, lady, I wish you had been anywhere else than here. You have entreated me in such a manner that I cannot refuse you, I therefore give them to you to do with as you please."

Five of the six burghers subsequently pledged allegiance to England and had all their possessions restored to them. The sixth refused and went into exile, so, with a fine sense of thrift, Philippa kept all his possessions herself.

Shortly after this episode she gave birth to her last daughter, Margaret, in 1347, and, with the Truce of Calais (Edward had again run out of money) the same year, peace was restored for almost a decade, although skirmishes continued. Philippa produced no more children during this time, and it was not until the war began heating up again in 1355 that she produced at Woodstock Palace her sixth son and last child, Thomas, Duke of Gloucester—ultimately the most unpleasant member of her large family. She was 41 years old.

Even when her long years of childbearing were through, life did not become easier for Philippa, as she had to cope with the increasing failings of her husband. Although Edward had inherited many of the virtues of the strong Plantagenets, he had also inherited some of the vices of the weak ones. Unlike his grandfather Edward I, whom he so strongly resembled in physique and who had been both faithful and thrifty, Edward was increasingly unfaithful and prodigal. He spent the vast revenues of the Crown and the equally vast booty acquired in the war, as well as borrowing heavily from Italian money-lenders. These monies went not only to fund his wars but also to fund a fantastically extravagant life-style. A case in point was his treatment of his eldest daughter Isabella, who from babyhood was as strikingly beautiful as her paternal grandmother and namesake, and of similar character, and on whom Edward doted. The household he set up for her was of a luxury verging on the absurd—gold cradles, jewel- encrusted clothing, and—as she grew up—any luxury her heart desired. On only a slightly lesser scale, he catered to her younger sisters Joanna, Mary and Margaret. Philippa hardly objected to living in the lap of luxury—after all, she had grown up in very pleasant and richly comfortable surroundings in Hainaut. In fact, she did much to "modernize" the royal palaces she favored, like Windsor, making them comfortable for family living.

Her husband's aspirations to the throne of France had a sad effect on her daughters' marriages, particularly those of her two oldest daughters, Isabella and Joanna, whose checkered matrimonial careers can be directly attributed to the fluctuating fortunes of the war. Isabella was first betrothed to Louis, son of the Count of Flanders, as Edward wanted to cement an alliance with the Low Countries. The Low Countries had other ideas, however, and Louis broke the engagement. Isabella herself then fancied a Gascon noble, but this alliance too was broken after a quarrel about his doubtful allegiance to the English cause. Finally, at the advanced age of 33, she fell in love with a French nobleman, Ingeram de Coucy, who was being held hostage in England. Since her father could deny her nothing, they were married with great pomp at Windsor in 1365. They were happy at first, and she had two daughters, Mary and Philippa; but when the war started again her husband decided to return to his allegiance to the French king. As the chronicler Froissart relates, she returned to England and "died of grief."

Joanna was even less fortunate. In 1338 at the age of five she had been shipped off to Austria as the affianced bride of Frederick of Austria, to be raised at the Austrian court. Then Austria decided to join France, and with considerable difficulty the poor child had to be rescued and brought home to England.

At the age of 13 in 1346 she was betrothed to another ally, Pedro, heir to the Castilian throne, and on January 9, 1349 set out for Gascony and the long trip south. But this was the year the Black Death swept across Europe, and Joanna was one of its first victims. She was deeply mourned by her family. The quiet and gentle Mary was married off to yet another ally, John de Montfort, heir to the duchy of Brittany, but in 1361 died only seven months after the wedding, of encephalitis; she was 17. In the same year her younger sister Margaret, who had been allowed to marry the man she loved, John, Earl of Hastings and Pembroke, died in childbed at the age of 16.

Ironically, all Philippa's sons—with one notable and important exception—made influential marriages from which they profited greatly. The one exception brought great grief to both Edward and Philippa, for it concerned Edward, the Black Prince, heir to the throne. Like Richard I, he was far more interested in war than in marriage, and in his early years had had many affairs and had produced at least two bastard sons, Sir Roger de Clarendon and John de Galeis; but at 30 he fell deeply in love, and insisted, in spite of all opposition, on marrying Joan, "the Fair Maid of Kent," daughter of the unfortunate Edmund, Duke of Kent, son of Edward I and Marguerite of France.

Though "fair" she was, Joan was far from being a maid, having been married twice (bigamously) and already having two sons. She was older than Edward and her reputation was far from spotless. His parents, who had hoped for a great marriage for their warrior son, were heartbroken. Joan tried hard to live down her dubious image and quickly bore him two sons—Edward, who died young, and Richard, who now, after his father, became Edward III's next heir. His ambitious uncles were not pleased.

Faced with increasing strife in the family ranks and depressed by her series of losses, Philippa did not accompany Edward when the war started again. Unlike Edward, she was feeling her age, and by 1367 was afflicted by a then-incurable disease: dropsy. That year saw two further blows: the overseas death of her best-loved son, the amiable Lionel, and the traumatic news that Edward, the Black Prince, was seriously ill. She became so weak that she could not move from her couch, and so lingered on for two more years.

In August of 1369 she felt she was dying, and sent for her husband, who luckily was in England. Of the rest, all her daughters and Lionel were dead; Edward, John and Edmund were off at the wars. Only her youngest son, the dark and brooding teenager Thomas of Woodstock, was at home with her.

Edward hurried to her bedside. He had reason to feel guilty, since his habit of recent years had been to choose his mistresses from among Philippa's ladies-in-waiting; his current favorite, Alice Perrers, had already had two daughters and a son by him. That Philippa was aware of this situation is suggested by her will, in which she left money to all her ladies *except* Alice. She even tried as she lay dying to save her jewels from Alice by giving them to another lady-in-waiting, Euphemia. This effort was in vain: Alice received them anyway.

The last meeting between husband and wife was poignant. Philippa did not wish him to see how bloated she had become, so received him covered up to the chin, with only one hand outside the covers. When he knelt by her bed she made three humble requests: payment of her debts, the fulfillment of the legacies in her will, and a wish that he be buried beside her in the cloisters of Westminster when he died.

"All this shall be done," he assured her, and she made the sign of the cross and died.

Despite his continuing infatuation with Alice Perrers, Edward quickly declined after Philippa's death. He became gray-faced and stooped, with little energy, increasing moodiness and a tendency to overeat and overimbibe to the neglect of affairs of state. After the further blow of the Black Prince's death (probably of cancer) and the realization that his favorite son, John of Gaunt, on whom he now depended for his continued military success, was not and never would be the equal of his dead brother, the king became prematurely senile. For a terrible interregnum, until John of Gaunt abandoned his overseas ambitions and returned home to take charge, the country was virtually in the hands of Alice Perrers and her cronies.

Edward paid a heavy price for his infatuation. His remaining sons turned against him, and when he died in the Palace of Sheen in 1377 he was attended only by his confessor; even Alice had deserted him, taking with her all his personal jewelry. He was buried, as Philippa had wished, beside her in Westminster Abbey.

Ironically, Philippa's great success as a wife and mother was also to cause great grief for England. From her many sons were to come the seeds of dissension that would lead to the disastrous "War of the Roses" between the descendants of John of Lancaster and those of Edmund of York, and to the final overthrow of the Plantagenet line.

Yet posterity owes her a great debt in that Philippa was a great patron of the arts—particularly of writing. She encouraged English writers like Geoffrey Chaucer to write in the English tongue, and perhaps even more importantly, employed a young writer named Froissart, who may be called the first reporter.

Attached to her household and accompanying her everywhere she went, he faithfully chronicled all the events, great and small, that happened in the royal circle, as an eyewitness. This is the reason we have such a vivid picture of this portion of England's history and such intimate glimpses of royal life. It is small wonder that through his pen Philippa appears in such a complimentary light—she deserved it.

ANNE OF BOHEMIA
(1366–1394)

m. Richard II   1382

No issue

DAUGHTER OF THE POWERFUL Wenceslas of Bohemia, who had become Holy Roman Emperor under the name of Charles, and his fourth wife, Elizabeth of Saxony, Anne was only 12 when her father died in 1378 and her half-brother Wenceslas succeeded to the throne of Bohemia. Tall, willowy and fair, nevertheless she was not considered beautiful. She was, however, very well educated and highly cultured and had an irresistible personal magnetism that was early noted and exploited by her brother. Already she had been sought by Charles V of France—an ally of her father's—for his young heir and namesake, but this match Wenceslas regretfully turned down because of political complications arising from the Avignon Papacy and Bohemia's firmer ties with the Roman Papacy.

At this juncture there arrived in Prague Sir Simon Burley, seeking a wife for the teenage Richard II of England, whose tutor he had been—and he fell completely under Anne's spell. He sent such glowing reports back to the young king that Richard insisted the marriage be arranged. Although France and England had technically been at peace since 1375, England was still "the enemy," so Anne's uncle, Duke Primislaus of Saxony, was sent to England to test the waters. When he reported back favorably to his sister Elizabeth, the Dowager Empress, Anne wrote a letter to Richard's Regency Council stating that she agreed "with full and free will" to become his wife.

The Bohemian negotiators of the marriage contract drove a hard bargain: Not only was there to be no dowry, but Richard had to pay Wenceslas 10,000 marks and all the expenses of her trip to England. The alliance would help England with its much-needed continental trade, so the stiff terms were agreed upon, though the news of it did not sit well with the English people. They were worn out from the long wars, and the peasantry was in a state of rebellious discontent. Indeed, the outbreak of the Peasants' Revolt in 1381 led to a postponement of the marriage, and Anne did not actually set out with her huge train of escorts until she had turned 15 a few months before Richard.

Still determined that she should wed his 11-year-old heir, Charles V of France was set to kidnap her in the English Channel and carry her off to his court. Her powerful uncles protested this move so vigorously that the ailing Charles called off his plans. "So be it," he said. "I shall order my vessels back to port. I do this out of love for my cousin Anne and not out of regard for the king of England."

She sailed out of English Calais and arrived in Dover the same day, December 18, 1381. After she landed, a storm hit Dover and most of the ships accompanying her, including the one she had sailed in, were sunk. To recover from this shock, she stayed three days in Dover, where Richard came to greet her. They were of such similar tastes and interests that there was an immediate liking between them, which was to deepen into love—on his part into complete adoration, equaled only by Edward I's love for his Eleanor. They proceeded to Canterbury, where they were met by the surly Thomas of Woodstock, Duke of Gloucester, who secretly loathed his nephew, and then to London, where they were wed on January 14, 1382 in St. Stephen's Chapel. Anne was crowned alone at Westminster Abbey a week later. So depleted were his resources that Richard had to pawn the jewels of Eleanor of Aquitaine to pay for the magnificent ceremony.

The citizens of London viewed with horror the large retinue of Bohemians the queen had brought with her; even when her main escort returned home after the ceremony a considerable number remained. However, Anne, whose undoubted charm was her strong point, soon won them over. She interceded vigorously for the peasants, against whom merciless retaliations were being carried out, and soon after the coronation a general amnesty was granted—with the result that the common people were shortly calling her "Good Queen Anne."

Her charm had an equal impact on her mother-in-law, Joan of Kent, who, once she saw that her only son was well pleased and that Anne was a good influence on him, lessened her own hold over him and even yielded up some of her holdings to the young queen.

The teenagers settled down to an idyllic and extravagant existence—for Richard, like his grandfather Edward III, was prodigal and even more of a peacock when it came to personal adornment than his great-grandfather Edward II. Anne conceived a preference for the spacious Palace of Sheen, where they settled, surrounding themselves with beauty and luxury. Their annual expenditures were fantastic: for food and drink alone, 18,000 pounds; for their wardrobes (including the servants' salaries), 15,000 pounds, with another 9,000 pounds going to their personal attendants. This at a time when the average wage in England was about five pounds a year. Thus the young couple disported in their own Garden of Eden, only dimly aware of the host of wily serpents gathering outside.

Anne was brought face to face with the cold reality that her husband was not in control and that their Garden of Eden was mere illusion in May 1388, when the "Merciless Parliament," led by barons headed by Richard's uncle and enemy Thomas of Gloucester and his cronies, the Earls of Arundel, Warwick, Nottingham and Derby (John of Gaunt's eldest son), accused and condemned as traitors four of Richard and Anne's favorites—Robert, Earl of Oxford; Michael, Earl of Suffolk; Sir Nicholas Brember, Lord Mayor of London; and— worst of all—Sir Simon Burley, who had brought them together and to whom they were both devoted. Many of the charges against the four were ridiculous, but some were taken seriously—namely, that they had manipulated the king against his barons; that they had encouraged his prodigality; and that they had committed treason by favoring peace with France. The accused were sentenced to be hung, drawn and quartered like commoners.

The desperate couple hurried to Woodstock Palace to Burley's chief enemy Lord Arundel to plead for his life. Anne went down on her knees to Arundel and remained there pleading for three hours—to no avail. The only answer she received was a veiled threat. "Let the request alone, Madame Queen. Pray for yourself and your husband. That is the best thing you can do." When they returned to the Duke of Gloucester, his reply to Richard was, "If you wish to be king, Burley must suffer." The only concession they could gain was that Burley should be beheaded, not hung, drawn and quartered. The brave old knight was executed that same afternoon, his only guilt being that he had loved his young charges too well.

At that time Richard was helpless to retaliate, but he neither forgot nor forgave, although, as long as Anne was beside him, he went about his revenge with intelligence and moderation. In May of the next year, 1389, he made his first move when, at the meeting of his Council of Regents, which included all the people who had been involved in the death of his friends, he turned to his uncle Gloucester and demanded, "How old do you think I am?"

"You are in your twenty-second year," Thomas of Woodstock replied.

"Then I am surely old enough to manage my own affairs. I have been longer under the control of guardians than any other heir in England, so I thank you, my lords, for your past services, but I need them no longer." He then demanded the Great Seal of England, which, perforce, they yielded to him and which he promptly handed over to William of Wykeham, the wise Bishop of Winchester. He then dismissed them all.

They had no recourse to this neat *coup d'état* short of open rebellion, and none of them was ready for such extremes. Richard quickly followed up by making a three-year truce with France, Scotland and Spain, actually achieving peace for eight years, thus leaving himself free to pursue his revenge quietly without outside considerations.

He was helped by the return of his oldest uncle, John of Gaunt, who had finally given up his attempts to gain the Castilian throne for himself and who disliked Gloucester and his friends as much as Richard did. Gaunt wisely urged his eldest son, Henry Bolingbroke, Earl of Derby, to go on a crusade against the Muslims; this would keep him safely out of harm's way. Anne continued her role of moderating Richard's fiery Plantagenet temper, as in 1393 when, after the city of London had enraged him by refusing to loan him money, Richard had threatened it with dire punishment, and she had intervened so that he pardoned the city.

In the following year, disaster struck. On June 7th, after a sickness of only two days, Anne suddenly died at the age of 28 at the Palace of Sheen. The cause is a puzzle, because no plague was circulating at the time and she was too well liked for anybody to want to poison her. Richard, who was with her when she died, was devastated. At first he could not bear to part with her even after death, and for two months, while he planned the most elaborate funeral England had ever seen, he kept her body with him in the palace where they had been so intensely happy. When the cortege set out, he ordered that the palace be razed to the ground. The order was not carried out, but he never set foot in it again.

At the funeral, to which all his barons had been summoned, all the old hatreds flared. The Earl of Arundel arrived pointedly late for the funeral service and then compounded the insult by asking to leave early "because of matters of importance." Richard completely lost control. Snatching a baton from an attendant, he felled Arundel with a single blow, then ordered that the earl, streaming with blood, be removed to the Tower. That area of the Abbey had to be cleansed and purified before the service could be finished. He kept Arundel imprisoned for a week and liberated him only after he had made a public (and grudging) apology.

The year 1394 was a bad one for royal wives. Not only did Anne die but so did John of Gaunt's unlamented second wife, Constance of Castile, and Henry Bolingbroke's first wife, Mary de Bohun. All of these deaths had repercussions on future events.

Anne had given Richard domestic happiness, but she had not given him an heir. Not only did she not have a child; there was never any sign of a pregnancy during their 12 years of marriage. Her death also removed the only effective moderating influence Richard had ever known, and from then on his own unfortunate and weaker instincts held sway. In the end, his failings would cause him to lose both his crown and his life.

ISABELLA OF FRANCE
(1389–1410)

m. Richard II 1396

No issue

THERE HAVE BEEN WIVES OF ENGLISH KINGS who were never crowned queen—like Berengaria of Navarre—but little Isabella is the only case of an English queen who was never actually a wife. Yet her betrothal opened a new era in Anglo-French relations, and her own attractive self led to a disastrous series of events for the Plantagenets.

Born in 1389 to Charles VI of France and Isabeau of Bavaria, she was the family favorite and the most like her mother, being black-eyed and fair-skinned. She was only three when her father had his first bout with insanity. This hereditary insanity (through Charles's mother, Joan of Bourbon) was to recur, drastically affecting the family. Her mother, Isabeau, started to take lovers, including Louis, Duke of Orleans, her husband's brother, and to neglect her young family.

Into this situation came the Earl of Nottingham, Marshal of England, seeking a second wife for Richard II. It was not that Richard, who would never cease to mourn his beloved Anne, *wanted* a wife—but, lacking a direct heir, he knew he would have no peace with his barons until he remarried, and so he was looking for a child bride with whom there could be no possibility of a real marriage for years. He also wanted to consolidate the peace he had established with France—hence the mission of Nottingham.

Isabella must have been a very precocious seven-year-old, for when interviewed by Nottingham she said, "Sir, if it please God and my lord the king that I be Queen of England, I shall be pleased thereat, for I have been told I shall then be a great lady." She was married by proxy, and the marriage contract, signed on March 9, 1396, included a 28-year truce between France and England. It did, however, have some provisions that would enrage the English, like the surrender of Cherbourg and Brest to France and the renunciation by Richard of all claims to the throne of France for Isabella's children. As an emollient, Isabella brought an enormous dowry of 800,000 francs, and the agreement that she was not to have any French entourage or attendants but would be brought up "as an Englishwoman."

Richard crossed to France, and the two kings met on October 27, 1396, with much display on both sides—particularly Richard's. When he met Isabella for the first time the next day she was, though so young, very impressed, being a materialist like her mother. The marriage took place on November 4th at the Church of St. Nicholas at Calais, and at a cost of 200,000 English pounds was an affair that impressed her even more.

Windsor Castle was designated as her home, and there the seven-year-old was taken to begin her English education. She was fortunate in immediately finding a friend in Katherine Swynford, John of Gaunt's third wife. Katherine, who was evidently good with children, was a remarkable and intelligent woman. Widow of a knight in John of Gaunt's household, she had gone on to be governess of his motherless children after the death of his first wife, Blanche of Lancaster, and his second ill-destined marriage to Constance of Castile. She had also become his mistress during this second marriage, and had borne him four children, three sons and a daughter, all given the name of Beaufort. In an unusually shrewd move on Richard's part, he not only welcomed their eventual marriage in 1396, but early in 1397 declared the four Beauforts "legitimate," both insuring John of Gaunt's friendship and endearing himself to Katherine.

But while Isabella learned her English lessons and played in the gardens of Windsor, Richard was advancing inexorably down the path to self-destruction. The sight of the French king's absolute power at their meeting during the marriage had brought to the surface all his arrogance. Increasingly he ignored his Parliament and assumed greater power. The year after the marriage he moved against three more of the men who had brought about Burley's death and had insulted his beloved Anne: His uncle Gloucester was seized and shipped off to Calais, where he "died" in prison. Arundel was executed and Warwick banished for life to the Isle of Man. The two remaining Lords Appellant, Derby and Nottingham, who had apparently sided with Richard, were made, respectively, Dukes of Hereford and Norfolk. But Richard had neither forgotten nor forgiven them, and in 1398, after a falling-out between the two dukes, he banished Norfolk for life and Hereford for 10 years, punishing with heavy fines the 17 counties that had supported them and the other Lords Appellant, his former overseers. In 1399, on the death of John of Gaunt, his last steadying influence, Richard confiscated for his own use all the estates that should have gone to Henry Bolingbroke, Duke of Hereford, as Gaunt's eldest son.

None of these events was apparent to or concerned the child Isabella, who looked forward eagerly to his frequent, present-laden visits to Windsor and who was very fond of him. At his last visit to her in 1399, with a gold crown he had given her on her small head, she presented prizes at a tournament at Windsor. Their final meeting was at Windsor Chapel, where they heard Mass together and shared a glass of wine at the church door. Then Richard lifted her up, kissed her repeatedly, and said "Adieu, madame, until we meet again." In May of that year Richard set sail for Ireland to avenge the death of his cousin and heir, Roger Mortimer, Earl of March, the grandson of Edward III's third son, Lionel of Antwerp. As Lord-Lieutenant of Ireland Mortimer had been slain by the rebellious Irish. Richard left his last remaining uncle, the vacillating Edmund of Langley, Duke of York, as regent.

This was Richard's final mistake, for Henry Bolingbroke, who had been waiting for just such an opportunity, landed at Ravenspur to claim his confiscated lands. Once in England, he found both the remaining barons and the country so hostile towards Richard that he decided to usurp the crown. Edmund of York was too weak to oppose him, and when Richard returned from Ireland in July it was too late. He submitted, was imprisoned, and on September 30, 1399, was formally deposed by the Parliament, and Henry Bolingbroke was recognized as King Henry IV. Of course, Henry had no legitimate claim; by hereditary right the crown should have gone to Edmund Mortimer, Roger Mortimer's son and great-great-grandson of Edward III, but Edmund was still a child.

Isabella was promptly removed from her kindly mentors in Windsor by Henry and put in the care of the Bishop of Salisbury at his manor at Sonning-on-Thames. Henry had his own plans for her. Her father, Charles VI, became so worried about her safety that he abruptly went mad again. It must have been a very traumatic time for the 11-year-old child.

But Richard still had his supporters, principal among whom were his half-brother and nephew, the son and grandson of Richard's mother, Joan of Kent, by her first marriage. They were the Earls of Kent and Huntingdon. Another supporter was the Black Prince's bastard son, Sir Roger de Clarendon. The three came to Isabella at Sonning with a plot to assassinate Henry and liberate Richard from his imprisonment at Pontefract Castle, and to this she eagerly agreed. It was a vain endeavor though; the whole rebellion was bungled, the ringleaders were executed, and for Richard it was a death sentence. Whether Henry actually had him starved to death or whether Richard, at this last catastrophe, starved himself is an unanswerable question. But in Pontefract he died, and his body was displayed publicly in London. As usual, there were no visible marks of violence on the body.

With Richard gone, Henry IV proceeded with his plan. Since Isabella's marriage to Richard had never been consummated, he wanted her for his eldest son, Prince Henry, who had met her and conceived an instant passion for her. But the 12-year-old Isabella would have none of it, in spite of heavy pressure. She hated the men who had brought Richard to his death.

In the face of her obstinacy, and with angry warnings being heard from France, the new king at last gave up on the idea, and in 1401 she left England. She was permitted to keep her jewelry, but her huge dowry was not returned.

Back home in her tormented family circle, she was eventually allowed to marry the man of her choice, a Valois cousin, son of Louis, Duke of Orleans, who had become her mother's lover and for that reason had been assassinated in 1407. They were wed in 1409, but her happiness was short-lived, for within a year she had died in childbirth at the age of 21.

Compared with first Isabella of France, the second Isabella was a lamb—but a lamb with considerable strength of mind. Her refusal of Henry of Monmouth, Henry IV's heir, and his continuing love for her, were to have important consequences in English history.

JOAN OF NAVARRE
(ca. 1370–1437)
m. (1) John de Montfort, Duke of Brittany
m. (2) Henry IV   1403

No issue

J OAN OF NAVARRE CAN BE CREDITED with two firsts in the chronicle of English Queens: She was the first widow to marry a king of England, and the first, and indeed the only, queen to be accused of witchcraft.

Although born in Spanish Navarre, she had been brought up to be more French than Spanish, for in the century preceding her birth that small kingdom had fallen more and more under the suzerainty of France; her father, the treacherous Charles the Bad, was partly French, and her mother was the daughter of the French king John the Good. Joan was shipped off at a very tender age to become the third and last wife of John de Montfort, Duke of Brittany, whose first wife had been the short-lived Mary Plantagenet, daughter of Edward III. Although John was old enough to be her grandfather, she proceeded to have nine children by him and, by all accounts, to be very fond of her cantankerous husband.

In 1398 there came seeking refuge in their court the widower, Henry Bolingbroke, newly exiled by Richard II. Henry was just three years older than Joan. His first wife, the heiress Mary de Bohun, had been dead for four years, and by her he had had four sturdy sons and two daughters; she had died in childbed with her seventh child. Joan was obviously very interested in Henry, who looked very similar to his cousin Richard II, being tall and strongly built and with the famous Plantagenet red-gold hair, but with a vastly different character. From what happened later the interest was evidently reciprocated.

In 1399 Henry went off to reclaim his rightful inheritance and ended up with the crown of England. In November of the same year Joan's aged husband died, and remarriage was already very much on her mind: She immediately wrote to the Avignon Pope asking for a dispensation to marry again, provided her husband not be a close blood kin. No name was mentioned, but when the dispensation was issued on March 20, 1402, she immediately sent word of it to King Henry.

Henry immediately married her by proxy. In fact he "married" her envoy, Anthony Rieze, then and there, even though the actual marriage ceremony did not take place until the following year. On his part he hoped to get the important Duchy of Brittany on his side against his enemies in France, who were threatening England with invasion against "the usurper." Joan, as Regent of Brittany for her 10-year-old son, the new duke, could assure this. On her part—for she was avaricious—the coffers of England looked better to her than the coffers of Brittany.

Henry was to be sadly disappointed, for when word of the marriage reached the Bretons, who wanted no involvement with England, they abruptly removed her from the regency, obliging her to flee with an enormous train of followers to England. In fact the Bretons were so enraged that they swooped down on the south coast of England and burned the town of Plymouth to the ground.

The marriage, which took place in Winchester Cathedral in 1403 when she was 33 and he 36, was unpopular with the English people. They did not want another grasping French queen. Still less did they want to support her horde of refugee followers. Reason was on their side, for Henry, who was tight when it came to money, was nevertheless constantly giving her the estates and hard cash she wanted. In 1404 Parliament ordered that all her Bretons, save for her two infant daughters by John of Brittany, be expelled. Henry, who was completely beholden to Parliament for his uneasy throne, was forced to agree— but Joan quietly went on amassing her own personal fortune.

Henry's constant struggles against his rebellious subjects meant that husband and wife did not spend much time together. He had made a quick job of liquidating Richard II's immediate family, but now most of his troubles stemmed from the relatives of England's legitimate heir, the boy Edmund Mortimer, whom Henry kept virtually a prisoner at his court. First the northern barons revolted, and were quelled by Henry at Homildon Hill in 1402 and again in 1405, after which he had to execute the Archbishop of York, Scrope, which did not endear him to the Church or the people. Then the Welsh revolted under the leadership of Owen Glendower, whose daughter had married Edmund Mortimer's uncle. Then the Scots grew troublesome, but were squelched by Henry when he captured the young Scottish king in 1405. In 1408 there was yet another uprising in the north, under the Duke of Northumberland, which ended with Henry's defeating and killing him at Bramham Moor.

By 1409 Henry had finally gained control over his kingdom, but by that time he was already a very sick man. To Joan's credit, she nursed him devotedly. He suffered from a terrible form of eczema (possibly due to the continual psychological stress he was under) and from 1408 onwards was subject to terrible fits (possibly the *grand mal* form of epilepsy). While praying at the shrine of Edward the Confessor in Westminster Abbey during the Christmastide of 1412, he was seized by a fit and was thought to be dead; he recovered slightly, but lingered on as a complete invalid until he died on the morning of March 20, 1413. After 10 years of marriage Joan was again a widow and her stepson, Henry V, was the new king.

After Henry's burial in Canterbury Cathedral the Dowager Queen retired with her two Breton daughters to one of her many estates in England, hoping to live out her life in peaceful luxury. This was not to be.

On the renewal of the Hundred Years' War by Henry V, he threw out the last of her Breton followers "who gave information to the enemy and carried much treasure out of the country." Worse was to come: In 1419 she and her confessor Friar Randolph were accused of having brought about the death of her husband "by witchcraft" and of having practiced "necromancy and witch-craft" against the life of her stepson, the king. The charge was trumped up, ironically made possible by Henry IV's own Act of 1401 against heretics. That act had been aimed mainly at the first "protestant" groups within the Catholic Church, like the followers of Wycliffe, but had brought in its train numerous accusations of witchcraft—particularly against rich widows. Henry V had no interest in seeing his stepmother burned at the stake—as the act permitted; what did interest him was acquiring her property for his own use in his expensive war against the French.

In any case, Joan was placed in rigorous confinement at Pevensey Castle in Sussex, and her estates and income confiscated. Friar Randolph, who had fled to Guernsey, was captured and imprisoned in the Tower of London. Henry V was not seriously interested in proving his case; he did not even take the obvious step of having Randolph tortured into confessing their guilt. But in prison Joan languished until 1422 when, on his early deathbed in the castle of Vincennes in France, Henry V repented his harshness to his stepmother and ordered her release and the restoration of her dower.

Joan retreated into the obscurity she craved, watching from afar the great successes of her sons, John the Wise, Duke of Brittany, and Arthur III, who became Constable of France, as the Hundred Years' War ground endlessly on. She died in her manor of Havering-atte-Bower in Essex on July 9, 1437, and was buried beside her husband in Canterbury Cathedral.

KATHERINE OF FRANCE
(1401–1437)

m. (1) Henry V   1420
m. (2) Owen Tudor

Children: *HENRY*
By (2) Jasper, Edmund, Owen, Janina, Katherine

THE YOUNGEST CHILD OF A MAD FATHER (Charles VI of France) and a dissolute and uncaring mother (Isabeau of Bavaria), Katherine had a miserable childhood. Her father's fits of madness, which had begun to show themselves in 1392, had become a well-established pattern by the time she was born in 1401, and her parents were living apart. She and her next-older sister Marie were almost totally neglected by their mother, who was bound up with her own love affairs and political intrigues. Life at the Hotel St. Pol in the Marais of Paris, where they lived with her, was poverty-stricken and insecure. They wore hand-me-downs from their older sisters, Isabella and Michelle, who had both escaped from the unhappy household into early marriages—Isabella being the cosseted child bride of Richard II of England, and Michelle having wed Philip, the son and heir of the powerful Duke John of Burgundy. But as Katherine grew into puberty and then young womanhood, she saw no sign of escape into marriage for herself. Her sister Marie had early found her own route of escape and become a nun, but this was not for Katherine. It was through her sister Isabella that her final liberation came about, even though the process was a long and agonizing one.

As a teenager, Prince Henry of England, the future Henry V, had conceived a great passion for the child-queen Isabella. She would have none of him, but he had never forgotten her, and there had been no other women in his war-torn life. Thanks to the efforts of his father he had succeeded to a secure English throne, and in 1414, taking advantage of the great weakness of the disorganized and divided French kingdom, he took up the Plantagenet dream and pursued the throne of France. He reclaimed the Angevin empire of Henry II and revived Edward III's claims to the French crown. Like his father Henry IV, he was a fine warrior, and quickly captured the important port of Harfleur, following it up with his smashing victory at Agincourt in 1415. For the first time in over 50 years it looked as if a Plantagenet did have a chance at the French throne.

Henry V also had another idea—to marry a French princess to solidify his claim. His beloved Isabella was untimely dead, but there still remained one available royal daughter, the 15-year-old Katherine. Negotiations were begun. Henry V demanded as a dowry the enormous sum of two million gold crowns. Charles VI had only offered a dowry of 600,000 crowns, which he subsequently raised to 800,000 (the amount of Isabella's dowry, which was "top dollar" for a French princess). Henry refused, and the haggling went on for years.

To whet his appetite for the marriage, in 1418 Cardinal Orsini was sent with a portrait of Katherine, and Henry "liked it well," but demanded a million gold crowns as well as Normandy, Aquitaine, and all the lordships named in Edward III's Treaty of Bretigny. Negotiations again failed, and Henry went on with his piecemeal conquest of France, taking Caen, Bayeux and Rouen. In 1419, after the assassination of John the Fearless of Burgundy by the Dauphin's party, Henry's cause received a great boost when John's son, Philip the Good, joined his cause.

The French were becoming desperate, and in June of 1419 Katherine was sent to meet Henry for the first time. She had been carefully dressed by the Duke of Burgundy, who had spent a large sum on her wardrobe, and it obviously did have an impact: A writer of the time recorded that "she was a very handsome lady to look at, of graceful figure and pleasing countenance." At the meeting it was evident that neither she nor Henry disliked the other.

But it was—despite the romantic picture Shakespeare has drawn for us in *Henry V*—the political situation that decided the matter. Following on Henry's military success, the Treaty of Troyes was drawn up in 1420. In it, both sides made important concessions, but the treaty guaranteed that the Plantagenet dream would at last be realized and that an English king would rule in France.

Henry gave up his demands for a dowry, but in return was to be regent to Charles VI during the latter's lifetime; Henry and his heirs would then succeed him. Katherine's brother, the Dauphin Charles, was expressly excluded from the throne. Katherine and Henry were married 12 days later, on June 2, 1420, by the Archbishop of Sens in the parish church of St. Jean in Troyes. At the age of 20 and after five agonizing years of uncertainty, Katherine was at last free of her family.

And it seemed she could not forget her parents fast enough. Henry and his bride made a triumphant entry into Paris on December 1, 1420, and occupied the Louvre Palace, where they kept "great state," though Paris was famine-stricken and Katherine's parents were miserably served and lodged in the Hotel St. Pol. Apparently, she did not care.

After Christmas came an urgent plea from England that Henry should return with his bride, for he had been away from home for over three years. At the beginning of February, 1421, they left Calais with an impressive entourage, including the captive King of Scotland; Henry's brother, the Duke of Bedford; and a coterie of earls. His other brother, the Duke of Clarence, had been left behind to oversee the crushing of the French opposition.

In England they were met with wild acclaim; the people no longer cared about Katherine's nationality, since their king would now also be King of France. On February 23 she was crowned queen in Westminster by Archbishop Chichele, and a magnificent coronation banquet followed. To be fawned upon and feted like this was very heady stuff for the neglected girl. The king and his new queen made a royal progress during March and April throughout the kingdom, partly to show her off but, more importantly, to collect much-needed funds for the royal coffers. Everywhere she was received with wild enthusiasm.

A sobering note was introduced when news came from France that the Duke of Clarence had been defeated and killed at Beauge by an army of French and Scots led by the Earl of Buchan. The war was far from over and, worse, demanded Henry's immediate return and martial expertise. But before he left her, Katherine had news for him that brought him great joy—she was pregnant. And on December 6, 1421 she bore him a son, Henry, "that filled his heart with great gladness," even though he was far away besieging Dreux and Meaux, both of which he subsequently took.

The delighted Henry summoned Katherine to France and, leaving the infant prince behind at Windsor, she joined him at the Castle of Vincennes on May 26, 1422. A few days later they moved back to Paris and the Louvre, where "they held great Estate and sat at Diner at a great Feast in Pomp crowned and the Queen also."

Brief as her glory had been, this was to be her last taste of the fruits of greatness, for on August 10 Henry was back at Vincennes, a dying man; by August 31, 1422, he was dead of dysentery.

It is clear that *something* had happened between the royal couple in the days leading up to his death. For three weeks Henry knew he was dying, and during that period he calmly and deliberately made provision for England and France, for the upbringing of the son he had never seen, and for the regency. He righted affairs with those he had wronged (like his imprisoned stepmother Joan of Navarre), begged forgiveness of his enemies—but said nothing about Katherine.

At his bedside were gathered his brother, the Duke of Bedford; his uncle, the Duke of Exeter; the Earl of Warwick; and others of his council—but not

Katherine. She did not even join the cortege of mourners accompanying his body back to England until October 5, 1422, at Rouen, and it did not arrive in Calais until November. It was not until November 7, 1422 that Henry was buried in Westminster Abbey, after a magnificent funeral. The mourners were led by James, King of Scotland, and Katherine. She herself paid for the magnificent silver-and-gilt-plated effigy of her husband to be placed on his tomb, even though Henry had made no provision for her to be buried by his side. There is no record that her name even so much as passed his lips as he lay dying.

So at 21, after two years of a marriage that so speedily and surprisingly had gone sour, she was a widow—but she had absolutely no interest in returning to her native France. Instead she moved restlessly around among her various dower houses and looked after her infant son Henry. But her most vital contribution to the history of England was still to come.

Three years after Henry died, Katherine fell in love with Owen ap Tudor, a handsome Welshman who was a clerk of her wardrobe and a humble squire. He was so far below her in station that they had to marry clandestinely—if indeed they married at all, for no proof of the marriage was ever found. Henry's brothers had been quarreling among themselves as to whom she should marry next, the most likely and suitable candidate being Edmund Beaufort, the grandson of John of Gaunt and Katherine Swynford—so secrecy was essential.

Married or not, she was soon in no position to deny the liaison, for she was again pregnant, and in the next 12 years would bear Owen Tudor five children—three sons and two daughters. Of these, one daughter became a nun and the other, Jacina, married Lord Grey of Wilton. Of her sons, Owen became a monk at Westminster; Jasper became 17th Earl of Pembroke and fought for his half-brother Henry VI and then for his nephew, Henry Tudor. Her second son, Edmund, married Margaret Beaufort (a great- granddaughter of John of Gaunt) and fathered Henry Tudor, Earl of Richmond, who as King Henry VII would bring the long succession of the Plantagenets to and end and bring in a new dynasty that, for England, would mean entirely new perspectives and directions.

That the regents of England were a little at sea as to how to handle Katherine is clear: They could scarcely sweep the Dowager Queen and mother of their charge under the rug. What measures they did take are almost a classic case of the proverbial shutting of the barn door after the horse is gone, for in 1428—six years into her widowhood and four years after the beginning of her liaison with Owen Tudor, and with two children already in existence from their "marriage"—the regents passed a statute forbidding her to marry without their consent, indicating that they did not believe she *was* married. But, aside from separating her from her son Henry, they apparently did nothing about her liaison, for she and Owen continued to live together and produce more children.

It was not until 1436, when young Henry VI was 15, that *he* finally did something about it. Owen Tudor was summoned from Daventry, where he and Katherine were living quietly, to explain himself to the king. He was fearful of this meeting and of Henry's intentions, and initially sought sanctuary in Westminster Abbey. Once enticed out of Westminster he was imprisoned in Newgate, and at the same time Katherine either sought sanctuary in, or was sent to, Bermondsey Abbey, where, either from the grief and stress of the situation or possibly as a result of another childbirth, she died on June 3, 1437 at the age of 36. Owen Tudor, in the meantime, had escaped from Newgate prison back to his native Wales, and no attempt was made to pursue him.

Katherine had come full circle. Born into "royal poverty" and misery, she died in it also; in a "rough coffin" she was laid in Westminster's Lady Chapel, with the corpse "badly apparelled" and open to public view, until she was finally buried under the altar of the chantry that was being built around Henry V's tomb, with an inscription on it that simply said she was the wife of the king. No mention was made of Owen Tudor.

Even in her tomb she was not allowed to rest in peace. When her grandson, Henry VII, became king, the chapel in which Henry V and Katherine rested was destroyed to make room for his own, grander chapel. At that time she was shifted to the right side of her husband, and the simple slab incised with an inelegant and absurd epitaph that concluded, "Therefore a happy wife this was, a happy mother pure. Thrice happy child, but grand dame she, more than thrice happy sure!" Anything further from the truth would be hard to imagine. Even Henry VII himself avoided mentioning her in claiming his right to the throne; instead he based his claim on his descent from John of Gaunt through his own mother, Margaret Beaufort.

And yet, after her death, the glib Owen Tudor must have persuaded her pious son Henry VI that the marriage *had* taken place, for not only was Owen not persecuted, but the king awarded him a state pension. Owen remained faithful to the royal cause, and died after fighting and being captured by the Yorkists at the Battle of Mortimer's Cross. He was beheaded on orders of Edward of York in 1460.

The Tudor children were taken out of his custody and placed in the care of the aristocratic Catherine de la Pole, Abbess of Barking, and were well educated and well brought up. Henry VI was markedly kind to his half-brothers and sisters, making the two boys earls and seeing that the girl married well. Much has been made of the fact that he never recognized their legitimacy, but this very fact argues in favor of the idea that Owen had convinced him that a legal marriage had taken place, so that there was no need for recognition such as, for instance, Richard II had given in the case of the Beauforts, John of Gaunt's children born prior to his marriage to their mother, Katherine Swynford, his third wife.

We shall probably never know what estranged Henry V so completely from Katherine at the end. What is undisputed is the terrible legacy of madness, recessive in the female, dominant in the male, that she bequeathed her royal son, Henry VI, and which would take him down the same painful path as his grandfather, Charles VI of France. That her Tudor sons showed none of this genetic taint is probably a tribute to the sturdy stock of the humbly born Owen Tudor.

MARGARET OF ANJOU
(1430–1482)
m. Henry VI   1445
Child: Edward

ALTHOUGH MARGARET OF ANJOU ranks high on the list of England's most unpopular queens, it has to be said in her defense that, considering the monumental and complex problems she was faced with, she could not have fought harder or done more for her husband and then for her son.

Margaret had a peculiar childhood, for though she came of distinguished lineage, her family had fallen on hard times and lived in genteel poverty. Her father was René of Anjou, titular King of Naples—a kingdom he had fought for but could not keep. Her mother, his first wife, was Isabella, heiress to the Duchy of Lorraine, where Margaret had been born on March 23, 1430. Her Aunt Mary, her father's sister, was married to the King of France, Charles VII, who was still fighting to get his kingdom back from the English. Their penury stemmed from René's adherence to the French cause, since he had been captured by Philip, Duke of Burgundy, an ally of the English, and had been forced to pay a huge ransom for his freedom. René was a man of many parts—a writer and musician himself, he was a great patron of the arts, and passed this enthusiasm on to his daughter, who was also noted for her witty tongue.

When the question of marriage to the 24-year-old Henry VI first came up Margaret was delighted, even though her father's motive for this unlikely alliance was to secure his own Anjou and to reclaim Maine for his brother Charles. The marriage meant she would be Queen of England and France; her husband-to-be had been crowned king in Paris in 1430, even though by this time the title was a hollow one, his uncles and cousins having lost most of the territories his father had won.

Margaret's portrait, showing her as being tiny and just a little bit plump, with very blue eyes, fair hair and a heart-shaped face, was painted and sent off to Henry, who approved enthusiastically. Accordingly, Michael de la Pole, Earl of Suffolk, and Edmund Beaufort, Earl of Somerset, two leaders of the English "Peace" party, arranged the marriage as part of a two-year truce with France, and Margaret's father was promised Maine as a reward. The marriage was bitterly opposed by Henry's last remaining uncle, Humphrey, Duke of Glouces-ter, and therein lay the seeds of all the misery that followed. The marriage went forward but, as one contemporary wrote later, "From this time forward King Henry never profited or went forward, but fortune began to turn from him on all sides."

The omens indeed were not good. As soon as the 15-year-old Margaret arrived in England she developed smallpox. Her wardrobe was found to be so skimpy and shabby that some hasty dressmaking had to be done before she could be presented to the people of England. Henry himself was so short of funds at this time that he had to pledge the crown jewels to pay for her wardrobe.

From the first, the marriage was highly unpopular in England. She came without dowry, and the brief euphoria about a French queen that Henry V's Katherine had engendered had long since dissipated, in view of England's heavy continuing losses in both men and money. But married and crowned she was, with due magnificence.

What she made of her new husband we can only conjecture, for anyone more unlike his warrior father than Henry VI would have been hard to find. He was kindly, gentle, studious and extremely pious. Like his half-brother Owen Tudor, he would have made an excellent monk: as it was, he made a poor king and a weak husband. He was nine years her senior, but she soon became the dominant partner in the marriage, although she would remain fiercely loyal to him to the end.

The trouble was that her marriage had acted as a catalyst to a dynastic war that had been in the making since Henry IV had usurped the crown—a war in which all the parties were both Plantagenets and descendants of Edward III. The descendants of John of Gaunt included Henry VI; his sole remaining uncle, Humphrey, Duke of Gloucester; children of John of Gaunt's first marriage; and the three mighty Beauforts from his third marriage: these were "the Lancastrians." Opposing them was Richard, Duke of York, whose father was Edmund of York, John of Gaunt's younger brother, but whose mother had been Anne Mortimer, descendant of Lionel of Antwerp, John of Gaunt's older brother. These were "the Yorkists." After the deaths of her Mortimer brothers and their children, Anne Mortimer stood in a more direct line of inheritance. Therefore, as Richard of York would make clear, his hereditary claim to the throne was stronger than Henry's. The quarrel theoretically was about heredi-tary right, but it eventually came down to military might. And this clash between the red rose emblem of Lancaster and the white rose emblem of York would plunge England into 30 years of civil war.

This was the situation that the teenage Margaret was catapulted into, and her only choice was to support her Lancastrian husband's closest kin, the

Beauforts, and their supporters—the amiable Henry being a mere cipher in what followed.

The situation became tenser when Humphrey of Gloucester died in prison—murdered, it was rumored, by the Lancastrian Duke of Suffolk, who shortly was murdered himself. Now Richard of York was one step closer to the throne; if Henry died without issue he was the next legitimate heir.

The endless quarrels between Richard and the Beauforts continued, but then in 1453 two events occurred that changed things completely. Margaret, after nine years of marriage, became pregnant for the first time, and on October 13th gave birth to a son, Edward, thereby crushing Richard of York's hopes of inheriting the throne. And two months before the birth, on August 10th, King Henry—like his grandfather Charles VI of France—had a bout of insanity. York immediately started a campaign labeling Margaret's son illegitimate. Both sides started to arm. War was inevitable.

The timing could not have been worse for the French-born and much disliked Margaret. That same year had seen the final defeat of English arms in France and the conclusion of the Hundred Years' War, with England completely stripped of *all* its French possessions save Calais.

The first Battle of St. Albans that opened "the War of the Roses" in 1455 was disastrous for the Lancastrians. Not only was the poor insane Henry wounded and captured, but Edmund, Duke of Somerset and the last surviving Beaufort, was killed. If Margaret was to save the throne for her infant son, she would have to take the leadership of the Lancastrian party herself—so she did.

Richard of York declared himself regent of the captive Henry, who had another bout of madness after St. Albans, and in 1460 forced him to agree that Richard, not Edward, should be his rightful heir. This was too much even for Richard's supporters, premier among whom was Richard Neville, Earl of Warwick, shortly to earn the title of "the Kingmaker"; it was certainly too much for Margaret, whose son was about to be disinherited. She rallied the Lancastrians in the north and west and ravaged the estates of York and his supporters. At the battle of Wakefield she gained a great victory that included the deaths of Richard of York and his younger son, the Earl of Rutland.

Unfortunately, she had scotched the snake but had not killed it, for Richard's eldest son, Edward, Earl of March and now Duke of York, had escaped the massacre, as had his brothers, George and Richard—all of them able fighters. And she made a mistake in vindictively allowing her armies to ravage the countryside, thus turning many against her cause.

As the seesaw battles went on, reprisals on both sides became progressively more cruel: At the Yorkist victory at Towton in 1461, 35,000 men were slaughtered. In the process Margaret became something of a monster herself, as when, after her success at the second Battle of St. Albans, she made her seven-year-old son pass sentences of death on all her prisoners. From that battle also we get a pathetic glimpse of Henry VI, who had been dragged along by the Yorkists. "The king was placed under a tree a mile away, where he laughed and sang throughout, and when the defeat of the Earl of Warwick was reported, he detained upon his promise the two princes who had been left to guard him. Very soon the Duke of Somerset and the conquerors arrived to salute him and he received them in friendly fashion and went with them to St. Albans to the queen . . . ."

The reunited royal family had not long to rejoice, for while Warwick had been losing at St. Albans, Edward of York had won a great victory at Mortimer's Cross in Wales. And after the subsequent Battle of Towton so many turned against the Lancastrians that Margaret and her son had to flee to Scotland.

Henry was subsequently recaptured and imprisoned in the Tower of London. Edward of York was crowned king as Edward IV in Westminster at the end of 1461. It seemed as if all was lost.

Margaret fled from Scotland to France, hoping to enlist the aid of her cousin King Louis XI, but he was only too thankful to have the English out of France and wanted no part in another war. For eight years she and her growing son led lives of unwelcome refugees in her homeland, until 1469 when hope revived once more.

In that year Richard Neville, Earl of Warwick, whose military expertise had been largely responsible for putting Edward IV on the throne, turned on the king, captured, and imprisoned him. When Warwick relented and released Edward, the king turned the tables on him and, rallying his supporters, defeated Warwick. He and Edward's rebellious brother George, Duke of Clarence, were forced to flee to France.

With an able English general on hand, Louis XI quickly reconsidered: He reconciled the erstwhile enemies, Warwick and Margaret, and to seal their bargain the now-16-year-old Edward was married to Warwick's youngest daughter, Anne Neville.

Warwick returned to England with an army, and this time it was Edward who was put to flight and who sought refuge in Burgundy. Henry was dragged from the Tower and restored to the throne. Up to this point Margaret and Edward had remained in France, because she still did not completely trust

Warwick, but now that victory seemed assured they returned to England and headed west to rally the pro-Lancastrian Welsh to their cause once more.

Their hope was short-lived. Supported by the Duke of Burgundy, Edward once more invaded the north with an army, his brother Clarence once again changed sides, and their joint forces met Warwick at the Battle of Barnet in 1471, during which Warwick was killed. Edward and his brothers then turned west, met Margaret and her army in battle at Tewkesbury, and there her hope was finally extinguished when the 17-year-old Prince Edward was slain in the engagement and she was captured. Shortly after this, in May, Henry VI was murdered in the Tower—probably by smothering. That very night she was brought to her own imprisonment in the Tower. With both husband and son dead nothing was left for her to fight for.

At first she was shunted from one dismal prison to another. Then in November of 1475, after four years, her desperate father, René, raised a ransom of 50,000 crowns for her liberation by selling his county of Provence to the wily Louis XI. In January of 1476, heartbroken, crushed in spirit and ailing in body, Margaret was allowed to cross the Channel to Dieppe, having first signed a document that began, "I, Margaret, formerly in England married, renounce all that I could pretend to in England by the conditions of my marriage, will all other things there to Edward, now king of England . . . ." She was allowed to settle in the manor of Reculée in Anjou.

There her father tried to ensure her a comfortable future by grants of land, but these were vetoed and revoked by the absolute power of King Louis, and further humiliation was heaped upon her when the king granted her a pension, but only after she had signed another document in which she gave up all rights of succession to both her father's and her mother's lands. Half the time Louis didn't furnish payments, so she lived, as she had in her youth, in genteel poverty.

After several years she moved from Reculée to an even-sorrier residence at the Castle of Dampierre, also on her father's lands; she was aged before her time and was suffering from disfiguring eye and skin diseases. There, on August 2, 1482, she made her will, bequeathing what little she had to her tiny household, and there, on August 25th, Margaret, "formerly in England and now in France, a widow," died at the age of 52.

THE YORKISTS

ELIZABETH WOODVILLE
(1434–1492)

m. (1) Sir John Grey
m. (2) Edward IV   1464

Children: *Elizabeth, Katherine, EDWARD, Richard, Mary, Margaret and four other daughters*

W AS ENGLAND'S FIRST QUEEN OF ENGLISH BIRTH in over 300 years a schemer who lured Edward IV into a secret marriage? Or was she merely a pawn in his own shrewd scheme to throw off the yoke of Warwick "the Kingmaker" and reunite the opposing elements of his kingdom?

The answer seems to be a little of both. Certainly she was a far cry from Henry I's consort, "Good Queen Mold," and the English, after their initial rejoicing at having at long last a queen of English birth, were soon to wonder aloud if they had not been better off with their foreign queens, as her relatives were extraordinarily greedy.

The first surprising fact about this second widow to wed an English king is that both by birth and by her first marriage she was in the Lancastrian camp that had opposed the Yorkists for so long. She was the daughter of the Lancastrian Richard Woodville, who had married (also secretly) Jacquetta of Hainaut, the widow of John, Duke of Bedford, Henry VI's uncle, and in whose household he had been as a humble squire. Elizabeth was also the widow of Sir John Grey, who had died fighting for Henry VI at the second battle of St. Albans in 1461, and by whom she had two sons. She also had 12 brothers and sisters, all of them looking for financial and social advancement.

Edward IV was an exceedingly licentious man, both before and after marriage, and noted for his cavalier treatment of his mistresses after he had tired of them, so that her snaring him into marriage—and a secret one at that—is all the more remarkable. There are several versions of how they met—some highly romantic—but the gist of them all is captured by the version of the Italian historian Dominic Mancini, who wrote (while Elizabeth was still alive), ". . . and when the king first fell in love with her beauty of person and charm of manner he could not corrupt her virtue by gifts or menaces. The story runs that when Edward placed a dagger at her throat to make her submit to his passion, she remained unperturbed and determined to die rather than live unchastely with the king. Whereupon Edward coveted her much the more and he judged the lady to be a royal spouse, who could not be over come in her constancy by an infatuated king."*

In any case, on May 1, 1464 they were married secretly at Grafton Regis, their only witnesses being her mother, the Duchess of Bedford; the priest; two gentlewomen; and a young man "who helped the priest to sing." Edward immediately bedded her and then rode off to fight yet another battle with the Lancastrians.

He realized that his marriage might not be well received by his Yorkist supporters, particularly the Earl of Warwick, who was abroad trying to arrange a "royal" marriage for him, the two leading candidates being Isabella of Castile and Bona of Savoy. Edward detailed one of his household, Sir John Howard, a Norfolk knight, to sound out the temper of his court and country. Howard saw this as a stepping-stone to greatness (as indeed it proved), struck a secret deal with the Woodvilles to take him under their wing, and reported favorably back to Edward, even though the reality was the reverse.

Five months after the marriage, Edward summoned a meeting of his leaders at Reading Abbey and there presented Elizabeth as his bride, with the announcement that she would be crowned queen in the spring of 1465. The reaction of the Yorkists was violent. His mother, the proud Cicely Neville, Duchess of York, was beside herself with rage that he should have married a Lancastrian widow, six years older than he, and one of such lowly birth. Her nephew, Warwick the Kingmaker, who had just struck a bargain with Louis XI of France for Edward to marry Bona of Savoy, was humiliated and furious. But it was all too late; the marriage was legal, and Elizabeth was pregnant.

The speed with which the Woodvilles were promoted and advanced by Edward took everyone's breath away; *he* was creating his own power bloc as a counterbalance to Warwick's. No sooner had his marriage been announced than he started to arrange advantageous marriages for the other Woodvilles. Elizabeth's sister Margaret was married to the Earl of Arundel's heir; her sister Catherine to the Duke of Buckingham; sister Anne to the heir of the Earl of Essex; sister Eleanor to the Earl of Kent's heir; and sister Mary to Lord Herbert of Pembroke's heir. But the least popular marriage was of her 20-year-old brother John to Katherine Neville, the very rich Duchess of Norfolk and sister of Edward's own mother, who was 80 years old.

In March of 1465 Elizabeth's father was made Treasurer of England and was created Earl Rivers, his eldest son becoming Lord Scales. Then Anne

---

*Anne Boleyn was to use exactly the same tactics to snare Elizabeth's grandson, Henry VIII.

Holland, the heiress of the exiled Lancastrian Duke of Exeter, was married off to Elizabeth's son by her first marriage, Sir Thomas Grey. Within a single year the Woodvilles had married into most of the kingdom's premier families, and with every marriage the gap between Warwick and his protégé Edward widened.

Warwick, of course, retaliated. He married his elder daughter Isabella, a considerable heiress herself, to George, Duke of Clarence, Edward's younger brother and next in line for the throne. With Clarence on his side, Warwick had a strong lever against Edward. The king naturally opposed the marriage, but to no avail.

The arrogance of the nouveau-riche Woodvilles, coupled with Warwick's own ambitions, led to a general uprising in 1469 against Edward, during which Elizabeth's father, Lord Rivers, and his son John were executed by Warwick and Clarence, the king was put to flight and Henry VI restored to his throne. But Warwick also, in coming to terms with Margaret of Anjou and marrying off his other daughter Anne Neville to Prince Edward, had managed to alienate Clarence, who saw his own dream of inheriting the throne, and worse, his hopes for the entire Neville inheritance, fading fast. So the shiftless George secretly shifted back to his brother's cause.

Elizabeth, who was heavily pregnant, did not accompany Edward on his flight into exile; instead she sought and was granted sanctuary in Westminster Abbey, so that her first son and heir to the throne, Edward, was born there in 1470 during his father's exile. She had already produced several daughters, including Elizabeth—a future queen—in 1466; and Katherine, who married William Courtenay, Earl of Devonshire. In total she would have seven daughters, some of whom died in infancy.

When her husband returned to triumph, first over Warwick at Barnet and then over Margaret of Anjou and her son Edward at Tewkesbury, Elizabeth was on hand to present him with his newborn heir Edward, and two years later would have another son, Richard, Duke of York, to solidify the succession.

With Warwick, his chief rival, dead; Henry VI and his son dead; and Margaret of Anjou his captive, Edward was at last secure on his throne. He was reconciled to his brother Clarence—at least on the surface—and his youngest brother, Richard of Gloucester, had always been fiercely loyal to him. Apart from the minor irritation of the continuously greedy Woodvilles, he and Elizabeth could settle down to rule.

They made a handsome couple. From his Plantagenet genes Edward had inherited great height (almost 6'4") and a strong physique; but in features he took after his mother, a Neville, being dark of eye and hair. Elizabeth, tall and slim, had long, wavy golden hair and blue eyes. Their children were also very good-looking. Although he remained fond of his wife, Edward was soon back to his old philandering ways and took a succession of mistresses, including the high-spirited Elizabeth Shore (often incorrectly called Jane). As Mancini wrote, "He pursued with no discrimination the married and the unmarried, the noble and the lowly: however he took none by force." There were also his bastards by Elizabeth Lucy, an earlier mistress—Arthur, Grace and Elizabeth, all of whom were raised at court; Arthur was a particular favorite of his father. So long as she got what *she* wanted—and she did—Elizabeth did not seem upset by all this.

The main troubles Edward now had to face were within his own family—namely his two brothers. No sooner was Warwick dead than George and Richard began to squabble over the Neville inheritance, for in spite of George's determined opposition, Richard had married Anne Neville, the widow of Prince Edward and joint heiress with George's wife Isabella. The rights of their mother, Warwick's widow, were totally ignored by their greedy husbands. Edward upset Clarence even more when he decreed that the inheritance should be divided equally. Then Isabella died in 1476, having presented Clarence with two children, the Earl of Warwick and a daughter, Margaret, who would marry the Earl of Salisbury. Clarence had really been in love with her and—already unbalanced by constant drinking— he accused one of her ladies of having poisoned Isabella, and had the woman killed. This behavior, combined with his plotting against the throne, was too much for Edward, especially in view of George's erstwhile betrayal. So he was arrested, placed in the Tower, and subsequently drowned there by Edward's orders, appropriately enough in a butt of wine.

Richard of Gloucester had returned with his rich wife Anne to enjoy the fruits of her inheritance on her estate at Middleham Castle, which his late father-in-law had made into a magnificent family dwelling, and there in 1474 Anne also presented him with a son, Edward. As long as his brother lived he would give Edward no trouble, but he disliked the Woodvilles, who loathed him in return. In particular, Lord Rivers, Elizabeth's oldest brother and her son Thomas Grey, Marquis of Dorset, were his avowed enemies. This, too, would bear bitter fruit.

As Edward became middle-aged he gave himself up more and more to the pleasures of the flesh and of the table. He grew fat and indolent, even giving up the athletic pursuits and hunting that had been so dear to him in his warlike youth. Overindulgence caught up with him, and in 1483 he died suddenly after a very short illness. To the dismay of Elizabeth and the Woodvilles he had decreed in his will that Richard of Gloucester should be the guardian of his 12-year-old heir, Edward V, "until his coming of age." They had all expected Elizabeth to be regent.

When his father died, Edward V was at Ludlow Castle with his guardian and uncle Lord Rivers, who tried to undo the damage by rushing the young king to London for immediate coronation. But the Woodvilles had underestimated Richard of Gloucester's own ambition and the speed with which he would act. He was in the north when news of his brother's death reached him, but hurriedly gathered a band of his own retainers, and intercepted the royal party on its way from Ludlow. He took the young king into his custody and escorted him to London, where he had himself confirmed by Parliament as "Protector" and sent Edward off to the Tower, from which he was never to emerge.

To further enforce his seizure of power he immediately had his former friend Lord Hastings executed on a charge of plotting with the Woodvilles to seize the king. The terrified Elizabeth had fled to the sanctuary of Westminster again, along with her daughters and her younger son, Richard of York, but was either menaced or cajoled into letting the boy join his brother just a few days later. He too disappeared into the Tower, never to be seen again. Both children were subsequently murdered there, although when exactly that happened is still a burning question.

The scene was now set for Richard's takeover of the throne—a goal he had probably had in mind all along. He mounted a vigorous campaign against the legitimacy of Elizabeth's children, claiming the marriage was never valid, because of a preexisting contract by Edward with the long-dead Eleanor Talbot, and the fact of the clandestine marriage. He even went so far as to impugn Edward IV's own legitimacy, reviving an old Lancastrian rumor that Edward, who had been born in Rouen while his father Richard of York had been fighting the French, was the son of an archer named Blaybourne. He was trying to create a smokescreen to ease his usurpation of the throne. Even if the propaganda were accepted as truth and Edward's children disinherited, the next legitimate heir would then be Clarence's small son, the Earl of Warwick. But the people of England knew the situation for what it was, and were probably remembering the disastrous regency of Henry VI, and so Richard was duly crowned on July 26, 1483 as Richard III.

As clever and able as Richard III undoubtedly was, he was not to know a quiet moment during the two years he reigned. Time after time he tried to tempt Elizabeth and her daughters out of their Westminster sanctuary. Having been tricked once, she stoutly resisted, although several of her daughters did join the court. In view of the Woodvilles's plight, she was wise to stay put, for Richard had executed both her brother, Lord Rivers, and her son, the Marquis of Dorset. He was even executing his own former friends, like the powerful Duke of Buckingham.

His aim initially was to marry off one of the royal princesses to his own small son Edward; but when the child died in 1484 he had to fall back on an even more desperate scheme. His own wife Anne was failing, and when she died in March of 1485, many thought he intended to make the young Princess Elizabeth, who had joined the court and now was the next legitimate heir to the throne, his next wife. This speculation may have been just more of the scurrilous gossip that beset him, for a dispensation from the Pope to marry his own niece would probably never have been given. Still, gossip was blackening his character.

A gleam of hope came to Elizabeth in her sanctuary when news reached her of the landing of the Lancastrian champion, Henry Tudor, Earl of Richmond, at Milford Haven in his native Wales on August 7, 1485. The gleam turned to a new dawn when the news came on August 22 that this new usurper had met Richard at Bosworth Field, and that in the battle Richard III had been killed.

A new era had begun, for Henry Tudor, now Henry VII, despite his feeble hereditary claims, was no Plantagenet. But he badly needed to mend all wounds in England and so needed Plantagenet support. He intended to marry the Princess Elizabeth and unite the red rose of Lancaster with the white rose of York into the Tudor red and white rose.

The Dowager Queen emerged from her sanctuary at this gladsome news, and on January 18, 1486, when Henry VII married her daughter, she must have thought that all was well and that the good days had finally returned. She was to be sadly disillusioned.

Henry VII had no intention of coping with "the Woodville problem," which would only be aggravated by the presence of his mother-in-law in his court. He also badly needed funds and, being canny when it came to money, had an eye on the extensive dower properties the queen had acquired during Edward IV's lifetime. He wanted her out of the way. Even though she was well along in her fifties, he thought of marrying her off to the young widower James III of Scotland, who was only 34. When that plan failed, Henry made his move. He appropriated her dower properties and ordered her to withdraw into the Abbey of Bermondsey—the same abbey in which his unfortunate grandmother

Katherine of France had died. Elizabeth protested vigorously—she had no taste for the secluded life. But the king was determined to keep her out of sight, so into Bermondsey she went, with a niggardly pension of some 400 marks a year. She was not allowed to leave the abbey without his express permission, which was rarely given. She lived in comparatively luxurious imprisonment.

Nevertheless, for five years she complained that she led "a wretched and miserable life" and died there in 1492 at the age of 58, virtually penniless. Without fanfare she was taken to Windsor and buried beside her husband, Edward IV. Her passing was barely noted by the people of England, to whom she had never endeared herself.

ANNE NEVILLE
(1456–1485)

m. (1) Edward, Prince of Wales   1470
m. (2) Richard III   1472

Child: Edward

N<small>O ONE ILLUSTRATES BETTER THAN ANNE NEVILLE</small> the fact that the position of women in England's patriarchal society had not improved in the more than 400 years that had elapsed since Matilda of Flanders had fought in vain against marrying William the Conqueror. Anne was England's second native-born queen in succession, yet she had no more power in her own life than any slave in Ancient Babylon, even though the Feudal Age was almost over and the Renaissance already well established in Europe.

Royal children of both sexes had always been raised with the recognition that their marriages were matters of state and not of personal preference, but Anne was not of royal blood. She was merely the daughter of a powerful noble, and still she was only a pawn to be manipulated by the men in her life: first her father, then her brother-in-law and finally her husband.

Her father, Richard Neville "the Kingmaker," was the younger son of the Earl of Salisbury, but by two fortunate marriages, both times to heiresses, had accumulated a huge inheritance. His very title, Earl of Warwick, he owed to his marriage to the heiress of Richard Beauchamp, 13th Earl of Warwick, who had died in France without male issue during the final stages of the Hundred Years' War. Richard Neville also was without male issue, so all this great inheritance was due to pass to his two surviving daughters, Isabella and Anne.

As part of Warwick's ongoing plan to reestablish his hold over the royal family of York, Isabella had been married off to George, Duke of Clarence, in 1468, and in 1470, after Louis of France had reconciled Warwick with his former enemy, Margaret of Anjou, Anne was married off to the 16-year-old Prince Edward, Henry VI's heir; she was 14. Warwick then had a foothold in both camps. Whether this marriage was ever consummated is unknown, but it was destined to be a very short one, as in 1471 her teenage husband was slain at the battle of Tewkesbury, and Anne became a 15-year-old widow.

Since her father had also been killed the same year at the battle of Barnet, Anne's care fell upon George, Duke of Clarence, her older sister's husband. Nevertheless, there was already another suitor for Anne, and one whose suit sat very ill with Clarence, for it was his younger brother, Richard, Duke of Gloucester. Richard had known Anne since her early childhood, for he had lived at Middleham Castle, Warwick's main family seat, under the guardianship of the Kingmaker for a number of years.

Clarence did not wish to lose his control over the entire Neville inheritance, so the extraordinary story is that he hid Anne from Richard, "disguised as a serving-maid," moving her around from castle to castle. Being cast in the role of Cinderella could not have been to the taste of the highborn Anne, so somehow she must have got word to Richard as to her whereabouts. He "rescued" her, removed her to sanctuary at St. Martin-le-Grand in London, and shortly thereafter, in 1472, he married her. She was 16, he was 20.

There began a monumental quarrel between the two brothers over the carving up of the Neville inheritance, which became so bitter that Edward IV had to intervene and decree that the wealth should be divided equally. The rights of the Dowager Countess of Warwick were disregarded, but Anne and her sister were helpless to do anything about it.

Since the historians of the next reign (not to mention Shakespeare) were to paint such a black portrait of Richard III, one wonders what sort of man Anne did marry. Tudor historians credited him with multiple murders: Henry VI; Prince Edward (Anne's first husband); his own brother Clarence; his nephews, Edward V and Richard of York, "the Princes in the Tower"; even Anne herself. Modern historians have proven that in the cases of Henry, Edward, Clarence and Anne the accusations were simply not true. The whitewashing has gone so far that the murder of his nephews has been blamed on his successor, Henry VII.

There they have gone *too* far. Blameless Richard may have been in the other murders, but the weight of the evidence against him points to the sad fact of the little princes being dead before Henry set foot in England. The confessions of the three purported killers, headed up by Sir James Tyrell, took place during Henry VII's reign and so may have been spurious; but the modern forensic examination of the bones found in the 17th century in the Tower reveals they belonged to a 13-year-old boy and an 11-year-old boy—the ages of the princes when they *entered* the Tower. Most telling of all are the subsequent actions of Richard and the boys' mother, the Dowager Queen Elizabeth.

Richard's elaborate schemes to marry first his son Edward and then himself to one of the royal princesses would have made no sense had their brothers still been alive. Similarly, the Dowager Elizabeth would never have been so eager to see her daughter Elizabeth marry the usurping Henry of Richmond had she had the slightest hope her sons still lived to claim the throne. On these two murder counts at least Richard must remain guilty as charged.

Tudor historians also credited Anne with loathing her second husband, who, according to them, had murdered her first, Prince Edward, just as they would have us believe he cared so little for her that he poisoned her to clear the way for his marriage to Princess Elizabeth. Again these theories are nowhere substantiated. She was apparently so attached to him that she would travel with him on his many journeys to oversee the business of his brother Edward, and they lived amiably and comfortably together for many years at Middleham Castle.

Immediately after their marriage they had, in fact, retired to be away from the court and the constant difficulties with brother Clarence and the Woodvilles, who resented Richard's good standing with his brother Edward. At Middleham Anne was to bear him their only child, Edward, born in 1474, two years after the marriage.

Neither she nor her sister Isabella were very robust women. In eight years of marriage to Clarence Isabella had only two children, and she died in 1476 at the age of 26. In 13 years of marriage to Richard, Anne only had the one child and died at the age of 29. Richard, like his brother Edward, was a sensual and virile man; before his marriage he had sired at least three bastard children—John de Gloucester, Katherine Plantagenet and Richard Plantagenet, and possibly a fourth, Stephen Hawes. Of these, John (his father's favorite) was imprisoned and finally murdered by Henry VII; Katherine married William Herbert, Earl of Huntingdon, in 1484, with a handsome dowry from Richard; and Richard Plantagenet, after the battle of Bosworth and his father's death, spent his life as a bricklayer and died in Eastwell, Kent, in 1550.

That Richard sired no bastards after his marriage supports his attachment to his wife, whom he always kept by his side—if he had disliked her he could easily have left her at home and continued his philanderings. And this pattern continued even after he seized the throne.

Indeed, this habit may have hastened Anne's end, for in the spring of 1484 Richard and Anne made a royal progress through the eastern counties, where she was remarked to have become very thin and pale, probably with the wasting disease of pulmonary tuberculosis that had already killed her sister. When they arrived in Nottingham, word reached them that their son Edward, also sickly, had died at Middleham. The griefstricken Anne was devastated that Edward had died without either of his parents' being present. By Christmas, which they celebrated at court in London, she was clearly fading fast. In March of 1485 she quietly slipped out of life during an eclipse of the sun.

It is noteworthy that immediately after her funeral Richard denied, before his ruling council, that he had any thoughts of marrying his niece Elizabeth. This was untrue, but he appears to have dropped the idea when he found it was so universally repugnant. But the accusation did not improve his already tarnished reputation, nor did nominating John de la Pole, Earl of Lincoln, the son of his sister Elizabeth, as his own heir endear him to anyone. Rather, it reinforced the belief that he had done away with his nephews. It also again disinherited the teenaged Earl of Warwick, Clarence's son, the only surviving male heir of the House of York.

The sole contribution Anne was allowed to make to the sweep of history was that of providing her husband the king with one child and a sickly one at that. Richard was to fight bravely to save his crown at Bosworth Field, but the fact remains that he had only himself to fight *for*.

THE TUDORS

Elizabeth of York

ELIZABETH OF YORK
(1466–1503)

m. Henry VII 1486

Children: *Arthur, Margaret, HENRY, Elizabeth, Mary, Edmund, Katherine*

Historians END THE PLANTAGENET DYNASTY with Richard II, but more as a matter of convenience than of reality, since both the Lancastrians and the Yorkists were as much Plantagenets as their predecessors. The last true Plantagenet to share the throne of England was Elizabeth of York, who not only united the warring houses into the single Tudor rose but was the last legitimate heir of the long and colorful royal line to reign. Henry Tudor *also* had Plantagenet blood, through his remarkable mother, Margaret Beaufort, daughter of John Beaufort, duke of Somerset, and wife of Edmund Tudor, one of the three sons of Katherine of France by Owen Tudor. But these descendants of

John of Gaunt's third marriage had only been legitimized long after their births, and had been expressly excluded from the legitimate line of succession in an act passed by Henry IV in 1407. Henry VII owed his throne to the strength of arms and to the fact that his usurpation was immediately legitimized by the English Parliament. Neither in physique nor in temperament, however, was he a Plantagenet.

Portraits of Elizabeth show her to have been a pretty woman, very like her mother Elizabeth Woodville in both features and coloring, having the same golden hair and blue eyes. But she was neither as robust nor as strong-willed as that determined lady. The oldest child of Edward IV, she had had, while her father lived, a luxury-filled childhood. She had been only four when her mother sought sanctuary for the first time in Westminster, after Edward had been forced to flee Warwick's onslaught on his crown, and Elizabeth would hardly have remembered that tense time in the halcyon days that followed her father's return. In her early teens there had been some talk of marrying her to the Dauphin of France (later Charles VIII), but her indolent father did not press the matter, so nothing came of it. Elizabeth was pleased to continue her privileged, tranquil life in the company of her sisters, of whom she was markedly fond, and her two young brothers. She was 17 when this pleasant world dissolved after the sudden death of her father in 1483.

The following two years were traumatic—they saw the usurpation of the throne by her uncle Richard, the kidnapping of her brother Edward V, the hasty retreat to sanctuary in Westminster with her mother and the rest of the family, the removal of her younger brother Richard by his uncle and then his disappearance. Elizabeth's life was suddenly in hellish turmoil. As early as Christmas of 1483 Margaret Beaufort had already approached the Dowager Queen with the proposition that a wedding of Elizabeth with her only son, Henry, Earl of Richmond, would "unite the Roses"—but Henry was far away, an exile in Brittany. Although the match was considered a possibility, its probability remained very uncertain, as, at home, an even more terrifying marriage prospect appeared.

Elizabeth and two of her sisters had rejoined the court, for Richard III had his heart set on marrying one of them to his nine-year-old heir Edward. With the death of his son and the failing health of Queen Anne, rumors circulated that Richard intended to make Elizabeth his second wife, even though he had already declared her and her siblings bastards in order to make his own seizure of the throne more palatable.

Her fears increased when she was separated from her sisters and sent away from the court to Sheriff Hutton, where Edward, Earl of Warwick, Clarence's son, was being kept as a prisoner. The news of Richard's death at Bosworth Field brought the relieved knowledge that at least she would not be forced into an incestuous marriage. At this point her mother, having abandoned hope that either of her sons was still alive, agreed to what Margaret Beaufort had been proposing all along—the marriage of Elizabeth to the conquering Henry Tudor.

Even then Elizabeth's worries about her future were not entirely over, for Henry made no move to rush to her side. He was, and would continue to be, an extremely cautious man. He methodically proceeded to work with England's Parliament, first to have his own right to the throne approved, and then to repeal the "bastardization" of Edward IV's children passed by his predecessor. Only then, when everything was legally settled, did he proceed with the marriage. The wedding was held at Westminster on January 18, 1486, and Elizabeth was crowned queen. She was 20, an advanced age for a royal princess to have remained unmarried; Henry VII was 29.

Their first son and heir to the throne was born, a month prematurely, in late September of 1486 at Winchester. To underline his break with the past and emphasize his own Welsh heritage, Henry named the boy Arthur after the ancient king of the Celts from whom he claimed descent.

They were to keep the custom of "intimate family" naming of their children as the others duly arrived: Margaret, named after Henry's mother, in 1489; another son, Henry (named for Henry himself) in 1491; a daughter, Elizabeth (named for her mother) in 1492; another daughter, Mary, named after Elizabeth's favorite sister, in 1495 (who was to be the spitting image of her mother); a son, Edmund (named after Henry's father) in 1499; and finally Katherine (named after Henry's paternal grandmother Queen Katherine) in 1503.

While Elizabeth was busily producing babies, Henry was even busier protecting their heritage. Like the usurping Henry IV and Richard III before him, he had to face multiple challenges to his throne. The first came in 1487 when Lambert Simnel, a boy who had been coached carefully in his part by Margaret, Duchess of Burgundy (a sister of Edward IV), and the exiled John de la Pole (Richard III's named heir) landed in Ireland, claiming to be the Earl of Warwick and the rightful king of England. The plotters had woefully miscalculated, for Henry VII had kept the real Earl of Warwick carefully penned up in the Tower—he had only to produce him, but not before he had had to fight what has been called the last battle of the Roses at Stowe with the Yorkist insurgents. He crushed them, and John de la Pole was killed in the battle. Henry spared the impostor, making him first a scullion in the royal household, later promoting him to falconer.

The second challenge was a more serious threat. Margaret, Duchess of Burgundy, Henry's avowed enemy, in 1495 introduced a new impostor, Perkin Warbeck, who claimed to be Edward IV's younger son, Richard of York. Henry was in no position this time to produce the real boy, whose bones had long been moldering in their hidden grave in the Tower. This time Margaret elicited the powerful support of Charles VIII of France, and a number of disaffected Yorkist nobles went to France to join the cause. Even more worrisome was the support given to the impostor by King James IV of Scotland, who even gave the pretender his kinswoman Lady Catherine Gordon in marriage.

King James invaded England on the Pretender's behalf, but soon had to retreat to Scotland, pursued by Henry's army. Henry VII hated war—it was expensive—so when James seemed amiable enough to talk terms, Henry offered him the hand of his small daughter Margaret in marriage. The offer was accepted. Although bereft of this strong support, Warbeck did not give up, but instead set sail for Cornwall and Devon in 1497, rallied supporters there and laid siege to Exeter. This scheme also failed, so he marched north to Taunton in Somerset supported by his Cornish army. There he deserted them on the eve of battle and took sanctuary in Beaulieu Abbey; the disgusted Cornishmen went home.

Henry respected the sanctuary but promised Warbeck clemency if he emerged. He did, and apparently convinced Henry that, though not Richard of York, he was (improbably) a bastard son of Edward IV. Henry sent him to the Tower, where Edward's other bastard son Arthur was already incarcerated, but treated Warbeck like a prince of the blood royal. Imprisonment, however luxurious, did not suit Warbeck, so in 1498 he escaped, only to be shortly recaptured and returned to the Tower, where he continued to plot. This time he drew the unfortunate Edward, Earl of Warwick into his web. Discovery of this plot was the last straw for Henry: Warbeck was condemned for high treason and hanged at Tyburn in 1499, having first made a full confession.

These events brought in their wake another incident that caused great pain to Elizabeth. Warbeck had inveigled the Earl of Warwick into his plot with the promise that, if Warbeck succeeded in becoming King Richard IV, Warwick would be freed and would have all his vast estates restored to him. The earl was by now 29 and had spent most of his life as a prisoner of the state. When the plot was revealed, he naively confessed his part in it. Elizabeth had shared some of his early imprisonment at Sheriff Hutton and was fond of her cousin, whose only fault was that by birth he stood in the way of too many people. Both she and the earl now depended on Henry's well-known clemency, but in this they were mistaken.

Henry VII was, on the whole, a merciful man, but he was also not a man to let sentiment impede political expediency. He was deep in negotiations with King Ferdinand of Aragon about the marriage of his son Arthur to Ferdinand's daughter, Catherine of Aragon. He was very eager for this Spanish connection, for Spain's star was rapidly rising along with the wealth accruing from its post-1492 conquests of New World civilizations. Ferdinand had no intention of saying yes to a man whose throne was not totally secure, so he demanded that all threats to Henry's throne be done away with, including Warwick's. So, in spite of Elizabeth's anguished pleas, the hapless earl, the last of the legitimate male Plantagenets, was beheaded in 1499 on the charge of treason.

Even on a mundane level, Elizabeth's life was not easy. Her parents had been lavish spenders and Elizabeth was equally generous and open-handed, but Henry was tightfisted—almost a miser—and she was constantly getting into trouble with him about her expenditures, particularly when it came to her sisters, on whom she lavished both affection and gifts. The only things Henry did not seem to mind spending money on were music (like a true Welshman he was very musical), dancing, and card- playing, which was coming so much into vogue in the courts of Europe. Court life was then not an entirely grim affair.

With her children she had help from an unexpected quarter in seeing to their upbringing and to the luxuriousness of their surroundings. The help came from her mother-in-law, Margaret Beaufort, who always had more influence over her only son than Elizabeth ever had. Margaret, who from her portraits had the Plantagenet red-gold hair, fair skin, and long straight nose, had, nonetheless, qualities that remind us of her forebear, the intelligent and kindly Katherine Swynford, mother of the Beauforts, She was very concerned about children, and was a great help to the young Elizabeth in all her confinements and in the setting up of the nurseries in regal style. Not that she interfered, for with the longed-for marriage of her son achieved she kept well in the background. But she was always on hand for her grandchildren whenever they needed her, and it was just as well, for Elizabeth had inherited her father's laziness. With the well-organized Margaret the royal children had better care and attention than was the lot of most royal children, either before or since.

Even good care, however, could not save the weaker ones; the little Princess Elizabeth died when she was three, her brother Edmund at 16 months, and another boy did not even survive long enough to be named. There remained Arthur, who had never overcome his premature birth and so was a weak child; the plain Margaret; the robust Henry; and the lovely Mary.

Henry pinned his hopes on his elder son, and all was rejoicing when in November of 1501 the 15-year-old Arthur was wed in St. Paul's Cathedral in London to the 14-year-old Catherine of Aragon. His grandmother Margaret "wept marvelously" with joy all through the ceremony. In January of 1502 there was further royal rejoicing when daughter Margaret was formally betrothed to King James IV of Scotland. A great banquet was held at Richmond Palace, where Elizabeth took her 12-year-old daughter by the hand and led her to the place of honor at the banquet as a future queen. Unfortunately, future sad events would delay the actual marriage for another 18 months.

The cycle of tragedy started in March of 1502 with the newly married Arthur dying of tuberculosis. It was a terrible blow to his parents, but from their grief we have telling proof that, in spite of the fact that theirs had been a marriage of state, this dissimilar couple had become truly attached. Elizabeth, comforting her distraught husband said, "Your mother had never no more children but you only and God has ever preserved you and brought you where you are, and we still have a fair prince and two fair princesses, and there might yet be more. We are both young enough." She then retired to her own chambers before breaking down with grief herself, whereupon Henry went to comfort *her*.

Following through on her suggestion, she immediately became pregnant again. In February of 1503 she delivered her eighth child, a girl named Katherine, and died in childbed; the baby died a few days later.

Elizabeth was greatly mourned: "One of the most gracious and best-beloved princesses in the world in her time being" was the verdict of her people. Henry mourned her also. He was so broken up by her death that, although he arranged a splendid funeral at the Abbey, he was too upset to attend it, and it was her sister Katherine, wife of the Earl of Devon, who was the chief mourner at the ceremony. He aged visibly after her death and his health began to fail. Although she could never deflect this outwardly cold and determined man from his purposes, Elizabeth, by providing him with a happy home life, had had a restraining and softening effect on him. After her death the worst traits in his nature were to surface in extreme form—particularly his miserliness.

His subsequent treatment of Arthur's widow, the young Princess Catherine, was abominable. He had no intention of giving up the Spanish princess or—more importantly—her very rich dowry, so he badgered, bullied and ill-treated the girl until she was forced to marry his younger son, Henry. He went still further. Avidly hunting for a rich wife, he proposed that he should marry her mad sister Joanna, the widowed Queen of Castile, and to marry off Joanna's son, the future Charles V of Spain, to his three-year-old daughter Mary. Fortunately, nothing came of this latter project.

He grew paranoid about his sole remaining son Henry, keeping the young man close by him and under strict supervision. When the prince was out of his father's sight, though, the story was quite different, for Prince Henry was very like his grandfather Edward IV in both physique and appetites.

As to his subjects, Henry VII mercilessly fleeced them, using unscrupulous lawyers like William Empson and Edmund Dudley. Only when he lay dying "of a wasting disease"—probably the same tuberculosis that had killed his elder son—did he repent and stop their depredations. He died, prematurely aged, in April of 1509 at the age of 52, and was buried beside Elizabeth in the splendid chapel he had had built for them in Westminster Abbey. His mother survived long enough to see her grandson crowned Henry VIII and married to Catherine of Aragon, but died in July of the same year.

A little footnote to Henry's affection for his wife Elizabeth is still with us. Before his death he ordered that the English deck of cards be standardized—the same deck of cards we use to this day. In it Elizabeth of York's portrait, clutching the Tudor rose, is still to be seen—she is the Queen of Hearts.

Catherine of Aragon

CATHERINE OF ARAGON
(1485–1536)

m. (1) Arthur Tudor
m. (2) Henry VIII   1509

Children: Henry, MARY & five others

PROBABLY THE VERY FIRST THING AN ENGLISH CHILD remembers about British history is the six wives of Henry VIII and the jingle that goes with them: "Divorced, beheaded, died, divorced, beheaded, survived." It was Catherine of Aragon's great misfortune to be the first of this unhappy group of women, unintentionally altering the entire course of England's history.

❖   128   ❖

National Portrait Gallery, London.

Born in December of 1485 at the palace of Alcala, the same year her future father-in-law Henry VII plucked the Yorkist crown from Richard III on Bosworth Field and established the Tudor dynasty, she was the youngest daughter of Ferdinand, King of Aragon, and his equally royal spouse, Isabella, Queen of Castile in her own right. She was not a particularly welcome sight to the royal couple, who already had three daughters but only one son; they had been hoping for another boy. Her parents were a remarkable duo: he, wily, cruel and flagrantly unfaithful; she, passionate and combative, more than a match for him. Both were ruthless and had come to their thrones by devious means: Ferdinand's elder brother had died "mysteriously" and Isabella had gained her crown by an even more startling route. Her brother Henry IV, who had reigned before her, had been pronounced impotent and deposed by the Castilians—even though he had a daughter, whereupon Isabella had seized the throne and exiled the inconvenient little princess to Portugal, where she became a nun. A streak of this ruthlessness was to be passed on to Catherine.

Having united their two kingdoms, the royal pair intended to rule all parts of Spain as a united country, and by the time of Catherine's birth only two provinces remained unconquered: the kingdom of Granada to the south, held by the Islamic Moors, and the kingdom of Navarre in the Pyrenees, which had strong ties with France. For the first six years of her life her parents' prime target was Granada. So the small Infanta, with her brother and sisters, was brought along on the campaigns, shifted from monastery to nunnery, surrounded by monks and nuns, obliged to hear three masses a day, and given endless religious instruction, while outside their parents conducted endless bloody warfare against "the Infidels." When she was six this existence came to an end as Granada was besieged, captured and added to their growing kingdom.

In 1492, when she was seven, an even more important event occurred that was to send her parents' fortunes soaring, when Christopher Columbus, backed by her mother's money (her father had considered it a harebrained scheme), discovered a whole New World for them and proceeded to lay it at the Queen's feet. The riches that would eventually flow into Spain's coffers from that discovery would catapult it from a minor, divided country to Europe's premier power. At the time, the seven-year-old was more interested in the "Red Indians" Columbus had brought with him to the Castilian court. And her father Ferdinand was deep in the acquisition of the only other Spanish holdout, the kingdom of Navarre.

Although Navarre was territorially in Spain, for a century the royal family of Navarre had been French and under the protection of the French king, so

Ferdinand made the fateful decision to bestow his daughters' hands *only* on the royal enemies of France. He married his eldest daughter Isabella to the King of Portugal; his second, Juana, to Philip the Fair, who was ruler of Belgium, Holland and many domains in France and who had his eye on rich Burgundy. He also married his only son Juan to Philip's sister Marguerite. But then the plan began to unravel. His son died without issue in 1497, making his eldest daughter heir to the throne. Then she died in childbed in 1498, and her baby Miguel (who could have united Portugal and Spain) died at the age of two in 1500. Her younger sister the Infanta Mary was sent to marry Isabella's widower. This left Juana as heir, and she had already produced a son by Philip (the future Emperor Charles V). Unfortunately, she was already showing signs of mental instability—brought on, it was said, by her beloved husband's flagrant infidelities. It was time to do something about Catherine.

Ferdinand had already been approached by Henry VII of England, seeking a wife for his elder son Arthur, Prince of Wales, and with an eager eye on the rich dowry that went with a Spanish Infanta. Ferdinand initially was not too enthusiastic: Henry was a usurper, and although England was the hereditary foe of France, all that remained of the vast English possessions in France was the port of Calais. But his own series of domestic tragedies made him reconsider, and in July of 1499 a treaty of alliance was signed, along with the marriage contract. To proceed this far, Ferdinand had already exacted a bitter price that had caused much pain to Henry VII's queen, Elizabeth: the execution of her cousin, the Earl of Warwick (the *legitimate* heir to the throne) and of the pretender Perkin Warbeck.

The treaty was ratified in 1500 and the 15-year-old Catherine officially betrothed to the 14-year-old Arthur. With her was to go a dowry of 200,000 gold crowns. Again, however, Ferdinand delayed, still uncertain of his new ally's motives, and not until September of 1501 did Catherine set sail on her long journey north, accompanied by a large retinue and her dowry in wooden chests.

Along with her sisters she had received the usual narrow and rigid education of a Spanish Infanta. She could read and write Latin—a language in which she had exchanged stilted letters with her fiancé Arthur. She could dance and do needlework, but overtopping everything was a heavy insistence on piety and religious duty. On the practical side, her passionate, embittered mother had well instructed her daughters that royal marriages were not love matches but affairs of state, and that their duty to their husbands was to provide them with heirs and not to expect love in return.

Even though this marriage had been evolving for two years, nobody had bothered to teach Catherine any English.

She was considered no beauty: dumpy, short-necked, sallow-skinned, with heavy features, she also had her mother's pale blue eyes and dull fair hair. Although some English chroniclers, enthusiastic about this Spanish marriage, would dub her "beautiful" when she arrived, her only really attractive feature was the freshness of youth, and this freshness would fade fast in what lay ahead. Unlike her sister Juana, who, although unbalanced, was vivacious, Catherine was solemn and staid and had been noted for her phlegmatic character even as a small child.

In October she landed with her train of ladies, priests and envoys in Plymouth. Henry VII and Arthur went part of the way to meet her and escort her back to London. The Spanish envoys were so alarmed by the young prince's emaciated appearance that they demanded a physical examination, but apart from his extreme thinness could find nothing wrong. They were right to be concerned, for, in fact, Arthur was already far advanced in the tubercular consumption that would shortly kill him.

Catherine was welcomed with wild acclaim by all London, and the marriage performed with due pomp in November, 1501 at St. Paul's Cathedral, followed by two weeks of celebration, during which the Princess Margaret, Arthur's sister, was officially betrothed to the Scottish king, James IV. Then the newlyweds departed for Arthur's residence at Ludlow Castle, where he went into a rapid decline and died in his young bride's arms on April 2, 1502. At the age of 17 the Princess of Wales, so lately a bride, was now a widow in a foreign land to whose language and customs she was a stranger.

The question of whether this four-and-a-half-month marriage had been consummated was to loom over her later in life. On the one hand we have the oft-quoted testimony of Arthur after his wedding night; he boasted to his friends "I have been in Spain all night." Consumptives can be sexually active—witness the poet John Keats and the composer Frederic Chopin. On the other hand we have Catherine's stout denial in later years that the marriage was ever consummated. She went to her second marriage seven years later dressed in virginal white and with her hair unbound, and no one protested.

English sources later became so polarized according to their prejudices that little account can be taken of them; Spanish sources have no definitive answer to this vital question either. A letter exists in the official Spanish royal records in which Isabella talks of the consummated marriage; but another, from Ferdinand, states that Catherine was still a virgin; and again there is a letter from her mother changing her mind and agreeing with him. Virgin or not, Ferdinand did not appear to want his slightly-used Infanta back on his hands because, in May, while instructing his ambassador to ask for Catherine and her dowry back, he also empowered him to arrange a match between Catherine and the new Prince of Wales, Henry, who was only 11 and so almost seven years her junior.

It was the beginning of long years of misery for Catherine. The grief-stricken Tudors were so busy comforting each other over Arthur's death that they had little time for her. Another tragedy struck the Tudor family circle in February of 1503 when Queen Elizabeth died in childbirth causing Henry VII even greater grief. In this dismal atmosphere Catherine and young Henry were officially betrothed in June of 1503. In the marriage treaty between Spain and England it was explicitly stated that a papal dispensation would be necessary because she had "contracted affinity" with Henry by her *consummated* marriage with Arthur. The dispensation caused further delay because at just about that time Pope Alexander VI died. Pope Julius II, who inherited the problem, hesitated, so it was not until March of 1505 that the dispensation was given. A further blow to Catherine came in June of that year when young Henry, now almost 14, protested the validity of the match. To add to her trials, in November her mother died, quickly followed by Ferdinand's remarriage.

Poor Catherine was in despair: Nobody wanted her in England and nobody in Spain wanted her back. Her letters to her father were full of her grievances: She complained about her clothes, her food, the meanness of her father-in-law, even about her confessor, who probably had not been sympathetic enough and had told her to be stoic about her problems. Henry VII, whose unpleasant traits were rapidly surfacing after the death of his moderating queen, badgered her to convince her father to allow him to marry the widowed Juana, Queen of Castile, even though she was insane and was roaming from place to place with her dead husband's embalmed body in a glass coffin accompanying her. Catherine did write the letter, but, since her father had no intention of letting Henry get a hold on Castile, nothing came of it. Despite her father's callous indifference, Catherine was still more concerned with Spain than England. As late as April of 1506, according to her own letters, she was still unable to write or speak any English.

The matter of marriage was settled only by the death of Henry VII in 1509. At this point the councillors to young King Henry VIII, seeing no other promising European royalty in the offing, advised him to go through with the marriage. On June 3, 1509, the faded Infanta was finally wedded to Henry. She was 24, he was 18.

Her second Tudor husband was a very different proposition from the sickly Arthur. In his great height and strong build, he resembled his maternal grandfather, Edward IV, and had the red-gold hair of the Plantagenets. Apart from a too-small mouth, inherited from his mother, he was extremely handsome. He also took after his grandfather Edward in his appetites: He was a glutton for food and drink, a dedicated womanizer, and a fanatic about hunting and all athletic activities. He had already enjoyed mistresses, and one affair, with an older, married woman, was particularly significant. The woman was Elizabeth Howard, a scion of the powerful nouveau riche Howard family, married to Sir Thomas Boleyn, also from a nouveau riche merchant family, and with a family that included two daughters, Mary Boleyn and Anne Boleyn.

At first the handsome king and the faded Infanta seemed happy enough, although they had virtually nothing in common; and she settled down to her royal task of bearing his children. She immediately became pregnant, and the birth was looked forward to with great anticipation, but she miscarried. She became pregnant again immediately, and this time carried the child to full term; it was a son, born on January 1, 1511. The parents rejoiced, along with the whole nation—and two months later the child was dead. Catherine would endure this miserable process no fewer than seven times—four children were boys—and by 1525, when she passed beyond the age of childbearing, all she had to show for all her agony was one daughter, Mary, born in 1516, who, though plagued by ill health throughout her life, did manage to survive among this series of stillbirths and short-lived infants.

Henry sorrowed with her through the first two or three disappointments, but after that sought solace elsewhere. By 1514 he was wondering aloud about an annulment, although the birth of Mary in 1516 apparently gave him renewed hope and he dropped the idea.

Catherine was not entirely passive about his affairs. She turned a blind eye when the woman was one of lowly birth, like Bessie Blount, who had provided him with a son, Henry Fitzroy, later to be made Duke of Richmond—or, for that matter, Mary Boleyn, who gaily followed her mother into the king's bed. Casting his eyes on ladies of noble birth was another matter, and when he started to pursue Lady Hastings, kin to the powerful Duke of Buckingham, Catherine objected so violently the whole court was in an uproar. Henry hastily backed down and Lady Hastings was removed from the court.

Although Henry was no longer physically interested in his wife, he retained a great respect for her, and he trusted her, so that when his wily father-in-law finally inveigled him into making war on France in 1513, he left her as Regent of England. During his absence his brother-in-law James IV of Scotland, an ally of France, invaded England and was soundly beaten and killed by an English army headed by the Howards at Flodden Field. Catherine was so delighted that she proposed to have the king's body preserved in brine and sent to her husband as a present. She was talked out of this project, and the body was bundled into a coffin and put in a cupboard, where it lay unsought for years—even by wife Margaret, who had hastily remarried. Catherine's ruthless streak reappeared the same year when Henry wrote to her advising the execution of Edmund de la Pole, Earl of Suffolk (a descendant of Edward IV), whom he thought had designs on the throne. She carried out his wish with celerity and without a flicker of regret.

With the French war settled and his unwilling sister, the beautiful Mary, packed off to be the wife of the aged and widowed Louis XII of France, Henry came home. The birth of daughter Mary cheered him, but she was succeeded by more short-lived children, so he became increasingly worried about the succession and started to root out all surviving Plantagenet descendants who were even remotely threatening to him. The Duke of Buckingham (a descendant of Thomas of Woodstock) was executed in 1521; Richard de la Pole (brother of the Edmund de la Pole Catherine had had executed) in 1525; Henry, Lord Montague (a grandson of Edward IV's brother George) in 1538; and, to Henry's eternal shame, Montague's mother Margaret, the aged Countess of Salisbury, daughter of George, in 1541. By 1525, when he realized Catherine was beyond childbearing, he cast around for ways to secure the succession. First he thought of his nephew the infant James V of Scotland for his daughter Mary; then he brought his bastard son Henry Fitzroy forward, created him Duke of Richmond and proposed *he* should marry his half-sister. Nothing came of that proposed bit of incest either.

In the meantime a complicating series of events occurred. Louis XII of France died and, to Henry's initial displeasure, his widow Mary hastily married her true love, Charles Brandon, Duke of Suffolk. Louis was succeeded by Francis I, whom Henry could not abide, partly because Francis was even more flamboyant than Henry. As a result Henry recalled all the young English lads and lasses who were being "polished" at the French court, among whom was Anne Boleyn, younger daughter of his ex-mistress Elizabeth Howard Boleyn and sister of his mistress Mary Boleyn. And Henry, probably for the first time in his self-indulgent life, fell in love to the point of obsession.

At first Catherine did not recognize this danger, thinking that in time Anne would follow the pattern of her mother and sister and that Henry would tire of her. But Anne held out for marriage, whetting Henry's appetite. So in 1527 Henry instructed Cardinal Wolsey, his *éminence grise* (and a butcher's son), to seek an annulment from the Pope on the grounds of Catherine's first marriage to his brother, and on May 31 Henry informed Catherine that they had been living in mortal sin and so must separate forever. His action had plenty of precedents, so he assumed success for his plan. But the timing was against him: just a year earlier Pope Clement would probably have acted with dispatch, but in 1527 Rome had been captured by none other than Catherine's nephew, the rising Emperor Charles V, son of the mad Queen Juana. the pope was to all intents and purposes the captive of a man who was not about to let his aunt be pushed aside or the honor of Spain be tarnished. The best Clement could do was to instruct his legate, Cardinal Campeggio, to persuade Catherine herself to enter a convent of her own free will and thus leave the way clear.

Catherine refused. She would not step aside or let her daughter be bastardized. As a good Catholic she did not believe in divorce. The stand she took from the start, and from which she never budged, was that she had done no wrong; she had never been Arthur's wife, for the marriage had not been consummated. She had been Henry's loyal and faithful queen for over 20 years and had borne him seven children, including a living heir, the Princess Mary. Daughter of a queen in her own right and sister of another, she saw nothing wrong with Mary's succeeding to the throne. Unaware of English history, she did not know of England's long discomfort with the idea of a ruling queen, or of the disastrous outcome of Henry I's daughter Matilda's attempts to reign.

When Campeggio suggested her retirement to a convent she wryly replied that she would retire to a convent the day husband Henry agreed to enter a monastery. Ironically, the desperate Henry was seriously discussing this strategy with Campeggio—he was considering joining a monastery and then having the Pope grant dispensation to come out again. Campeggio thought not.

In May of 1529 Catherine was summoned before the legates at a court in Blackfriars, where she stated her views, adding that she would not consent to appear before them again; she appealed directly to the Pope. Even Henry was touched, and some of the bishops, including the important Bishop Fisher, courageously supported her. Her appeal did not save her in the long run, but it did result in the Cardinal Wolsey's disgrace and downfall, since he had failed his anxious master. Before he could be executed he solved his own problem by dying, and was replaced in the king's councils by his own chief aide, the equally lowborn and even more intelligent Thomas Cromwell.

Henry next tried all sorts of ploys to make her leave him, such as keeping Anne and Catherine in the same palace—a ploy which did not disturb Catherine but exasperated Anne. Not until July of 1531 did he permanently forsake her. He began to shunt her from one palace to another, reducing her household at each shift. By this time Anne felt she had the upper hand, and with the prospect of an imminent marriage before her, finally entered the king's bed.

In 1532 Thomas Cromwell suggested that the only means to make way for this marriage was for Henry to render himself independent of the papacy by declaring himself the head of the English Catholic Church. The Protestant Bishop Cranmer would be summoned back from Germany, where he had espoused the new separatist religion. The superstitious Henry still hesitated to take such a drastic step, but by the beginning of 1533 Anne was pregnant, and with the prospect of the son and heir she had promised him Henry could afford to dither no longer. Cranmer was summoned back and made Archbishop of Canterbury. In January, Anne and Henry were secretly married, and on May 23, 1533 they were publicly married by Archbishop Cranmer, who formally pronounced Henry's marriage to Catherine null and void on the old grounds of her first marriage to Arthur. After 24 years of marriage Catherine was put aside.

Feelings ran high at court, particularly among the women, and brave men like Sir Thomas More and Bishop Fisher went to the block rather than agree to this solution. When Anne was crowned queen in June 1533 some ladies, loyal to Catherine, absented themselves from the ceremony—among them the Duchess of Norfolk (a Stafford by birth who did not approve of the overly ambitious Howards) and the Marchioness of Exeter, who was Spanish ambassador Chapuys' chief pipeline into the court.

Henry was not a magnanimous winner. He separated Catherine from her 17-year-old daughter Mary and saw to it also that Mary was parted from all her former mentors and ladies. He restricted visits to Catherine, and this isolation was increased as Queen Anne, not having produced the promised male heir but merely another girl—Elizabeth—became increasingly insecure herself and forbade the ex-queen *any* visitors. Her faithful friends, however, still managed to smuggle messages to her, and it must have afforded Catherine a certain grim satisfaction to hear of Anne's miscarriages and of the king's waning interest in her.

In 1535 Anne was reported as being pregnant again, and in December Catherine fell violently ill with nausea and excruciating pain in her stomach and bowels. Much to Henry's and Anne's dismay, she recovered. Immediately after Christmas she again fell ill with the same symptoms, and Chapuys managed to sneak into Kimbolton where she lay dying. She thanked him with the words, "I shall at least have one friend beside me, I shall not be left to die alone like a beast." Still she lingered, and Chapuys had to leave, but one of her Spanish ladies, who had married an English aristocrat, talked her way past the guards. She and a priest were with Catherine when she died at two o'clock in the afternoon of January 7, 1536. Henry and Anne were overjoyed at the news, but that very same day Anne miscarried—a stillborn son—and sealed her own fate.

Catherine's death brings up the question of murder. Two Spanish doctors whom Chapuys had left with her were so suspicious of her symptoms that they demanded an autopsy. The request was denied and one of the Spanish doctors who persisted was spirited away to the Tower, never to be seen again. An autopsy of sorts was performed, albeit not by a doctor, resulting in the report that her heart was "blackened and shrivelled." Combined with her other symptoms, the condition of the heart could well point to arsenic poisoning.

Looking around for a suspect one has to eliminate Henry, who could have killed her years before and spared himself much agony. The most likely suspects are the Howard family, who had easy entree into the queen's household and were known to have tried poison on her long-time supporter, Bishop Fisher. The poisoning had failed, although several of the bishop's household had died, and the actual poisoner (the cook) was caught and boiled alive on Henry's orders. Their motive was undoubtedly Anne's own faltering relationship with Henry and the awful prospect that he might change his mind and take Catherine back.

Catherine died thinking she had failed, yet what she had fought for did come to pass: Her daughter Mary was to reign as England's first successful queen, even though that reign was besmirched by Mary's attempts to put England back into the Catholic fold and by her ruthless persecution of all those who had harmed her mother and herself.

Catherine's real importance grew out of her determination. Through it, she forced her erring husband into breaking with the Catholic Church, thereby detaching England from the continuous internecine struggles of southern Europe and forcing the nation to look to northern Europe and its burgeoning Protestant Reformation, and ultimately to the northern New World. Catherine had sounded a drum the repercussions of which would be heard through the whole course of England's future.

Anne Boleyn

ANNE BOLEYN
(1507–1536)

m. Henry VIII 1533

Child: ELIZABETH

OFTEN CALLED "ANNE OF A THOUSAND DAYS," Anne Boleyn has been portrayed as an arch-villainess by her detractors and as an arch-heroine by her supporters. She was neither: If anything, she was just as much a victim of her time as Anne Neville had been. Caught between a spoiled monarch's obsessive love and her family's ambitions, she would be crushed and annihilated.

Her father, Sir Thomas Boleyn, came from a well-to-do merchant family whose rise to riches had culminated with his grandfather's becoming Lord Mayor of London. Later, the family retired from commerce and settled down to be "country gentlemen." Like most of the rich merchant class, he had looked to make a socially advantageous match and had married into the influential Howard family, whose own rise to riches had begun when Edward IV had deputed the young Sir John Howard to survey opinion about his own marriage to Elizabeth Woodville. Howard had presented a favorable (and false) report to the king, and consequently received a handsome reward from the Woodvilles. The Howards had a tenuous claim to royal blood themselves as descendants of Thomas of Brotherton, the fruit of Edward I's second marriage to Marguerite of France, but they too were considered to be nouveau riche and not true members of the old nobility.

The Howards were masters at political maneuvering, having easily changed their allegiance from Richard III to the usurper Henry Tudor. High nobility had eluded them until the joint victory by the father-and-son team of Howards at Flodden in 1513, when Henry VIII gave the father back the title of Duke of Norfolk and the son became the Earl of Surrey. Since Sir Thomas Boleyn's wife, Elizabeth, was the new Duke's sister, their standing was also enhanced. They had three surviving children, one son George—later Lord Rochford—and two daughters, Mary and Anne.

Anne was born in 1507 at Bullen Hall in Cheshire according to some, and to others at Bicklington Hall in Norfolk—both family estates. Certainly she spent part of her childhood at Bicklington before being shipped off at the age of 12 to the court of Louis XII along with sister Mary for "polishing" at the most civilized and cultured court in Europe. There her sister Mary, considered the prettier of the two, shortly earned a notorious reputation, her lovers including the heir to the French throne, Francis, who referred to her as "my hack, my mule."

But Anne, while learning all the courtly graces and playing at courtly love, managed to keep herself intact. In 1521, when she was 14, Henry prepared to go to war with France and summoned back all the English from the French court. Anne joined this exodus and returned to her parents' home, now at Hever Castle in Kent. It was probably there that Henry first set eyes on her when he came in pursuit of his new mistress, Mary, who had succeeded her own mother as Henry's mistress.

The female Howards were already well entrenched at court; both Anne, the Dowager Duchess of Norfolk, and Elizabeth, the current Duchess of Norfolk, were ladies-in-waiting to Queen Catherine. Mary Boleyn was soon added to this Howard clique, who deeply appreciated having another *maîtresse en titre* or, roughly, "official mistress" in the king's bed as an added fillip to their fortunes. Her father also obtained for Anne a position in the queen's household, and off she went to court. There, from the start, she was a smashing success, and many men fell in love with her, including the king.

What was Anne's secret? Her physical characteristics included a large dark mole on her neck (which she hid with high collars) and a sixth rudimentary finger on one of her hands (which she hid with long sleeves). Her only claims to physical beauty were her lustrous black hair—so long she could sit on it—and her large, sparkling black eyes. Her great attraction was her personality. Stylish, vivacious and accomplished, she had what we might call sexual magnetism.

One of the men who fell in love with Anne, and whose love she may well have returned, was young Henry Percy, heir to the earldom of Northumberland, who was attached to the household of Henry's chief advisor, Cardinal Wolsey. Anne wanted this marriage for she would become part of one of the oldest noble families in England—a match that would please even the ambitious Howards. But the king had already marked her for himself and would have none of it. Although Henry Percy begged and pleaded with the Cardinal to be allowed to marry Anne, he was shipped back to the family seat in Northumberland and quickly married to someone else.

Bereft of this hope, Anne turned for consolation to her cousin, Sir Thomas Wyatt (their mothers were sisters). Wyatt was a sensitive soul, a poet, and though married was himself in love with Anne. He was certainly sympathetic, and often she would sneak away from Hever to his home near Maidstone in Kent to tell him her troubles. Again Henry intervened: A word in Wolsey's ear and the Cardinal told Wyatt to go to Italy on a long visit "for his health."

By 1525 Henry was openly pursuing Anne, writing impassioned letters—still extant—making all manner of promises if only she would become his mistress. Although she must have realized that he would resist marriage, Anne would not yield. She had seen what happened to his former mistresses, like Bessie Blount, Jane Popincourt and her own sister Mary. After he had tired of them (Mary had lasted two years) he would marry them off to some obscure and accommodating minor gentleman and forget them. That fate was not for her.

One cannot help but think that possibly the progenitor of the Howard fortunes, John, had handed down to the family the tale of how Elizabeth Woodville captured Edward IV by playing "hard to get," and that this had given Anne the idea. Her family was horrified that she should dare to reject the king, fearing for their own fortunes, and the only support she received was from her brother George, who despised his parents and the Howards as much as she did. In spite of their pressure she held out.

Gradually Henry realized that she meant what she said. Already desperate for an heir, he slowly put the machinery in motion that would dissolve his marriage and clear the way for a union with this elusive young woman, who had many years of childbearing ahead of her and could provide him with the sons he lacked.

With a family member who might indeed have a chance at being queen, many of the Howards now changed sides and came out in her active support—among them the Dowager Duchess of Norfolk, who deserted Catherine and was one of those who testified at Blackfriars Court in 1529 that Catherine's marriage to Arthur had been consummated. Other Howards, however, were incensed by Anne's pretensions, among them Elizabeth, present Duchess of Norfolk, a Stafford and an ally of Catherine's, who publicly chastised Anne for her behavior.

If those eight years between 1525, when Henry's pursuit began, and 1533 when it ended, were hard on Catherine, they were equally hard on Anne, who was taking a desperate gamble. Over the years she could not continue to keep the king at arm's length, and it is evident from their letters that bit by bit she was yielding. All the court regarded her as his concubine; only Henry and she knew she was not, in the full sense of the word.

What made her yield finally in 1532 is obscure. Possibly, with Catherine and her daughter Mary both banished from court and Thomas Cromwell urging the king to take the final step and break with the Roman Pope, she may have felt secure enough to play her last card and demonstrate that she was fertile and could give him the son he so badly needed. Or maybe she feared that his roving eye would light on some younger, fairer face and that all would be lost. At any rate, yield she did and immediately became pregnant, thus literally pushing him into the final fateful decision to break with the Roman Catholic Church and grant his own divorce.

On January 25, 1533, they were secretly married by Archbishop Cranmer so that the child she carried would suffer no hint of bastardy, and the marriage was publicly celebrated on May 23 after Archbishop Cranmer had declared Catherine's marriage null and void. A magnificent coronation followed on June 1, with Queen Anne and her family triumphant. Her father was created Earl of Wiltshire and Ormonde and made Lord Privy Seal; his heir George was created Lord Rochford. Anne's thousand days had begun.

The first few months were outwardly all joy and gladness. Unlike Catherine, Anne had numerous interests in common with Henry. She could hunt and hawk with him. She could dance and loved music as much as he did. They kept a gay and witty court full of young people that gave back to the 42-year-old Henry a temporary illusion of recaptured youth. But it *was* all an illusion.

After 24 years of marriage, Catherine probably knew Henry better than he knew himself, and realized that once Henry's desires were sated, he would go philandering again. Even before the birth of the child the Spanish ambassador Chapuys reported with relish a public row between Anne and Henry because of the king's attentions to another lady, when Henry had told her "that she must shut her eyes and endure, as those who were better than herself had done"—this from a man who had written to her but two years previously, "I will never, ever, leave your side."

Then on September 10, 1533 the long-awaited child was born—not the son of his dreams but another daughter—the future Elizabeth I. In her own disappointment, Anne became almost frenzied in her efforts to get Henry to adopt harsher measures with Catherine and Mary, thus further alienating him. She became immediately pregnant again, but by the autumn of 1534 she had gone through three miscarriages and the disgusted Henry turned to a new mistress, whose name has not survived but whose sympathies were with Catherine and her supporters. Increasingly insecure, Anne hatched a plot to get rid of her rival with the help of her sister-in-law Lady Rochford. It failed, and Henry found out. He was furious and banished Lady Rochford from the court. Anne tried another ploy, introducing a compliant Howard cousin, Madge Shelton, who replaced the intruder in Henry's bed; but she too was soon replaced, because Henry's eye had fallen on someone else.

A brief respite and reconciliation between the battling royal pair came in June of 1535 with yet another pregnancy, and they were both delighted when news of Catherine's death at Kimbolton reached them in January of 1536. But that same day Anne went into premature labor and was delivered of a son—stillborn. Her thousand days were fast running out.

Here a pause must be taken to note a remarkable pattern. Catherine's unhappy record of miscarriages, stillbirths and only one sickly child was followed by Anne's with one live birth, three miscarriages and a stillbirth—in both cases happening to young and healthy women. The pattern, of course, points toward Henry.

In the 1920s a medical doctor wrote a book entitled *Mere Mortals*, an in-depth study of the health problems of the Tudor dynasty, in which he made a very strong case for Henry's having contracted syphilis as a youth. The immediate and hereditary effects would explain all the subsequent health problems of the Tudors: the sterility of his two surviving daughters, the continuous ill health and early deaths of his two sons, Henry Fitzroy and Edward VI, the sterility of his last two marriages to women of childbearing age (his fourth marriage was never consummated), and his own death, which the doctor ascribed to syphilis in its tertiary stage. Recent historians have rejected this diagnosis, reasoning that if Henry had contracted syphilis, his doctors would have prescribed mercury, already known to be a palliative—though not a cure—for syphilis. We know that they did not. But in rejecting the theory these historians are overlooking a very important point.

Although other venereal diseases had been known since ancient times, syphilis had not made its appearance in Europe until the end of the 15th century—so late, indeed, that it has been blamed by some on Columbus's sailors bringing it back from the New World and spreading it in the Old. Perhaps they did, or perhaps it was just a deadly mutation of an existing virus. Whatever its origin, "the great pox," as it was called, spread throughout Europe, especially the courts of Europe, with deadly speed and catastrophic results, and was regarded with as much fear, shame and ignorance as AIDS is now. There was no cure for it, often it was fatal, and it had horrendous hereditary effects that would bedevil European successions from then on.

Since Henry was notorious for his high-handed treatment of those who crossed or upset him—innkeepers, fortune-tellers, cooks, even bearers of bad tidings—it would have been a very brave doctor indeed who would have dared to tell His Majesty that the fault in those births lay not in his wives but in himself—and that he needed a good dose of mercury because he had "the pox." No such brave doctor came forward, and so the king remained untreated, living and dying in happy ignorance.

As for Anne, she quickly recovered from the premature birth, but it was too late; the king had turned his back on her and was in active pursuit of another coy lady-in-waiting, Lady Jane Seymour. He wanted Anne out of his life, and for the first time she realized that Catherine's death had weakened rather than strengthened her own position—if he retreated back into the fold of the Catholic Church, he would now be considered a widower and free to marry anyone he liked. She could easily be put aside and her daughter bastardized. Still, she did not fully comprehend how dramatically Henry's feelings had changed.

Unfortunately, in her rise to power she had made many enemies by her arrogance and by the ambitions she had openly showed. Many of her most dedicated enemies were ladies of her court: Gertrude, Marchioness of Exeter, Catherine's chief proponent; the "near royals" like Charles Brandon, Duke of

Suffolk and Henry's widowed brother-in-law, and his new wife. Most threatening of all was Thomas Cromwell, always swift to sense what the king really desired, who, behind the scenes, was compiling evidence to charge her with high treason. She had made his task easy when, in her growing insecurity and in the hope of bringing her unfaithful husband back through jealousy, she had flirted openly with some of her male courtiers, many of whom had for years loved her from afar.

The politically careful Howards, with the exception of her brother George, turned completely against her—even her own father and mother. Her uncle, the Duke of Norfolk, was in fact to be Cromwell's chief aide in investigating Anne's alleged misconduct. Cromwell knew his job, so he attacked at the weakest point—a court musician, Mark Smeaton, who, not being of noble birth, could be tortured not only until he confessed to adultery with the queen but also named others. On May 1, 1536, Henry Norris, Sir Thomas Weston, William Brereton and Anne's faithful brother George were arrested—the last on the strength of his own wife's accusations of incest with his sister and treasonable utterances. In return for her testimony, Lady Rochford was to be rewarded by restoration to her position at court, from which Henry had formerly banished her. On May 2, Anne herself was committed to the Tower, where she was surrounded by spies, including her own mother, who faithfully reported her every word to Cromwell.

On May 15, 1536 Anne and George were both tried in the Tower. The trial was a travesty, and although they both stoutly denied all the charges, both were convicted. It was their uncle, the Duke of Norfolk, who pronounced the sentence of death. On the 17th of May, George and her four other supposed lovers were executed on Tower Hill. On May 19th Anne herself was executed within the Tower, the sole concession she had obtained being that she was beheaded by the French executioner with a sword rather than the customary axe. She was 29 years old.

Her headless body was bundled into an old arrow chest and hastily buried under the floor of the chapel of St. Peter-in-the-Tower. Small wonder the unhappy shade of the queen is still supposed to haunt its precincts, as well as those of her old homes at Bicklington Hall and Hever Castle—if ever a woman was framed, she was.

Like Catherine before her, Anne probably died thinking her life a failure, ruing the day she had set eyes on the king, and believing she had borne him a hapless female child. Yet that daughter—surviving against all odds and with no memory of her tragic mother—would go on to become England's most powerful queen, quite possibly the most successful monarch of either sex England was to know.

JANE SEYMOUR
(1509–1537)

m. Henry VIII   May 20, 1536

Child: EDWARD

IF ANNE BOLEYN HAD BEEN AN EXOTIC FLOWER, Jane Seymour was an English rose. By the time Henry noticed her, she had already been at court for years, first as lady-in-waiting to Queen Catherine and then to Anne. She was 26 and still unmarried at a time when most gentlewomen of noble birth were married off in their late teens or early twenties. In portraits, she looks the caricature of the maiden aunt—plumpish, and slightly dull. She was excessively pale, with light blue eyes and fair hair. And she was virtuous in a court which, while by no means as licentious as the French court, was certainly no prim and proper place. Some accounts trace the beginning of Henry's interest in her in 1535 to the time he visited her ailing father, Sir Thomas Seymour, at his home at Wolf Hall, Savernake in Wiltshire, where Jane was not lost in a crowd of courtiers. She did have siblings, though, and if Jane was not dynamic or ambitious, they were: particularly her eldest brother, the serious and power-hungry Edward, and Thomas senior's fourth son, the dashing and charming Thomas. The others included her younger sister Mary, who, significantly, was to marry Geoffrey, son of the powerful if lowborn Thomas Cromwell, who always had his own eye on bettering his family's position.

Henry probably made the customary advances, and the virtuous Jane firmly declined. The family, scenting possible advantage, returned with her to court and, while encouraging her virtuousness, quickly joined the opposition to Queen Anne.

By the time Cromwell had engineered Anne's downfall, Henry was already set on marrying Jane as quickly as possible. Anne was executed on the morning of May 19, 1536, and, as is recorded in Wriothesley's contemporary chronicle, "on the 20th day of May the king was married secretly at Chelsea in Middlesex to one Jane Seymour, daughter of Sir John [sic] Seymour knight, late departed of this life, and she was brought to White Hall by Westminster the 30th day of May and there set in the Queen's seat sat under the canopy of estate royal. Also the fourth day of June the said Jane Seymour was proclaimed Queen at Greenwich and went in procession after the king . . . ."

We have no reason to suppose Jane was anything but delighted by this swift turn of events: She was at last being waited on and fawned on by those on whom she had lately been waiting. She loved exotic food, rich clothing and fine jewelry—now, her prerogatives as Queen. Since she knew all the domestic pitfalls from her years as lady-in-waiting, her own household was soon meticulously arranged to her own satisfaction.

Her coronation was scheduled for October, but an outbreak of the plague in London canceled the ceremony and no further mention was made of a new date. Henry was learning caution, and since the first few months of marriage had passed without any sign of a pregnancy he was not about to sanctify his new queen until he was sure she could produce his children. Thus Jane was destined never to be crowned.

In the meantime Jane tried her hand at the wider sphere of diplomacy, with mixed results. Mary Tudor, sick of her exile at Hunsdon, had begged Cromwell to intercede with her father to let her return to court, indicating she was willing to make some concessions. Jane thought this a very good idea and pleaded with Henry to let her come. She was only partly successful, for Henry sent the Duke of Norfolk and a band of nobles to his elder daughter, and not until she had abjectly acknowledged her father's supremacy, abjured Rome and declared her birth illegitimate was she allowed to return. Bitter as she was, her capitulation probably saved her life; the vindictive Henry had been poised to execute her.

Jane tried to exert her influence again when Henry and Cromwell decided to move forward with a plan they had been formulating ever since Henry had declared himself Head of the English Church—the dissolution of the monasteries and nunneries, tied to Rome. The step was hailed by the nobles and lesser gentry, for, although the bulk of the spoils went into the royal coffers—and were used wisely by Cromwell to set up a civil service that would stand England in good stead from then on—they also greatly benefited in this huge land grab. But what was good for the nobility was catastrophic for the poor and the lower classes, for at one fell swoop they were deprived of their hospitals, what education had been open to them, and their sole means of charity and shelter during a crisis—all of which had been provided by the religious houses. It would take centuries before alternate systems replaced them. On her knees Jane implored Henry to halt this dissolution of the monasteries, and was sternly told to mind her own business.

At this point Jane decided that she was not cut out for statecraft, and she was never heard from on any issue again. Indeed, she was so shy that she cut a rather poor figure at court, stuttering or merely gazing stupefied at flatterers when they paid her fulsome compliments; and Henry often rushed into the breach to cover her social awkwardness. He seemed at least briefly to find it charming. Fortunately for Jane, by February of 1537 she knew she was pregnant, and Henry and the court went wild with excitement. She was cosseted and pampered throughout the pregnancy but, just before she was due, there came another outbreak of the plague in London. Henry withdrew to Esher in Surrey, while she remained behind at Hampton Court awaiting the birth.

She went into labor the 11th of October: "And the morning after, being Friday and the even of Saint Edward the Confessor, at two of the morning the Queen was delivered of a man-child at Hampton Court." Henry at last had the son of his dreams—promptly named Edward after Henry's grandfather, whom the king now so closely resembled in girth and appetites. Henry rushed to her side, joyful that plain Jane had succeeded in giving him a healthy son, where his previous wives had failed. She became his "best-beloved."

Yet here begins a medical horror story. Jane had had a very difficult labor—one source has it that the baby had had to be delivered by Caesarean section, a terrible undertaking in the 16th century. Everyone was excited looking after the welfare of the new prince and preparing for the celebration of the birth, the christening, the "churching"* of Jane, and the forthcoming Christmas festivities when she would undoubtedly be crowned. With all the complicated arrangements and the elaborate new gowns to be made, no one paid much attention to the new mother, who probably did not want to miss the excitement either.

So, three days after the birth, on Monday the 15th, Jane was propped up on a throne in Hampton Court Chapel, where she alternately shivered and sweated under her royal robes, to see her son christened "Edward, son and heir to the King of England, Duke of Cornwall and Earl of Chester." His godmother was the Princess Mary; his godfathers, Archbishop Cranmer, the Duke of Suffolk and the Duke of Norfolk (the Howards could never be kept out for long). Four days later Jane was again propped up to witness the triumph of her brothers: the investiture of sober Edward as Earl of Hertford, and the knighting of her younger brother, the rascally Thomas. The next day the court belatedly realized that the queen was very ill. In another four days, just 12 days after the birth, she was dead at the age of 28 of either septicemia or puerperal fever.

---

* It was customary after a birth to "church" the mother in a sort of cleansing ritual.

By dying in her moment of triumph, Jane was probably saved a lot of grief. Although Henry was genuinely shocked and grieved at her loss, and probably would never have put aside the mother of his heir, she would doubtless not have had long to wait before facing his continuing infidelities, just as her predecessors had done.

Henry sorrowed for this virtuous wife who had never let him down, and by enshrining her memory extended his favor and thrust to her family throughout the rest of his reign. On his deathbed—and to everyone's surprise—he appointed her brother Edward as Regent and Lord Protector of the boy Edward, also giving him the title Duke of Somerset. Since the Duke, during this Protectorate, would steer the English Church firmly into the Protestant fold under Edward VI, this appointment was very important to the future of England, even though Jane herself was clearly a Catholic of the old-fashioned kind.

Romanticists have claimed that Henry truly loved Jane and did not love again. What is certain is that even before her burial in November of 1537, inquiries were being made by the ever-busy Cromwell for another bride for the bereaved Henry, who himself quickly warmed to the idea of the foreign marriage-mongering that would go on for two full years.

Henry decreed that Jane be buried in his newly refurbished chapel in Windsor Castle and that a magnificent tomb be built that would house both of them when he departed this life. The tomb was never completed, but he *was* eventually buried beside his shy queen.

Anne of Cleves, by J. Houbraken after Hans Holbein

ANNE OF CLEVES
(1515–1557)

m. Henry VIII Jan. 6, 1540
divorced July 9, 1540

No issue

ANNE OF CLEVES WAS NEITHER CROWNED QUEEN nor fully a wife to the king, but her short marriage has comical overtones and is the only one of this sad roster that had a happy ending. It also had one very important outcome.

This Anne was not even on the original list of possible brides that Cromwell and the king had first compiled after Jane Seymour's death. Both saw the sense of a foreign match: The English people might approve of queens of English blood but, as such marriages had recently proved, in royal circles they had their drawbacks. English queens also had English families only too eager and ambitious for their own advancement. This situation had been true of the Woodvilles and the Greys in the time of Henry's grandfather Edward, and was even more true of the Howards, and now the Seymours. In addition was the possibility of a good foreign alliance or, failing that, a hefty dowry with a foreign princess.

Here, however, they met an obstacle: Henry's reputation as a husband was hardly impressive, with one divorce, one execution and one death, so the royal families of Europe were not eager to send their daughters to his bed. Henry and Cromwell had to set their sights a little lower, but even then the candidates were reluctant. The impoverished Mary of Guise hastily decided she would rather marry the widowed James V of Scotland; Christina of Denmark, widow of the Duke of Milan, also quickly declined. The total came to nine women who either refused or were not exactly to Henry's taste.

A new factor entered in when in 1539 Henry became convinced that his two enemies, Francis I of France and the Holy Roman Emperor Charles V, were cementing an alliance to attack Protestant England and that he needed Protestant allies fast. This fear suited Thomas Cromwell: If the Catholics regained a foothold in England his own head would be the first to roll, so he suggested an alliance with William, Prince of Cleves—who like Henry was a Protestant but not a Lutheran—and a marriage with one of William's unwed sisters, Anne or Amelia, to cement the pact.

Henry thought this a good idea, and so the painter Holbein was dispatched to Cleves to paint their portraits, as he had done for five other suggested "brides." When Henry saw the portraits, on the strength of the winsome picture Holbein had created (and which makes her look more attractive than all the previous wives), his choice settled on Anne. It was a big mistake—a fatal one for Cromwell, who should have heeded a letter that he had received from England's envoy John Hutton, just after the search had begun in 1537: "The Duke of Cleves hath a daughter, but I hear no great praise of her personage or beauty." Nicholas Wotton had written later "She is a dull girl with few accomplishments." In fact, as Henry learned later to his dismay, the portrait had been highly misleading.

Born in 1515 to the impoverished Duke of Cleves, she had grown up in a frugal and depressing household with little education and less fun. She could speak only German, knew no music or dancing (only considered fit for "light women") and had not a single courtly grace. At two she had been betrothed briefly to the Duke of Lorraine, but nothing had come of the arrangement and so she remained at home, ungainly, overweight and flabby, until Holbein's magic and Henry's need gave her hope of release. She was also a complete innocent.

The marriage compact and alliance was signed late in 1539, and at the end of December she landed in England with a large train, all hoping to better their lot. The royal escort sent to greet her at the coast were so dismayed by her looks and deportment that they did not know what to do, other than delay the moment of truth as long as possible. The Earl of Southampton and Geoffrey Cromwell hastily taught her some of Henry's favorite card games, which delighted her (such frivolity was unknown in Cleves), and dallied so long that Henry, afire with impatience to meet his new bride, rode out in disguise to intercept the party on December 31 at Rochester in Kent. It was his turn to be dismayed, as he took in her ungainly figure and odd clothes, her sallow, shiny-skinned, pockmarked face with its large upturned nose. Anne did not know who he was and could not communicate with him, since he knew no German and she no English.

Henry returned to London ahead of her in a fury, which was the beginning of the end for Cromwell, whom he had so lately ennobled as Earl of Essex. To him Henry roared, "If I had known as much before as I know now, she would never have come into this realm!"

Desperately he postponed the marriage, hoping to find escape, but if he backed out at this late date he might drive the Duke of Cleves into the arms of his enemies. Besides, Cromwell could find no loophole for him. On Twelfth Night, January 6, 1540, he knew he could procrastinate no longer. Before the wedding, he told Cromwell grimly, "If it were not to satisfy the world and my realm I would not do that I must do this day for none earthly thing." Several weeks later he admitted that he could "never be provoked and steered to know her carnally." Anne was such an innocent that she thought his hesitant fumblings were all there was to marriage. When she was informed otherwise, she was thunderstruck.

The Howards, never slow to spot an opportunity, saw a golden one. Knowing the king's frustration and his previous weakness for Howard women, they introduced to court a likely candidate for his bed, the teenage Catherine Howard, a coarser version of his formerly beloved Anne Boleyn. The bait worked; by April the king had deserted his wife's bed and was in full pursuit of the merry, vivacious Catherine, although this time the Howards saw to it that she was chaperoned by her uncle, so Henry could only look.

The tantalized king determined to divorce Anne and marry Catherine as quickly as possible. He ordered Cromwell, against whom the Howards and the licentious Bishop Gardiner were already plotting, to find a way out of the marriage. "But what and how" cried the desperate Cromwell, knowing full well that to do so would bring the Howards back in full strength and make his own downfall a certainty.

Early in June his enemies had contrived such a good case against Cromwell that he was taken to the Tower, still under orders from the disgruntled king to dissolve the marriage. A few days later Henry had Anne removed from court to the royal palace of Richmond "for her health." Henry was delighted when the "Catholic coalition" of Francis and Charles did not come to pass. Henry no longer needed Cleves as an ally and Anne was in a potentially dangerous position. In what was to be his final official act, Cromwell sent the proposed divorce to Henry, along with an impassioned plea for mercy and clemency for himself. All the divorce needed was Anne's consent.

Henry dispatched Wriothesley and the Duke of Suffolk to Richmond to obtain that consent, and when Anne saw them and their entourage she was so certain they had come to take her to the Tower and chop her head off that she keeled over backwards in a dead faint. The concerned councillors revived her, propped her up, told her the king meant her no ill and indeed was only desirous of "doing right" by her if she would only give her consent to the divorce, and spelled out the terms of the settlement. Anne was not only willing, she was delighted, and so the pact was made.

Anne seems to have had one great gift: she brought out the best in people by arousing their compassion. The courtiers who met her train at Deal, instead of dissolving in laughter at the sight of her, were anxious to guard her from the wrath they knew would come; the cynical and sophisticated Southampton taught her to play Henry's favorite card games and postponed the meeting as long as possible. The English ladies of her short-lived court, who could have made her life an endless misery, instead were astonishingly supportive and protective. Henry himself, who so hated to be crossed or disappointed, was astoundingly generous when it came to the divorce settlement.

She was granted a large annual income for life, assigned Richmond Palace and the manor of Bletchingly for her town and country residences, and allowed to keep everything she had received as queen; also she could retain all the Cleveans she still had around her. In addition she would be welcome at court as Henry's "sister" and would take precedence over everyone there except the royals themselves.

When her furious brother—who never did accept the divorce—demanded that she return to Cleves, Anne politely declined. She had no intention of returning to dull and frugal Cleves; she knew when she was well off. "Now I can have a new dress every day!" she declared happily. She amused herself with her gardens, gambling, pets and frequent visits to court, where she became a welcome friend to the royal children—particularly the young Elizabeth—and was on good terms with Henry's two subsequent queens. In short, she lived happily ever after. There is even a rumor, impossible now to substantiate, that, as the years went on, she had a "great, good friend" among the gentlemen of her household. Nobody seemed to mind.

She outlived Henry as well as his short-lived son, and lived to see the first queen regnant of England, Mary, safely installed on the English throne, riding to the coronation with her favorite, Princess Elizabeth. She died in London on July 16, 1557 at the age of 42, and by order of Queen Mary was buried with royal honors in Westminster Abbey—the only one of Henry's queens to be so honored.

There was one very important political outcome to this tragicomedy of a marriage, in which Anne was just an innocent bystander. The king had broken Cardinal Wolsey because of his failure to secure his divorce from Catherine; he broke his successor Cromwell for spearheading the marriage to Anne of Cleves, even though no one had served him better. In spite of his pleas for mercy, Cromwell was executed on July 28, 1540, the very same day Henry took a new wife, Catherine Howard. The Howards and their supporters rejoiced, thinking that now the power behind the throne was theirs. They were wrong; from here on, and helped by the bureaucratic machinery Cromwell had brought into being, Henry would rule alone and with increasing despotism. They were all now at risk.

Catherine Howard, in a painting after Hans Holbein

CATHERINE HOWARD
(1521?–1542)

m. Henry VIII   July 28, 1540

No issue

WITH HENRY'S FIFTH WIFE we move from comedy back into tragedy. Born to Lord Edmund Howard, a younger brother to Thomas, Duke of Norfolk, and Elizabeth Boleyn, Catherine had the advantage of high birth but not of the money that usually goes with it. Her father, a younger son with no striking abilities, always needed funds and did not improve his financial position by fathering 10 children by four wives. Catherine was one of the fruits of his second marriage to a widow, Joyce Culpeper Leigh, who already had four children by her first husband and proceeded to bear Edmund eight more, three sons and five daughters, of whom Catherine was probably the oldest girl. She died when Catherine was still a small child. Lord Edmund, who was stationed overseas at Calais, promptly remarried another widow, Dorothy Troyes, who had eight children of her own, so the children of his former marriage were considered redundant and were shipped off to Horsham, the house of Catherine's step-grandmother, the Dowager Duchess of Norfolk. Here they joined a crowd of Howard cousins also abandoned by parents in similar circumstances—not that the Dowager Duchess was a very attentive guardian, for she was far too busy as a lady-in-waiting at court, where she was furthering the Howard interests.

Catherine spent her childhood in the Duchess's household with very little discipline and less instruction and education. When these children reached their teens, apparently a kind of sifting process took place, and the more promising ones were shifted to the Duchess's town house in Lambeth, London, where they received some rough polishing in courtly ways. Catherine's uncle, the Duke of Norfolk, was still Lord Treasurer of England in spite of all the Howard family upheavals, and he could still usher his relatives into that hotbed of opportunity, the royal court. But for impecunious Catherine there would be none of the fine polishing or instruction received at the French court by her rich Boleyn cousins, Mary and Anne.

It was at Lambeth that the first act of this tragedy began, for, as at the Duchess's country house, there was little in the way of discipline or supervision over these rambunctious teenagers. As Catherine learned deportment, music and dancing, she was also learning other lessons. Her music master, Henry Manox, later admitted to sexually molesting her as a young teen and, although the boys and girls of the household were separated into dormitories, there was much surreptitious coming and going.

Catherine, as vivacious and attractive as most of the Howard women, was soon experimenting, and then having an actual affair with Francis Dereham, who would sneak into her bed. They were eventually caught by the Duchess, and Dereham was banished temporarily from the scene, while plans were made for Catherine, who had been given a beating, to be shipped off to court as quickly as possible.

But matters external to the Lambeth household were shortly to raise the curtain on act two. Her neglectful father died in 1539, so Catherine was now a penniless orphan and at the mercy of her Howard relatives. The same year, the king's impending marriage to Anne of Cleves was announced, and the Duke of Norfolk, needing a place for his headstrong and attractive niece, obtained a position for her as lady-in-waiting to the new queen. At 18 or possibly 19

Catherine was tiny but full-figured, with Titian hair and with the same cast of feature as her late cousin Anne. She also had much of Anne's vivacity and natural grace, but, alas, none of her intelligence.

Her uncle, the Duke, when the farce of the king's marriage to Anne of Cleves was revealed, reviewed the list of eligible Howard women for a suitable candidate and lighted on Catherine as the most promising. At a banquet given for the king by his friend and coconspirator Bishop Gardiner, the duke made sure that Catherine, who was a good musician and an excellent dancer, was brought to Henry's notice. Apparently, this was all that was needed to spark the interest of the frustrated king; the Howard charm had its usual effect and he was off in hot pursuit.

Having gained the queenship once by Anne Boleyn's withholding of sexual favors, the Howards made sure that Catherine was unavailable to the king's desires. Henry rid himself of Anne of Cleves with dispatch, and on July 28, 1540, the day he also rid himself permanently of Thomas Cromwell, he rode out from Hampton Court and he and Catherine were married privately at his manor of Oatlands in Surrey. But Henry, more cautious than ever after his fiasco with Anne of Cleves, did not announce their marriage or pronounce her queen until Catherine had proved herself satisfactory in bed. On August 8 she was proclaimed Queen of England.

It was an overwhelming experience for a 19-year-old orphan, and she clearly reveled in the dresses and jewels, estates and properties and costly gifts her infatuated old husband lavished upon her from then on. But as someone who had suddenly been catapulted from obscure poverty to high position and riches, Catherine was anxious that she receive the "deference due her." She quarreled with Princess Mary, her senior by several years, who sulked away from court, not willing to pay homage to her father's parvenu bride. On the other hand, Anne of Cleves, delighted that she herself was free, gave the young queen respect as well as gifts and so became a valued friend.

There was also the problem of Henry, who at 49 was far from "the handsomest prince in Christendom" that the first Catherine had married. He was enormously fat, his face an ugly swollen mass; in constant pain, limping from his ulcerated legs that would never heal; and increasingly concerned about his health and well-being: not a very appetizing bedmate for a 19-year-old girl. She was "too much for him"; after the first few months he would slip away alone for a few days to recoup his strength. Although during the Clevean marriage his doctors had reassured him that he was not impotent, by this time he may well have been sterile, for throughout the two-year marriage Catherine, who came of such fertile stock herself, showed no sign of a pregnancy.

Mostly threatening of all were the people with whom Catherine was forced to surround herself, for young queens of aging kings should not have skeletons in their closets, and Catherine had a plenitude. The companions of her girlhood descended on her like a flock of vultures, seeking preferment. Their pleas often were thinly veiled blackmail, as in the case of Joan Bulmer, who had helped her to write love letters to Francis Dereham (Catherine was only semiliterate); she wrote, "I know the Queen of England will not forget her secretary."

Catherine did her best to take care of them all, swelling her retinue, already packed with Howards. Joan Bulmer, Margaret Mawton, Alice Restold and Katherine Tylney—all "dorm-mates" of hers at Lambeth—were added to her ladies. But Catherine had enough sense to know that she could not trust any of them, and so for a confidante she turned to an older kinswoman, Lady Rochford, thereby arousing the jealousy of the others. She should have known better than to trust a woman who had regained her place at court by betraying her own husband George and his sister Anne Boleyn. Then, perhaps again to head off further blackmail, Catherine brought Francis Dereham into court as her private secretary, and he was stupid enough to boast openly that "if the king die, I will marry the queen"—high treason in itself. He was also wrong; Queen Catherine no longer cared for him. She did care for someone else.

After many years of separation she met again at court Thomas Culpeper, a gentleman of the King's Privy Chamber and her first cousin on her mother's side. She had known him during a brief, happy interlude in her childhood when she lived with her mother's brother, Sir John Culpeper, before being sent to the Howards. Thomas was of her age and tastes, and although they were both to deny later that there had been an affair, if their claim is true they behaved with astounding stupidity.

The trouble apparently started in March of 1541, when the ailing Henry suddenly canceled all court festivities, and the bored Catherine, deprived of her entertainments, looked around for other means of amusement. She began seeing Culpeper on the sly and in private, and, worse, writing him love notes. To compound their stupidity, they used Lady Rochford as their watchdog at their private meetings. This continued after Henry recovered sufficiently to embark on a progress through Yorkshire, Lincolnshire and Lancashire to check on his kingdom and show off his new queen. Culpeper was in his retinue, and their clandestine meetings continued throughout the journey.

It was not the danger from within that was to prove Catherine's undoing, but the danger from without. She had not been able to take care of *all* the people who had known about her youthful indiscretions, and one of those, a Mary Lasells (who had discovered her relationship with Manox and knew of her affair with Dereham), was not at court. When her brother John Lasells taunted Mary about this lack of preferment, she declared hotly that "she would not serve anyone so light both in conditions and living," and on being pressed, supplied the damning details. Now brother John was a strong Protestant and hated the pro-Catholic party headed by the Howards, so he informed the leader of the Protestant party, Archbishop Cranmer, of these deadly secrets. The curtain on the final act of the tragedy had risen.

Cranmer, a rather timorous soul, was terrified by this turn of events, so in turn he consulted the Earl of Hertford, Edward Seymour, also anti-Howard and cautiously pro-Protestant. And Seymour grimly pointed out that, if the allegations were true, and if the new queen produced a child, it might well be illegitimate—"a cuckoo in the royal nest"—and might put the Tudor succession in jeopardy, because, after his own frail nephew Edward, this child would be the next in succession; Mary and Elizabeth still being classified as "bastards." The king would simply have to be told.

The quaking Cranmer carefully picked his moment. After the king had returned and was in chapel at Hampton Court, on November 3, 1541 Cranmer handed the document containing Lasells's revelations. As anticipated, the king was furious and refused to believe them. He was so sure that the charges were groundless that he immediately ordered an investigation to "clear the Queen's name."

What followed was like a recurring nightmare for Henry, as statement after statement made clear that the allegations about her early indiscretions were indeed true. Further, Dereham, under torture, implicated Culpeper as the man who had succeeded him in Catherine's affections. On the sixth of November Henry left Hampton Court and Catherine was removed to Syon House. It was the Duke of Norfolk who confronted his niece on November 7 and extracted a confession from the hysterical girl of her earlier indiscretions, although both she and Culpeper (who had also been tortured) stoutly denied any misdoing and tried to shift the blame to Lady Rochford and her sinister machinations. And, once more, that untrustworthy woman tried to save her own skin by saying that "she believed Culpeper to have known the queen

carnally, considering all things that she hath heard and seen between them."
To Henry, history was repeating itself: Twice he had loved Howard women and
made them his queen; twice he had been betrayed. He saw only one and the
same solution—Catherine had to die on the block, just as Anne had done.

The Duke of Norfolk, trying to save his own neck and what he could of
Howard influence in this debacle, not only threw Catherine to the wolves but
all the Howard females who had been with her: "guilty of misprision of treason
for having concealed Catherine's ill-behaviour prior to her marriage." On
December 2, 1541, the Dowager Duchess of Norfolk and Catherine's aunts,
Lady Bridgewater and Lady William Howard, as well as all her companions from
her Lambeth days, were sentenced to life imprisonment and forfeiture of their
possessions. And, despite her efforts, Lady Rochford's many sins at last caught
up with her: She was executed on February 13, 1542.

Of the principals involved, Dereham and Culpeper were tried at the
Guildhall on December 1, 1541 and Dereham was sentenced to be hanged,
drawn and quartered; Culpeper was allowed the greater leniency of beheading.

Catherine, unlike Anne, was not accorded a public trial. She remained
in custody at Syon House while Parliament debated her guilt in January of 1542.
On February 11 the death sentence was passed on her and on Lady Rochford,
and she was transported from Syon House to the Tower in a closed barge. The
21-year-old girl did not submit stoically; she alternated between fits of wild
hysteria and deep melancholy, although she did finally summon enough courage to die with dignity when she was beheaded inside the Tower on the 13th.
Her body was bundled into a rough coffin and buried beneath the floor of St.
Peter-in-the-Tower beside her cousin Anne. And, like Anne, her unhappy
shade is still said to haunt Hampton Court, as she runs down the gallery to the
chapel screaming to the king for mercy.

Although Henry was to show surprising leniency to the remaining
Howard women by releasing them after her execution, Catherine's death
shattered Howard hopes and would soon drive them to desperate measures.
Henry too was shattered; from this point on his life would be a vast downward
slide both mentally and physically.

Catherine Parr

CATHERINE PARR
(1512–1548)

m. (1) Sir Edward Burroughs   d. 1529
m. (2) John Neville, Lord Latimer   d. 1542
m. (3) Henry VIII   July 12, 1543
m. (4) Sir Thomas Seymour   m. 1547

No issue

HENRY'S SIXTH WIFE AND THIRD CATHERINE is in some ways the most interesting of them all, representing the "new woman" of the 16th century, born of the twin forces of the Renaissance and the Reformation. She was intellectual and well-educated—a true rarity in royal circles both then and now. Henry holds the record for having the most wives of any English monarch, but Catherine

National Portrait Gallery, London.

had the most husbands of any queen consort—four in all, of whom Henry was number three. She is also the first queen, indeed the only queen up to the present day, to write and publish a book in her lifetime—albeit a dull one.

Born in 1512 to Sir Thomas and Maud Parr from Kendall in Cumberland, she came from a family dedicated to royal service. Sir Thomas was an official of the royal household, and Catherine's sister Anne served as lady-in-waiting to all six of Henry VIII's wives (including Catherine herself), indicating that she must have been a woman of extraordinary tact. Sir Thomas died when his children were still very young, but his redoubtable wife Maud saw to it that they were all very well educated in the "New Learning," all serious-minded and, above all, devoted to duty and not pleasure.

Catherine may have been ahead of her time, but she was far from a liberated woman. In 1528, when she was 16, she was married off to a rich old man, Sir Edward Burroughs, who died the next year, leaving her a 17-year-old widow. She was quickly snapped up by another elderly man, John Neville, Lord Latimer, a widower himself with several young children, to whom she was to prove an excellent stepmother, instructing and educating them; her efforts did not go unnoticed. She nursed her elderly husband tenderly at the end, and when he died in March of 1542, after 13 years of marriage, found herself a rich widow.

After two marriages of obligation, the serious-minded Catherine proceeded to fall in love with a most improbable suitor, who possibly had his eye as much on her fortune as on herself. The suitor was the charming and dissolute Sir Thomas Seymour, young uncle of the heir to the throne, Prince Edward, and they were betrothed.

But the wedding was not to be, for Henry VIII, after over a year of self-inflicted widowerhood, was ready to marry again, and his eye lighted upon Catherine. Two years earlier he would not have given her a second look or thought, but after the blows to his ego of the past year he had given up on youthful passion and, to him, Catherine seemed a paragon of virtue: sober, sensible, an interesting talker, good with children and tender with aging, ailing husbands. He did not think her much to look at, having a long hooked nose and round black eyes under bushy eyebrows. She was not interested in fine clothes or jewelry either, but he was past caring about such things.

So, feigning ignorance of her attachment and engagement to Sir Thomas Seymour, Henry informed her that he wanted her as his wife. Catherine was shocked, reportedly going white and crying out in astonishment, "I, your *wife*!"

Duty was duty, however. The king had gotten Sir Thomas out of the way by sending him overseas as an ambassador, so in Hampton Court chapel the

52-year-old Henry and the 31-year-old Catherine were wed on July 12, 1543 and she was proclaimed queen. They honeymooned at Oatlands, where Henry had passed his last honeymoon with the late Catherine. Then they made a long progress through the south of England, accompanied by Princess Mary, to whom Catherine would become a true and much-needed friend.

As was customary by now, her own family profited by Catherine's marriage. Her brother William was given Cromwell's old title, the earldom of Essex, and was later made Marquess of Northampton; her uncle, Lord Parr of Horton, was made Lord Chamberlain; and her sister, the long-lasting Anne, was made Lady of the Bedchamber and shortly thereafter married the rich Earl of Pembroke. Even her stepchildren were recognized, Margaret Neville becoming her maid of honor.

On Catherine's return the royal court was transformed; gone were the dancing and gaiety, the jugglers and tumblers, although serious music remained; instead the court was flooded with scholars and intellectuals of all kinds, like Roger Ascham and Sir John Cleke of Cambridge, the latter becoming tutor to young Prince Edward in 1544. So great was the change that one of the new courtiers thanked Catherine, "for her rare goodness has made every day a Sunday, a thing hitherto unheard of, especially in the royal palace." The new atmosphere evidently suited the aging and ailing Henry well enough, but it must have bored his old-style courtiers.

Despite her sobriety, Catherine had her weaknesses. Although not interested in clothes, she was the Imelda Marcos of her time when it came to shoes, investing in a new pair almost every week, and often giving shoes as presents. She was also passionately fond of flowers, particularly roses, and would spend large sums on fresh flowers in season for her quarters, and for flower perfumes to scent them out of season.

Henry so revived after his marriage that he even went on an overseas campaign against the French—his last, as it turned out—leaving her as Regent of England, indicating he had great trust in her. But he soon fell sick and returned to England and to her care, leaving his armies under the command of younger men, first Henry Howard, Earl of Surrey, and then Edward Seymour, Earl of Hertford. His fighting days were behind him, but Catherine was soon to find out that he still could be very dangerous.

Snakes lurked in the Garden of Eden she had created at court, and they were shortly to show their fangs. The pro-Catholic party headed by the Howards and Bishop Gardiner were alarmed by all the Protestant thinkers who now swarmed at court, and deeply suspicious of Catherine's ties with the pro-Protestant Seymour family through her attachment to Sir Thomas Seymour. In their plotting, they were greatly aided by the king's conservative tendencies. Although head of his own church, which titularly was Protestant, Henry remained at heart, and doctrinally, a conservative Catholic. He hated extreme Protestants as much as he hated extreme Catholics; for years he had been impartially executing both, often at the same public spectacles.

Judging from Catherine's own book, *Lamentations of a Sinner*, she was clearly very conservative herself, but, good scholar that she was, she owned many Protestant books and had more liberal-minded Protestant friends at court. Here was her one vulnerable spot, so Gardiner, Lord Chancellor Wriothesey and the despicable Sir Richard Rich (the betrayer of Sir Thomas More) hatched a plot, going to such unheard-of lengths as torturing the highborn Anne Askew, another serious-minded friend, with their own hands, trying to get her to implicate the queen. Anne died a martyr's death without uttering a word against the queen, but the plotters continued to drip poison into the king's ear, working him up to such an extent that in 1546 he ordered her arrest.

Fortunately, Catherine was forewarned of her danger, and flattered and cajoled the king by declaring that she had disputed with him on religion to take his mind off his sufferings and that "the wisdom of her spouse, Supreme Head of the Church, was her sole anchor under God."

"And is it even so, sweetheart, and tended your arguments to no worse end?" said Henry, believing as usual what he wanted to believe. "Then perfect friends we are again as ever at any time before." When Wriothesey turned up to arrest her—on Henry's orders—the king sent him packing, calling him "an arrant knave and a fool." The episode was a close shave, but Catherine was safe from then on, and turned more and more to the Seymours, whom she knew she could trust.

Gardiner and the Howards grew increasingly desperate as the king visibly failed and power seemed to swing towards the queen and the Seymours. After the debacle of Catherine Howard, they had recouped their position by doing what they did best—fighting: the Duke of Norfolk by invading and defeating the harassing Scots at Solway Moss, and his son Surrey by fighting and winning against the French. But after his first defeat in 1546, Surrey was replaced by a man he hated, Edward Seymour, who was given all the credit for the war, and a furious Surrey returned to England.

More hot-headed than his crafty father, he ranted openly against the Seymours, suggested himself as a mate for Princess Mary, and when he was snubbed tried to inveigle his sister into becoming the mistress of the dying king.

Her more cunning father had been trying to marry her off to Sir Thomas Seymour to gain a foothold in the opposition camp, but Thomas, with the king's end in sight, was waiting for Catherine. In December of 1546 Surrey went one step to far—among other offenses he was accused of plotting to seize Prince Edward—and was arrested and tried for high treason, his judges headed by Edward Seymour. Sentenced to death, Surrey remained arrogant to the end. "I know that the king wants to get rid of the noble blood around him and employ none but low people," he spat at his judges. He was executed on Tower Hill on January 19, 1547.

His father, as usual, tried to save himself and in typical fashion, stating "The malice borne me by both my nieces, whom it pleased the king to marry, is not unknown to such as kept them." But his enemies were in control now, and he also was sentenced to death and carted off to the Tower, his immense wealth forfeited. Most of that eventually ended up in Seymour coffers. But again his incredible luck held, for on January 28, 1547, the very day that Norfolk was due for execution, Henry VIII died in Whitehall Palace, with only Cranmer at his side, the Queen and his children being kept away. Although the Seymours tried to keep the news of the death from leaking out for as long as possible, they did not quite have the nerve to go through with the execution, and Norfolk was saved again. He remained in prison throughout the reign of Edward VI, though, dying there in 1554. The power of the Howards was in eclipse—temporarily.

When Henry's will was read, although he treated his wife generously in giving her precedence at court, much to everyone's surprise she was not named as Protector and Regent to the young King Edward. That plum went to the boy's uncle Edward, shortly to be Duke of Somerset. Probably Henry thought the job would be too much for a woman, able though that woman was. And possibly he might have been clearsighted enough to realize that she would marry Sir Thomas Seymour at long last, and that this match would bode ill for his son.

Scarcely was Henry safely buried beside Jane Seymour at Windsor, than Catherine fell into Thomas's waiting arms and they were secretly married in May of 1547, less than four months after Henry's death. At last she had everything she had dreamed about—riches, high position and the man she loved, and, to her added joy, was almost immediately pregnant with a child of her own.

But, unlike Anne of Cleves, for Catherine there was no happy ending. With all his charm, Thomas was unstable and a dedicated rake, already intriguing against his more powerful brother Edward, the Regent, even though

Thomas had himself been made Lord High Admiral of England. In addition he became involved with Princess Elizabeth, now a sprightly teenager with much of Anne Boleyn's charm, and Catherine caught him "sporting" with the young princess in her bedroom. She was deeply hurt and sent Elizabeth away, although she never blamed her.

Catherine also had to endure the spite of her sister-in-law the Duchess of Somerset, who resented Catherine's ordained precedence and tried to make her life at court miserable. Catherine did not have to bear these trials for long. She was 36 when she went into her first labor, a long and difficult one, and was finally delivered of a baby girl—but the trauma of birth had been too much for both of them, and after lingering for a few days both she and the child died on September 7, 1548.

At least she was spared the grief that followed for her headstrong husband. Thomas continued to conspire against his brother until Somerset was forced by his own followers to take action in January of 1549 against him. He was imprisoned in the Tower, and because he refused to answer to the council was not even given a hearing. He was beheaded on March 20, 1549, only six months after Catherine's death.

Perhaps Catherine's greatest influence on her times was that during her short marriage to the cantankerous and ailing king she had succeeded in reconciling and bringing him close to his two daughters, so that in his final testament he strictly laid down the order of succession, in which he finally recognized the legitimacy of them both. The order was to be Edward first, then Mary, then Elizabeth. Interestingly, he went even further, ordaining that in the absence of heirs to any or all of these, the succession should pass to the heirs of his *younger* sister Mary, late Duchess of Suffolk, specifically excluding the heirs of his older sister, Margaret of Scotland, a bequest that would soon make for bitter times.

INTERLUDE I
(1547–1603)

Mary I, by Master John

EDWARD VI, MARY, ELIZABETH

The first long break in the continuity of queen consorts was a result of the death of Henry VIII's only son Edward before reaching marriageable age and the reigns of England's first two queens regnant: Mary I, who married her cousin Philip II of Spain but who had no children, and the long reign of Elizabeth I, who never married; she had at least two long-term lovers but without issue. Since events of great moment to the future history of England occurred during these three reigns, they require a brief summary.

The sickly Edward VI was only nine when he became king under the regency of his uncle Edward, Duke of Somerset, who, along with Archbishop Cranmer, hastened to further the Protestant Reformation of the Church.

Cranmer produced the Book of Common Prayer in 1549, which brought uniformity of worship to the fledgling Anglican Church but widened the gulf between the Protestant and Catholic segments of the population. Somerset soon fell from power and was executed, his place taken by the ambitious, but not very able, Duke of Northumberland, who so mismanaged the country that when Edward died of tuberculosis at the age of 16 in 1553, it was in chaos. Northumberland then attempted to override the Order of Succession by making the Protestant Lady Jane Grey (a granddaughter of Henry VIII's sister Mary, Duchess of Suffolk, and wife of Northumberland's son, Lord Guilford Dudley) queen in place of the Catholic heir, Mary. The attempt failed after nine days and all the principals were executed.

When the bitter Queen Mary ascended the throne in 1553 at the age of 37, she had many old scores to settle after the neglect and persecution she and her mother, Catherine of Aragon, had suffered. But her methods instilled in the people of England a positive phobia against Catholicism that was to bedevil the English crown and country for the next two centuries.

She repealed all the religious legislation of Edward's reign and attempted to put England firmly back in the Catholic fold. She burned as heretics all the major Protestant leaders, like Archbishop Cranmer and Bishops Latimer and Ridley, then spread the bloodbath to lower Protestant echelons throughout the country.

To compound her offenses she insisted, in spite of vigorous opposition from Parliament, on marrying her cousin, the widower Philip II of Spain and England's most implacable enemy. Philip did not care at all about Mary, but was very interested in acquiring dominance over England, particularly over its growing sea power. Although the country erupted into rebellions, he came to England in 1554 and the marriage was celebrated in Winchester Cathedral in 1556. He stayed in England only 14 months before returning to Spain, leaving Mary bereft and childless, although she experienced an entire "false" pregnancy, even to the labor pains.

In 1558, England's last territorial possession in Europe, the port of Calais, fell to the French. This loss, though traumatic at the time, was a blessing in disguise, for it finally turned England away from the endless wars occasioned by its European territorial claims and towards the new lands opened by the 16th-century explorers. The loss, though, was the ultimate blow to the ailing Mary, who died shortly thereafter declaring "Calais will be found written on my heart." The immediate cause of her death was attributed to dropsy or edema. In her five-year reign, she had well earned her nickname "Bloody Mary."

Elizabeth I

National Portrait Gallery, London.

When the 25-year-old Elizabeth ascended the throne in 1558 she inherited a bankrupt country in complete disarray; at her death 44 years later it was strong, secure and on its way to becoming a major world power. This remarkable offspring of Henry VIII and Anne Boleyn was extremely intelligent—an intelligence welded to a strong personality endowed with great common sense and an absence of fanaticism.

She reestablished the Anglican Church on a firm foundation, but only persecuted those Catholic dissidents who directly threatened the Crown. With the aid of wise councillors like William, Lord Burghley, and his son Lord Robert Cecil, she did her best to keep England at peace, to bring back prosperity and, indeed, to bring about a "Golden Age" in English life, letters, art and architecture. Her captains, like Sir Francis Drake, Sir John Hawkins and Sir Walter Raleigh, sailed the seven seas in endless voyages of exploration and established trade with far-flung lands. Shakespeare was in his prime.

Throughout most of her reign she had to face the implacable enmity of Philip II of Spain, who felt he had been cheated out of a kingdom, and this enmity culminated in his sending his great invasion fleet, the Spanish Armada, to take England back. In 1588 the destruction of that Armada, partly through the prowess of Elizabeth's seamen, partly by a fortuitous storm, ended the Spanish threat, although to the end Elizabeth was never safe from Catholic plots against her life.

A passionate woman, she never dared marry, but used the prospect of marriage as a powerful diplomatic tool. She might have been tempted to marry the one man she truly loved, Lord Robert Dudley, Earl of Leicester, but the mysterious murder of Dudley's wife, Amy Robsart (not by him, but possibly by someone paid by him), made her realize this match was impossible, although they remained lovers until his death in September of 1588. Her later affair with Robert Devereaux, Earl of Essex, was a younger man–older woman relationship which, through his own folly, led to his execution in 1601.

Probably the most difficult situation she faced during her long reign was deciding the fate of her cousin, the feckless Mary, Queen of Scots, granddaughter of Henry VIII's sister Margaret and, since Elizabeth was childless, the next heir to the throne. After a tempestuous six-year rule in Scotland, during which the Catholic Mary had managed to enrage the Protestant Scots to the point of rebellion, she had been forced to abdicate, seeking asylum in England in 1567.

This posed a terrible dilemma for Elizabeth, for immediately Mary became the focus of Catholic hopes and Catholic plots in England. Elizabeth tried to minimize the machinations by keeping Mary securely out of the way in remote

Fotheringay in East Anglia, but the strategy did not work. By 1586, when the Catholic Babington plot to kill Elizabeth and make Mary queen was exposed—and Mary implicated—Elizabeth could no longer ignore the situation. With considerable reluctance, after Mary had been tried and convicted of treason, she ordered her execution in 1587. It is typical of Elizabeth's pragmatism that, later, with Mary's Protestant son James VI of Scotland now her heir, she should bombard him with wise letters and advice preparing him for his future role as King of England.

When she died in Richmond Palace on March 24, 1603 at the age of 70, having outlived lovers, friends—Lord Burghley had died in 1598—and enemies—Philip of Spain had died earlier the same year—the aged queen left her successor a prosperous kingdom that was on the verge of exploring new vistas and new settlements, both in the New World of North America and beyond.

THE STUARTS

Anne of Denmark

ANNE OF DENMARK
(1574–1619)

m. James VI of Scotland & I of England   1589

Children: Henry, CHARLES, Robert, Elizabeth, Margaret, Mary, Sophia
& an unnamed son

T HE FIRST DANISH QUEEN OF ENGLAND, Anne has three other firsts
to record: She was the first to be "attacked by witches"—at least according to
her husband; the first to convert to another religion in the teeth of her
husband's wishes and to his great embarrassment; and the first to start out as
queen of one realm and end up queen of two. If this all gives the impression of

great accomplishments, that is an illusion. Unfortunately, Anne lacked the character, intelligence and drive to influence her husband. In her defense, it must be said that she was in many ways a victim of circumstance. But the fact remains that, because of her own upbringing and personal foibles, she had a negative influence on both James and the subsequent history of the Stuart dynasty.

Born December 12, 1574 to Frederick II of Denmark and Norway and his wife Sophia, daughter of the Duke of Mecklenberg, Anne was brought into a world of turbulent upheaval in northern Europe, with Denmark involved in a life-or-death struggle against Sweden. As a consequence of the struggle, her father had become a despotic monarch, and Anne grew up with the idea that absolute monarchy was the right and only way. When she was 14 her father died and was succeeded by her brother as Christian IV. The next year, 1589, while still 14, she was married by proxy on the 20th of August to the 23-year-old James VI of Scotland, who was so anxious for this marriage that he settled for the relinquishing of claims by the Danish crown to the Orkney and Hebridean islands and only a very small dowry.

Here is where the witches come in. Anne and her wedding party set sail from Denmark, only to be driven back to Norway by an unusually violent storm. This, James was to claim, was the work of Scottish witches under the direction of his stepcousin, the "warlock earl" Francis Bothwell, and was aimed at killing his bride. The episode marked the beginning of his private obsession with witches and witchcraft—about which he wrote two books—as well as a violent and merciless witch hunt in Scotland that continued for years. It did not thwart his wedding plans, however, for like some ardent romantic he sailed off to Norway, where they were officially married in Oslo on November 20, 1589. They spent a long honeymoon in Denmark and did not sail back to Scotland until the following spring, arriving on May 1, 1590 in Edinburgh, where she was subsequently crowned. There the teenager was in for a shock when she found that James was bisexual.

James was an extremely complex man. As the great historian Lord Macaulay wrote, "He was made up of two men—a witty, well-read scholar, who wrote, disputed and harangued, and a nervous drivelling idiot who acted." And the horrendous upbringing that James had received does much to explain and excuse his many failings.

Before Anne he had had virtually nothing to do with women. He hardly knew his mother, the foolish and unfortunate Mary Stuart, who was said to have murdered his father, Lord Darnley, and from whom he had been torn as an infant to be brought up by a series of regents, all bent on their own ends rather than his needs. That he remained intact and managed to acquire something of an education is a wonder in itself. At the age of 16 and old before his time—and after nine attempts to kidnap him—he still had enough spunk to take the reins of government and to hang on to them and govern his turbulent kingdom. Small wonder that he was abnormally nervous and eternally suspicious.

The only emotional bonds he had known were with men, starting with his cousin Esme Stuart, Earl of Lennox, who came straight from the French court of the homosexual Henri III with its riotous ways. After Esme fell from favor, he was replaced by Patrick, Master of Gray, then by George Gordon, Earl of Huntley, who was still the favorite when James married Anne. All of them had tried to dominate the king, but to James's credit, although he lavished affection and gifts on them all, in the public sphere he was still his own man.

It did not help Anne, who was regarded with suspicion by the stern Scottish Calvinists because she was a Lutheran and already openly sympathetic to Catholics, that for five years there was no sign of an heir to the throne. She was railed against for her "light ways"—dancing, singing and card-playing being considered sins. When finally she did become pregnant in 1594 and gave birth to their first son, Henry, the event did nothing to help the marriage. Anne may not have been a very fond wife but she was certainly a fond mother, and James alienated her when he removed the infant to be raised by the stern John Erskine, Earl of Mar. She next produced a daughter, Elizabeth, in 1596, and another son, Charles, in 1600. In total she would give birth to eight children, two more sons and three more daughters—Margaret, Mary and Sophia—but only her first three would survive into adulthood.

In 1603 their lives changed. Elizabeth I of England was dying, and the only feasible Tudor heir remaining—despite Henry VIII's deathbed orders—was James, with his double dose of Tudor blood, his mother Mary being the granddaughter of Margaret Tudor and James IV, and Mary's first cousin and James's father, Lord Darnley, being the grandson of Margaret Tudor by her second marriage to the Earl of Angus. Robert Cecil, Elizabeth's chief minister, was so aware of James's tastes by this time that he sent Lord Henry Howard, himself a flagrant homosexual, to make the arrangements for an easy transition of power.

After Elizabeth's death James left for England in the early spring of 1603, and Anne saw this as a wonderful chance to retrieve her son Henry. She went to Stirling Castle and demanded her son from the Earl of Mar, who flatly refused. She was so upset that she miscarried—she was carrying a son—and almost died in the process. James was sufficiently alarmed to order Mar to "pleasure the queen" by surrendering the boy.

The delighted Anne hastily went south with her two older children and settled in Windsor Castle. A further strain on the marriage, however, occurred at their joint coronation in Westminster Abbey in July of 1603, when Anne refused to accept communion at this Anglican service—a slap in the face to James, who, as king, was now also head of the Anglican Church.

Both experienced culture shock in England, for life there was a very different proposition from life in Scotland, and there was one vital issue that neither of them ever did understand or handle correctly—the role and rights of a king in a *constitutional* monarchy. In their respective ways they both believed in the divine right of kings, and unfortunately—and fatally—would pass this belief on to their children. In Anne's case divine right took the form of spending extravagantly on whatever she fancied, be it buildings or baubles, which kept her husband in almost constant battles with Parliament, who held the purse strings. She also saw nothing wrong in following her own religious bent, which would lead to her eventual adoption of Catholicism—again a terrible political mistake in Anglican England.

James had an even more drastic adjustment to make. Governing in Scotland had been largely a question of controlling the heads of the clans, who in turn controlled their people. Successful rule therefore boiled down to personal control over a small body of men, with the ultimate power still very much with the king. In England he was faced with Parliament—a large body of men, most of whom he neither knew nor saw, but who held considerable power. Although James tried to rule in his previous fashion, mainly through young favorites and their partisans, the method did not work, and his problems boded ill for future Stuarts.

As for the English, they found Anne easier to accept than James. By now they were used to foreign-born queens, and, besides, she was decorative, gracious and tactful, making a very good public impression. James they found considerably less palatable, for England was dealing with its first "foreign" king since William the Conqueror, and for many of the insular English this Scotsman was a bitter pill. James also did not cut an impressive figure, with his curious padded clothes (he was afraid of assassins), his broad Scots accent made worse by a speech impediment, his odd demeanor—he was so nervous that his eyes rolled constantly and his head twitched—and his coarse manners and general lack of tact. And, last but not least, there were his romantic involvements.

This last is what probably led to Anne's final physical separation from him, for their last child, the short-lived Sophia, was born in 1607 at the time of James's heavy involvement with his new favorite, Robert Carr, whom he created Earl of Somerset. Anne despised Carr, who allied himself with the Protestants and who achieved, at least for a while, a dangerous psychological and physical dominance over James. The separation was amicable; they occupied the same palaces, only in separate quarters. He led his life and she led hers, with no bitter quarrels. He treated her with great respect and, in small matters, with great indulgence.

The separation did, however, alter the nature of the court around her. Anne had displayed unusual tact in bringing only a few Scottish ladies-in-waiting with her, and so there was the usual scramble by highborn English ladies for places in her court. In Elizabeth's time this strategy had been one of the premier ways to advancement and influence. But soon her ladies realized that the queen had no influence whatsoever; the reason most of them stayed was that she paid them extravagantly and also that, because of her own love of lavish and continuous entertainment, her court was a merry place.

Indeed England does owe its first Danish queen a debt of gratitude, for she was a tremendous patron of the arts. She imported the great architect Inigo Jones from the continent, thereby introducing a great wave of building in the elegant Jacobean style, and supported great playwrights like the aging Shakespeare and Ben Jonson, who wrote for the royal court. Many lesser artists, writers, costumiers and jewelers benefited as well from her bounty. Anne did try to influence the king in matters of importance to her, particularly those concerning their children. She bitterly opposed her daughter Elizabeth's marriage to the Protestant Elector Palatine Frederick V in 1613, as much as she had favored the proposed marriage to the Spanish Infanta of her adored Henry, Prince of Wales, who looked so like her and who was equally adored by his father. Henry's tragic, premature death of typhoid fever in 1612 at the age of 18 put an end to that project, leaving both his parents prostrate with grief. She even tried to save Sir Walter Raleigh from his unjust execution, and to mitigate her husband's harsh imprisonment of his cousin, the foolish Arabella Stuart. In none of these matters did she have the slightest success: James would indulge her extravagances and grant small boons for her ladies and their kin, but on the big issues he simply ignored her.

Anne was so limited in her understanding of the larger political framework in England that she reacted to events solely on a personal level. She positively supported and encouraged the rise to power of handsome George

Villiers, later Duke of Buckingham and James's last favorite, because she hated the disgraced Robert Carr and because Villiers (an even more dangerous man than Carr) was pro-Spain and therefore more pro-Catholic. Many of these preconceptions she would pass on to the only child remaining near her, the heir to the throne, Charles, the least gifted of her children.

In 1618 she started to sicken with the breast cancer that would finally kill her on March 2, 1619. True to form, James, fearful of any illness, did not go near her and was not present when she died. She was buried in Westminster Abbey with due ceremony, and was mourned more visibly by her English subjects than by her husband of 29 years.

Henrietta Maria of France, in a painting after A. Van Dyck

HENRIETTA MARIA OF FRANCE (1609–1669)

m. Charles I 1625

Children: *Charles, CHARLES, JAMES, Henry, Mary, Elizabeth, Katherine, Henrietta*

UNLIKE HER SOMEWHAT PHLEGMATIC Danish predecessor, Henrietta Maria was a spirited woman and a born fighter.

England had not had a French queen for almost 200 years, the last being the ill-regarded and unfortunate Margaret of Anjou, Henry VI's queen. So, from the first, Henrietta had two strikes against her in popular opinion, being both French and Catholic. Worse, she was an afterthought on the part of her husband-to-be, who had planned to marry a Spanish Infanta until he was turned down. At the urging of his principal advisor (and his father's last favorite), the wily Duke of Buckingham, he had negotiated this French marriage in the hope of helping his beloved sister Elizabeth and her husband the Emperor Frederick, who had lately been dispossessed of their crowns by the Catholic coalition in Europe and were at the beginning of the terrible Thirty Years' War between Catholic and Protestant Europe. Henrietta, in the usual way of royal princesses, was merely doing as she was bidden by her elder brother, the foppish Louis XIII of France.

So off she was packed to England with the usual large entourage of French ladies, having already been wed by proxy in May of 1625, just after Charles had succeeded to the throne. She was officially married to him at Canterbury in June, with the usual fanfare and a dose of suspicion on both sides. She was 16, he was 23, and their first sight of each other did not please either of them.

Though a small woman, Henrietta found she overtopped her diminutive bridegroom, the smallest of all English kings at four feet ten inches. He was sensitive about his height, which he disguised by wearing high heels and tall hats. He didn't quite fit in with his own family, worshipping his intelligent and forceful brother Henry and doting on his sister Elizabeth, again far more intelligent than he. He had been a sickly child and had grown up shy and reserved, with many of his father James's nervous mannerisms and a stammer. Now that he was king he disguised his feelings of inferiority with arrogance and aloofness, neither of which endeared him to the pretty, sprightly Henrietta.

Charles soon found he had married a really spirited woman. Henrietta was unforthcoming in the fulfillment of her wifely duties; Charles desperately applied to her older ladies-in-waiting to encourage her. She refused to learn English and would sit all day prattling to her circle of French ladies, ignoring everyone else. Worse, although her own rights to continue Catholic practices had been guaranteed under the marriage contract, she actively mocked the Protestant Anglicans. The serious Charles had respected her wish not to be included in his coronation in February of 1626—no doubt also fearing that she might embarrass him, as his own mother Anne had James I at *their* coronation— and was understandably upset when he emerged from the ceremony to see Henrietta watching the proceedings from a nearby house, with her ladies having a huge party in the room behind her. She had similarly upset many of his Protestant clergy, interrupting a service by breaking in with a pack of hunting dogs and, with her ladies, uttering wild hunting calls.

By the summer of 1626 Charles was so exasperated that he determined to get rid of her French entourage, and applied to her brother Louis for permission to do so; since Louis had just similarly disposed of his own wife's entourage, he could scarcely say no. Henrietta did not take this action at all kindly. Removed by the king to a room in St. James's Palace and locked in while he dismissed her ladies, she broke out the windowpanes with her bare fists and screamed for help to the departing entourage, also in an uproar, below in the courtyard. They were replaced by English ladies, including the voluptuous and utterly unscrupulous Countess of Carlisle, the Duke of Buckingham's mistress, whom Henrietta had previously loathed. But the Countess had a wicked wit, and the two eventually became the closest of friends. To Charles's consternation, the queen was obviously influenced by this sophisticated older woman, "who has already brought her to paint and in time will lead her into more debaucheries," it was darkly observed. Then in 1628 the Duke of Buckingham, returning from his unsuccessful campaign to aid the French Protestants' revolt against Henrietta's brother Louis, was cut down by the assassin Felton. Although, unlike his father, Charles had never had a physical relationship with the Duke, he had depended absolutely on this ruthless and unscrupulous man. Adrift and totally demoralized by this blow, Charles turned, in the clamor of power-seekers that followed, to his wife. This was all, apparently, that Henrietta needed. As he started to confide in her, the most unexpected thing happened— the royal couple fell in love.

Between 1629 and 1644, she would produce nine children by him, even though she had a slightly deformed spine which in turn had effected her pelvis and made every birth a long torture for her. In succession she produced a son, Charles, who died in infancy in 1629; another Charles in 1630 (the future Charles II); a daughter Mary in 1631; James (the future James II) in 1633; then Henry, Duke of Gloucester; Elizabeth; Anne; Katherine; and, finally, in 1644, Henrietta, destined to be the family favorite and Charles II's beloved "Minette."

They settled down to a loving and decorous family life, mirrored for us in the paintings of Van Dyck, whom Charles had imported from Holland, and confirmed by all court reports. But during those happy years, in which Henrietta was wrapped up in her children and her husband, heavy storm clouds were gathering over England—storm clouds which she herself inadvertently created. She would take her older sons to Mass with her—anathema to the Protestant English, whose kings they were destined to be. She loved and participated in court theatricals—again anathema to the extreme Puritan Protestants. And since Charles would not tolerate criticism or threats to her, he persecuted her critics viciously.

Accustomed to the autocratic rule of the French crown, she saw nothing wrong in the ideas of "divine right" that Charles had learned from his parents, and which led to his trampling of all those rights that the English held most dear. He dismissed Parliament, surrounded himself with men like Archbishop Laud and the Earl of Wentworth, and while tolerating the Catholics (because of her) he persecuted the extreme Protestants, many of whom left for the New World of North America at this time. England was coming to a slow boil of anger.

Ironically, it was in Scotland that the spark of rebellion was lit, when Charles stupidly tried to impose the high Anglican Church on his Calvinist Scottish subjects. To fight them Charles needed money, and to obtain money he had to recall Parliament. Laud and Wentworth were both executed in the ensuing bloody vendetta, but it was still not enough. The Puritan Parliament wanted to get rid of Charles and his Papist wife, and England quickly became polarized between the Royalists, who wanted reforms but who also wanted to keep the king, and the Puritan "Roundheads," who wanted him gone for good.

Once Henrietta realized that her beloved Charles and her family were in danger, all the fighting spirit she had inherited from her father Henry of Navarre (who had won the crown of France by force of arms), rose in her blood. She became a dynamo of action—appealing to the Pope and her undependable brother Louis XIII for help, rushing off to Holland with the crown jewels to pawn them and buy much-needed arms for the Royalist cause, charming her way back into England (the Puritan commander of Bridlington in Yorkshire where she landed converted to the Royalists under her spell) and pushing her way through to Oxford, where her husband had established his headquarters. She even took to the field herself, as Margaret of Anjou had done in the long-ago fighting for *her* husband, to encourage the Royalist troops to greater efforts.

But in 1644 she was pregnant again, and Charles, concerned for her welfare, especially since the Royalists were losing ground, wanted her safe. He sent her to the Royalist stronghold at Exeter in Devon, where in June she gave birth to her youngest daughter and namesake Henrietta. But the Roundhead General Fairfax was making great inroads into the Royalist west country, and in July, although Henrietta had still not recovered from the birth, she was escorted to Falmouth and sailed into exile to her native France. She was never to see Charles again.

For Henrietta there followed five years of hell. Not only was Charles in danger, but all her children were in England, with the exception of her eldest daughter Mary, who had married William III of Orange in 1641, and the baby Henrietta. Charles and James, not yet in their teens, were fighting alongside her husband, and the younger ones were either with Charles or with Royalist supporters. Desperately she applied again to the Pope and to Cardinal Mazarin, for her brother Louis had died in 1643 and Mazarin was the chief advisor to her nephew the young Louis XIV. Nothing came of her appeals.

In 1645, when the battle of Naseby crushed the Royalists, the first phase of the Civil War ended. Her son Charles managed to escape, but James was captured at Oxford with the rest of the younger children. Charles I fled to Scotland, but his subjects there handed him over to the victorious Oliver Cromwell in return for a cash payment.

Although Charles was now a prisoner, he did not stop his scheming; from his prison in Carisbrooke Castle on the Isle of Wight, he persuaded the volatile Scots to rise against their new masters, whom they found no more to their taste than he had been. So in 1648 hope flared briefly for Henrietta when the second half of the Civil War began, during which her son James managed to escape and make his way to join the family circle in France. It was a short-lived hope, for the Scots were no match for Cromwell's Roundheads, and this time the reprisals were bitter. Scotland was ravaged, English Royalists were exiled as slave labor to the Barbadoes, and the king, after a tragic farce of a trial, was condemned to death. He was executed in front of his own Palace of Whitehall on January 30, 1649; meeting his death with such dignity and courage that the people of England underwent a revulsion of feeling against their new rulers.

When the news of Charles's death reached Henrietta, she withdrew from Louis XIV's court. She took no further part in politics and devoted herself to raising Henrietta and young Henry, Duke of Gloucester, her only other child to have escaped the holocaust in England. Her spirit was not entirely broken; she had a quarrel with her son Prince Charles over the Catholic upbringing she was giving young Henry, and they were estranged for several years. But she took no part in the endless wanderings of her penurious older sons, who went all over Europe seeking support for their lost cause and leading the sad lives of royal exiles. She had no role in Prince Charles's abortive invasion of Scotland and the raising of the Royalist flag again in 1650. This episode, too, ended in disaster, and he escaped by the skin of his teeth after the Battle of Worcester in September of 1651. Later he tried fighting the Roundheads on the high seas with the help of his father's nephew, Prince Rupert of the Palatine, but that also ended in defeat.

Then in 1660 the fortunes of the Stuarts changed dramatically. England's "Great Protector" Oliver Cromwell had died late in 1658 and had unwisely named his inept son Richard to succeed him. "Tumbledown Dick" was not up to the task and resigned in 1659. England was without a leader and in near chaos, and at this juncture the people of England made their wishes known: A republic was not for them. They wanted their king back, good or bad.

After long negotiations, Charles II landed in Dover to the wild acclamations of his people on May 29, 1660, his 30th birthday. The Puritan revolution had failed. The Roundheads had taken from the common people all of their simple and customary pleasures; they had disgusted them with the senseless vandalism of their churches and cathedrals by Roundhead soldiers, and, above all, had shown them that a military dictatorship was even more arbitrary than the rule of a constitutional monarch.

Once Charles was sure of his kingdom he sent for his mother and made up their quarrel (little Henry, alas, was long dead). She was established in great luxury in Somerset House with a vast income of 60,000 pounds a year and a royal entourage.

In 1661 she returned briefly to France for the wedding of her beloved Henrietta to her first cousin, Philip of Orleans (Louis XIII's younger son), and in 1662 she welcomed Catherine of Braganza, Charles II's Portuguese bride, of whom she approved. She outspokenly disapproved of her younger son James's bride, Anne Hyde, who, already pregnant, had married him secretly in September of 1660. The royal Henrietta thought her common and presumptuous, but Anne was a witty and tactful woman and managed to win her mother-in-law's good will over the years.

Henrietta also strongly disapproved of the life-style of her two elder sons and the dissolute court they kept. Her dead Charles had always been faithful and considerate to her and an excellent father. Her sons were flagrantly unfaithful to their wives and indifferent fathers, and, in her view, the court was a maelstrom of vice and corruption. After a while her health began to fail, and in 1665, she returned to France, retiring to Colombes; at least there she could offer some support and comfort to the child of whom she was fondest, her namesake the Duchess of Orleans, whose husband had turned out to be a dissolute villain. There she died where she had begun 60 years before, on August 31, 1669.

Even if the English had never really warmed to her, she had been a good wife and a good mother, but she had left a troublesome legacy to her sons—a predisposition to Catholicism that would bedevil both of their reigns, and which, in the case of James, would prove fatal.

Catherine of Braganza, in a painting after D. Stoop

CATHERINE OF BRAGANZA
(1638–1705)

m. Charles II   1662

No issue

HOW ENGLAND CAME BY ITS ONLY PORTUGUESE QUEEN is tied up with the history of Portugal itself, for first and last the marriage was Portugal's idea—a marriage it desperately needed. The sequence of events had been started by Catherine of Aragon's parents, after the discovery of the New World in 1492, when they united Spain with the riches of the New World. Under their successors, Spain had become a dominant power in Europe and between 1580 and 1640 had annexed and absorbed its smaller Iberian neighbor. With help from France the Portuguese had revolted against Spain's domination, and in 1640 the Duke of Braganza, Catherine's father, was crowned king of the "new" Portugal as John IV and established the long-lived dynasty of Braganza, which would continue to rule there until 1910.

Portugal itself had been foremost in the 16th-century voyages of world discovery and had established colonies in Africa, China, India and Japan. Brazil had been awarded to Portugal by the Pope and was just beginning to send its natural wealth into Portuguese coffers. Hence Portugal was an extremely rich little country; but it was not a mighty country militarily, and it needed allies—preferably allies with a lot of sea power—to help it stave off further attempts at Spanish domination.

John IV had gained his crown with help from the French, but he was understandably alarmed when France started to negotiate with Spain for the hand of one of its Infantas, Maria-Teresa, as the young Louis XIV's bride. Swift to see this possible threat, John looked to England and its considerable sea power as a counterbalance, and as early as 1642 had made a treaty with Charles I in which the idea of a marriage between daughter Catherine and Charles, Prince of Wales, was first mooted. Charles I's execution naturally put an end to this hope, but on the restoration of the monarchy in 1660, John IV's wife, Luisa de Gusmaon, who was acting as regent for her 17-year-old feeble-minded son Alfonso (John having died in 1658) was even more desperate for the marriage, so she offered Charles not only her 24-year-old daughter Catherine but a truly enormous dowry: two million gold crowns as well as the important trading ports of Tangiers in North Africa and Bombay in India. In return Charles would provide men and arms to help Portugal fight Spain—and he proceeded to do so, with great success.

As a result of the economic disaster caused by the English Civil War and his own extravagant life-style, Charles II needed money and was only too eager to oblige. So in 1661 a treaty of alliance was signed, and on May 13, 1662, Catherine of Braganza landed in Portsmouth. She and Charles married there on May 21, first secretly by Catholic rites and then publicly in an Anglican ceremony.

Again it is astounding to us how nonchalant royal families were about sending their daughters to strange lands and strange beds without any kind of instruction or preparation. The English marriage had been talked about in Portugal for 20 years, and yet Catherine landed at Portsmouth not knowing a word of English or, for that matter, the *lingua franca* of European courts, French. Of England's history, politics and religion she was equally ignorant—sad preparation indeed for her future role.

She arrived with the usual large entourage of Portuguese ladies, obviously intended as a buffer to her strange surroundings, but the English took an immediate dislike to these ladies, pronouncing them "for the most part old, ugly and proud." Catherine was hardly considered a beauty herself, but she was undoubtedly thought the best-looking of the bunch, and Charles, even though they could not communicate, pronounced himself well pleased with her. In fact, he took a positive delight in teaching his bride English, and luckily Catherine learned and adapted quickly.

But after they retired to Hampton Court Palace for their honeymoon, Catherine soon found she was in for far greater surprises. Her husband was as unlike his sober and faithful father Charles I as it was possible to be. He was almost a reincarnation of his maternal grandfather, Henry IV of France: tall, dark and swarthy, he had basically the same character—swashbuckling, cynical, intelligent, extremely amusing and charismatic, and a noted womanizer.

The cynical Henry had declared that "Paris is well worth a Mass" and had given up his Protestantism for Catholicism to win France; his grandson, equally cynically, was to go in the opposite direction. England was worth being Protestant for, even though in sympathy and upbringing he was Catholic. But he would jealously and against all opposition guard the rights of his devout Catholic queen to worship and think as she pleased throughout their marriage. No woman had been able to resist the charismatic Henry IV, and no woman could resist Charles either. Catherine was no exception; she fell in love with him and then found to her dismay that she would have to share him with a small multitude of others.

Her introduction to her husband's character was particularly brutal and humiliating. Charles's current favorite was the venomous Barbara, Lady Castlemaine, who had already had one child by him and was about to have a second at the time of his marriage. She delivered in June and proceeded to Hampton Court, demanding to be made Catherine's Lady of the Bedchamber. The phenomenon of royal mistresses was not unknown to Catherine; even in her sheltered upbringing she knew of them, but in Portugal they were kept discreetly in the shadows and certainly not underfoot. So when her confessor broke the news of Castlemaine to her, Catherine resolved never to receive her. Hence, when Charles submitted a list of proposed ladies-in-waiting to her, she scornfully crossed off Lady Castlemaine's name. Charles then presented Castlemaine to her at a reception. When the unsuspecting Catherine realized who the stranger was, she had a violent nosebleed and fainted.

That night she and Charles had a battle. But Charles did not like to be made to feel guilty, and the more Catherine cried and threatened, the more obstinate he became. He retaliated predictably: Castlemaine remained, but all

Catherine's attendants, save one, were sent back to Portugal, leaving her homesick and lonely, with an estranged husband and a pack of English ladies who paid far more attention to his favorite than they did to her. She held out as long as she could, and received support from other royals, including Charles's mother, who was furious with him. Even his sister Henrietta, nicknamed "Minette," to whom he occasionally listened, wrote from France chiding him for his ill-treatment of Catherine. But it did no good, and in October Catherine swallowed her pride and acknowledged Castlemaine, who did nothing to help the situation by treating the queen with contempt.

Once she had accepted the situation Catherine proved the most accommodating of wives, earning for herself the respect and then the affection of his dissolute court and endearing herself to Charles. She even began to enjoy herself with cards and music, picnics and riding. Perhaps surprisingly, Charles was jealously possessive of her, so that when her Master of the Horse became obviously enamoured of her, Charles kicked him out in double-quick time.

Unfortunately for Catherine, she did not fulfill her primary purpose, the production of a legitimate heir to the throne. Not until they had been married six years did she become pregnant, but in May of 1668 she miscarried in her third month. The next year she was again pregnant in May, but miscarried after only a month. After that there were no signs of further pregnancies. Although her barrenness was to cause endless trouble for Charles and for England, it may have been ultimately a blessing in disguise for, genetically, something was seriously wrong with the Braganzas, particularly with the males. Catherine's brother Alfonso was feeble-minded, and her brother Pedro, who deposed his brother, was also mentally unstable at the end of his life. Charles, however, would produce a round dozen strong and healthy bastards who lived (about the same number died), and the court was positively aswarm with them, all ennobled by their loving father. Among them was his eldest son, whom Charles had sired at the age of 19 and while he was in exile by his mistress Lucy Walters, and whom he had created Duke of Monmouth. Catherine became particularly fond of Monmouth.

After her last miscarriage, pressure mounted on Charles to divorce Catherine, sterility being sufficient grounds for annulment by any church. Charles adamantly refused. In 1673 the question resurfaced when the Duke of York, whose first wife, Anne Hyde, had died, remarried the Catholic Mary Beatrice of Modena. Since he was still Charles's only legitimate successor, this incensed the Protestant English, and the cry for the king's divorce went up again. Charles even considered legitimizing Monmouth, now 23 and married, but Charles's brother James understandably opposed the move and Charles did nothing. For the first time mention was made of William III of Orange, son of Charles's sister Mary and married to James's daughter Mary, both firmly Protestant.

But the more his ministers harped the more Charles turned to Catherine, so that by 1679, Lady Sutherland, one of her ladies, would write that "Catherine is now a mistress, the passion her spouse has for her is so great." Sheer goodness was finally winning out, and in the ensuing 18 months this growing love of Charles for his childless wife was to reach remarkable proportions.

In the Popish Plot of 1678 (instigated by Lord Shaftesbury, the head of the Whig Protestant Party, and spearheaded by the nefarious Titus Oates) the queen was accused of high treason because her doctor and Mary of Modena's secretary had conspired to poison the king to make way for Catholic James.

By this time the English were so fond of Catherine that no one seriously believed she was involved, but Charles was taking no chances and sprang to her defense. In the face of anti-Catholic fury he could not save all the accused, like poor old Lord Stafford, who was condemned on perjured evidence and executed in December of 1680; but Charles went after all those who had attacked his queen—and catch them he did. Shaftesbury was forced into exile, Oates given his quietus for the perjurer he was, and the Whigs, in desperation, played right into Charles's hands by plotting to murder him and James at Rye House on their way back from Newmarket races in 1683. The leaders of the Whig party were all tried and executed, and its power broken.

And in what were to be the last two years of his life Charles became a devoted husband to his long-suffering queen. In 1685, he had a massive stroke. His pious and grief-stricken wife was terribly concerned about his immortal soul, and so on his deathbed Charles, as a final gesture of love, became a Catholic convert, receiving the last rites from Father Huddleston, the priest who had saved his life after the Battle of Worcester over 34 years before.

With all his faults, Catherine had truly loved him, and she retired from court to mourn him in seclusion. She soon had many other things to mourn as well. Her favorite of Charles's bastards, the Duke of Monmouth, supported by Whig Protestants, invaded the west country from Holland to oust the new king, the Catholic James II. Monmouth was roundly defeated at Sedgemoor in Somerset in 1685, executed, and his followers viciously punished. The tactless and intransigent Catholic James, who had inherited a peaceful England from his brother, proceeded in three short years to so alienate his subjects that in 1688 they invited the Protestant William of Orange (half-Stuart himself) and his Stuart wife Mary to take over the throne, and threw James and his family out of the country in a bloodless revolution. The temper of England changed to a markedly Protestant bent, and Catherine was irked by the constant squabbles between the new Queen Mary and her sister and heir, Princess Anne. Much as she had come to love her adopted country, Catherine no longer felt comfortable or welcome there, so she decided it was time to go home to Portugal.

In 1692 she returned to Lisbon and was received with wild acclaim. Although she continued to live quietly, she used her contacts in England to good effect by bringing about the important Anglo-Portuguese trading alliance in the Methuen treaty of 1703, benefiting both countries. Soon she was called to assume greater responsibilities as her brother Pedro became increasingly unbalanced. She was appointed Regent of Portugal in 1704 and proved an amazingly able stateswoman, achieving several Portuguese victories over their old enemy Spain. Then, after 20 years of widowhood, she herself died suddenly, "of a colic" in December of 1705. Although she had had no political influence in England, her personal hold on Charles's affections certainly influenced what came after. Ironically, it was not she but her dowry that had the most lasting effect, for it had given the English a firm foothold in India—which was to become the jewel in the crown of the British Empire.

Mary Beatrice of Modena, by William Wissing

National Portrait Gallery, London.

MARY BEATRICE OF MODENA
(1658–1718)

m. James II 1673

Children: *Charles, James, Catherine, Charlotte, Louisa*

NO WOMAN WAS EVER WORSE PREPARED for her future role than England's only Italian queen: When the marriage was first proposed, Mary did not even know where England was.

Mary was born to Alfonso IV, Duke of Modena, of the erstwhile powerful Este dynasty, former Dukes of Ferrara. In her grandfather's time the Estes had been forced out of Ferrara and had set up their new headquarters in the quiet university town of Modena in northern Italy, described by a contemporary as "a vast sea of monastic calm." This deeply religious atmosphere had already made its mark on Mary, who at 14 had decided to become a nun of the Salesian Order in Modena. As her father's only daughter, however, it was put to her that she could do more good for her faith by marrying the secretly Catholic widower, James, Duke of York, to reinforce his faith and to carry the "torch of Rome" to heretic England. So she was wed, by proxy, in September of 1673, and arrived in England in November, where she met her 40-year-old bridegroom for the first time. She was 15, much closer to the ages of his two daughters by his first marriage to Anne Hyde—Mary, who was 11, and Anne, who was eight.

James, unlike his jovial and charismatic brother Charles II, had inherited much of Charles I's solemnity, his aloofness, and, unfortunately, his tactlessness. He had been dubbed by Charles's witty Cockney mistress, Nell Gwynn, "Dismal Jimmy," and the name was apt. He was thought handsomer than Charles, being fair of hair and skin, and must have had some of the Stuart charm because Mary fell in love with him and became a devoted wife. To him she came as a pleasant surprise, being truly beautiful in a sultry, dark Italian style, tall with a slim and graceful figure. She already looked like a queen.

All the same, like Catherine of Braganza before her, the teenager was in for some rude shocks. For instance, James *did* share with his brother an insatiable appetite for women.

At the time of his marriage he had an official mistress, along with any other court lady he could get his hands on. And his mistress was probably more influential on the future history of England than poor Mary Beatrice ever could have been. Her name was Arabella Churchill; she was the daughter of a humble Dorset squire, Sir Winston Churchill, and it was through her that her brother, John Churchill, and his equally remarkable wife Sarah Jennings, were brought to the royal court to start their amazing careers: John, destined to become Duke of Marlborough and one of England's greatest generals, Sarah to be the "Svengali" of the future Queen Anne, and together to found a formidable dynasty. Arabella had already given James four children, including his eldest son, James, Duke of Berwick, who, like his uncle John, would become a great general—but for France, not for England. He would probably have made an excellent king.

But by the time Mary came along Arabella's power and attractions were already on the wane, and James's next prime favorite was to be the plain but highly intelligent Catherine Sedley, Mary's particular *bête noire*. Mary was to be no more successful at turning James from his wicked ways than Catherine of Braganza was with Charles, but she never stopped trying.

Some things in her new country delighted Mary—such as snow, which was virtually unknown in Modena. An idyllic little episode is recorded of her first winter in England, in which the vivacious little teenager and her solemn husband pelted each other with snowballs. But most things about England mystified and terrified her, for this Catholic marriage was highly unpopular and she was treated to spectacles of anti-Popish riots outside the royal palace and effigy-burning. Her carriage was pelted with mud and stones. Within the confines of the court she felt safe and secure enough, but even there certain things puzzled her, like the steadfast Protestantism her two step-daughters maintained even though both of their parents had been Catholic. She, who in Modena had never even seen a "heretic" Protestant, let alone understood what Protestantism meant, was at sea as to why the English so reviled Catholics.

Mary settled down to do her chief wifely duty, and between 1675 and 1683 had three miscarriages and bore five children, all of whom died as infants. In 1678 came the "Popish Plot," in which her secretary, Edward Coleman, was one of those named as being about to poison the king. Although he had been corresponding with Louis XIV, he was innocent of the specific allegations but, unlike Catherine of Braganza, whom no one believed was involved, there was deep suspicion of Mary. Her unpopularity grew, even though all her Catholic attendants were banished from court.

Then came Charles's death in 1685, and the reins of power passed to James, who was allowed to assume them with surprisingly little complaint or opposition. The English were at peace and had done well under Charles II; they obviously hoped that this prosperity would continue and that James's kingship would matter more to him than his Catholicism. Trouble was not long in coming, for in June the Duke of Monmouth, with support from William of Orange, landed in the west country and raised his Protestant banner. He was soundly trounced, however, and the magnificent coronation of Mary and James took place in July.

Mary was queen now, and as such felt she had things to do. Most of them added to her unpopularity. She at once brought back all her Catholic ladies, and, in addition to the Catholic chapel that had been installed in St. James's Palace, she ordered another one built in Whitehall Palace. Up until then she had also been popular within the court circle, being beautiful, charming and witty, but now she became more regal and aloof, alienating many of her former supporters. She also felt that the time had come to do something about James's mistress, Catherine Sedley, and, backed by a whole battalion of priests, she demanded that James send her away. James apparently submitted: He created Catherine Countess of Dorset and sent her off to Ireland. Mary became noticeably more cheerful, but her mood was to be of short duration because, a few months later, Catherine reappeared and James took up where he had left off. This time, however, he was more discreet about the affair, and Catherine was never to regain her ascendancy at court.

Meanwhile, with classic Stuart tactlessness, James was alienating his subjects, by favoring and promoting all his Catholic nobles to official positions and by packing the universities of Oxford and Cambridge with Catholic heads of colleges, making enemies of the very people who had been most disposed to be his friends. Although he did wish to suspend the laws that had been passed against Catholics *and* Dissenters, most of which were grossly unfair, the country was facing an almost certain return to Catholicism, and it was soon in no mood to listen.

Mary had problems of her own, for since 1685 she had shown no sign of further pregnancy and James still needed a legitimate son and heir. In 1687 she went to take the waters of Bath Spa, and James to pray at the shrine of St. Wilfrid. The joint effort apparently worked, for she was immediately pregnant again. Then in May of 1688 James reissued the Declaration of Indulgence to Catholics and Dissenters (first issued then rescinded by his brother Charles) and gave orders for it to be read in all the churches. Seven of his bishops, headed by the Archbishop of Canterbury, refused, and James promptly had them locked in the Tower. At their trial in June the people showed their might in riots and the bishops were acquitted, to wild rejoicing, on June 30. The next day Mary went into labor and was delivered of a son. The royal couple thought their troubles were over, as the excited James, carrying the baby, raced through Whitehall Palace bellowing "Make way for the Prince of Wales!" In effect, the reverse was true. The English may have been resigned to tolerating James for the rest of his life, but the prospect of a son of the same Catholic ilk was too much for them. Parliament promptly sent an invitation to William of Orange and James's elder daughter Mary to come over and assume the English throne.

Meanwhile the wildest stories were put in circulation about the new baby, even though Mary had had it as publicly as it is possible to have a birth.* It was not her child, the rumors went; it had been smuggled into the royal bed in a warming-pan; her baby had died and another had been substituted. Most of the rumors were fanned by Princess Anne, who was jealous of her beautiful stepmother and did not want to lose out on her own chance of succeeding to the throne. The rumors were palpably false, but the people of England wanted to believe them. Prince James would prove himself all Stuart in later years, and Mary would demonstrate her continuing fertility by producing another daugh-

---

* Many of the court were present in the chamber at the time of the birth.

ter, Louise, four years later, but the death knell of their dream of a Catholic England had been sounded.

In November William of Orange landed at Torbay in Devon with his troops and advanced at a snail-like pace towards London, for the last thing he wanted was to capture James or the royal family and have royal martyrs on his hands. Although James immediately sent Mary and the baby to France, he dallied so long that he almost got caught anyway before finally escaping in December. James and Mary would never again set foot in England.

At first the sun shone upon them in friendly Catholic France. Their host, and James's cousin, Louis XIV, was extremely generous to the exiles, giving them the beautiful royal palace of St.-Germain-en-Laye as their residence, a bounteous pension, and royal carriages and equipage. The schemes and plots to restore James to his throne began, although Mary took little part in them, as she was busy pampering her little son and then in June of 1692 giving birth to a daughter, named Louise Marie, who was to be a great solace to her.

In 1690 James made an abortive invasion of Ireland and was soundly beaten by King William. He returned to France to try again. The death of James's daughter Queen Mary in 1694 of smallpox at the age of 32 gave the Jacobites (supporters of James) fresh hope, and another invasion was planned in 1696, but that also came to nothing. With hope of return gradually fading, Mary took to spending long periods of retreat at the Salesian convent of Chaillot in Paris, the same order she had once planned to join and where Queen Henrietta Maria, in her exile, had gone to mourn her Charles. James was also becoming increasingly religious and was already showing signs of premature senility.

Then in 1697, when the eight-year war between France and the Grand Alliance (which included England) ended with the Peace of Ryswick, real hope arose. William III was without an heir, and did not think much of Princess Anne, who also lacked an heir, though she had tried through *eighteen* pregnancies. So, he proposed, through Louis XIV, that, if James would cease pressing *his* claim to the throne, William would name young Prince James as his heir; no mention was made of the religious issue. Here is where Mary of Modena made her fateful contribution to history. Louis made this offer in front of James, James's illegitimate son the able Duke of Berwick, who had followed him into exile, and Mary. The men approved the plan, but Mary declared stoutly, "I would rather see my son dead than possess the Crown to the prejudice of his father." The subject was dropped, and by her rash retort Mary doomed the Stuart dynasty.

In 1700, when the childless William III was failing and Princess Anne's only surviving child had just died, the question of a successor again came up. William looked around for a suitable candidate, but found that Henrietta Maria had done her work only too well and that all 42 of the remaining offspring of Charles I's descendants were Catholic. He had to look further back in the family tree, to the descendants of Charles I's sister Elizabeth—namely to her elderly daughter Sophia, who had married the Elector of Hanover. Sophia was a sensible and intelligent woman, and firmly told William to do the obvious and adopt James's son as his heir. "Having learned and suffered from his father's errors, he may yet make a good king." William again made the offer without strings—and again it was refused.

So the die was cast, for in June 1701 the English Parliament approved the Act of Settlement, whereby, after the death of Anne, the crown would pass to the Protestant Sophia and her descendants, and no future English king would be allowed to marry a Catholic. By their obstinate single-mindedness, Mary and James had deprived their son of his rightful inheritance.

Shortly after the passage of this bill in 1701 James II was cut down by a stroke, and in September he had another, from which he died on the 16th. The grief-stricken Mary was left with her 13-year-old son and nine-year-old daughter, and for five years would be Queen Regent for her son James III, the king without a kingdom.

Possibly she now realized how foolish she had been, for she published an important statement on her son's religious policy, that in effect said that the Anglican Church would have the power left in its hands and not the king's, and that Parliament would be left to decide the matter of religious tolera-tion. But it was all to little and too late. With the weighty Act of Settlement backing him, William III was no longer interested in James, and in 1702 passed the Act of Attainder, whereby James III was liable to execution, if captured in England, and, more importantly, that those helping him in any manner would be liable to lose their property, their titles and possibly their lives. This would seal the fate of countless faithful "Jacobites" in the years ahead. Shortly afterwards, in March of 1702, William died after a fall from his horse and Anne ascended to the throne.

There followed a tranquil period for Mary—perhaps the happiest in her life—as her grief for James dimmed and she watched her pleasant and promising children grow up, well received at the French court and with able and willing assistance from the Duke of Berwick, of whom she had grown fond. This tranquillity lasted until 1708.

In 1707 Queen Anne had passed an Act of Union which abolished Scotland as a separate country and made it one with England. This infuriated the Scots, and so James III saw a great opportunity to win back his lost kingdom with the aid of his loyal Scottish subjects. With Louis XIV's enthusiastic backing, the 19-year-old set out in March of 1708 to claim his kingdom.

Whether James had the attributes to make a successful king is a moot point; what he certainly did not have was luck. In fact he seemed to be bedeviled throughout his life by falling ill at the wrong moment. Before the invasion fleet even set out he came down with a bad case of measles (caught from his sister Louise) and had to be carried on board. It hardly mattered in the long run, for the French fleet got within sight of Scotland and were so intimidated by an English fleet that they retreated to Dunkirk, and so James never got to set foot in his native land. Throughout the rest of Anne's reign he had to content himself with trying to placate her and to change her mind about making him her heir. But he refused to change his religion and she refused to leave her crown to a Catholic.

In 1712 fresh tragedy struck the exiled family. James, who had been off fighting for France as a soldier, returned for a visit to St. Germain and came down with smallpox. He was so ill that extreme unction was given; then, to Mary's horror, Louise came down with the same disease, and on the morning of April 18 she died. She was 20. James was still so sick that he could not be told of her death, although he did eventually recover. Further woe was heaped on Mary at the end of the long War of the Spanish Succession in 1713, when Louis XIV, in exchange for the recognition of his grandson as King of Spain, was forced to accept the Hanoverian Succession in England. This meant he *had* to withdraw his support from the exiled family, and James III, now "The Pretender," had to leave France.

He was given a final chance by the dying Anne to change his religion for the crown—and turned it down. She died in August of 1714 muttering "My poor brother!" and the cruel and gross George of Hanover, the Electress Sophia's son, became George I of England.

Again James had another chance, for the Scots wanted to see the Scottish Stuarts have their rights and the throne. The Stuart standard was raised in the highlands in September of 1715, and the call to arms was quickly answered by English Jacobites as well. Had James moved quickly, he might have had a chance, but he hesitated, and not until Christmas was he carried onto Scottish soil. (This time he had been deathly seasick.) Already the English Jacobites had been defeated at Preston, the Scottish Jacobites at Sheriffmuir, and by the time he arrived most of the disgusted clansmen had returned to their homes. A government force of 10,000 men was advancing on him. James retreated north, and was then talked into embarking for France in February of 1716. The terrible reprisals George I took on the Jacobites so upset James that he never tried again.

To Mary this result meant fresh pressures, with penniless exiled Jacobite refugees crowding the French court, begging for aid. Her own plight had been worsened by the death of the aged Louis XIV, who had always been so supportive, and the throne was now occupied by his small great-grandson Louis XV, under the regency of the Duke of Orleans, who was no longer interested in the Stuarts. He made it plain that James was no longer welcome in France, so James started on his European wanderings, far from his mother. Mary's hopes rose for a while when he stopped in Modena and fell in love with his cousin Benedicta, the daughter of Mary's uncle Duke Rinaldo. Mary pleaded with her uncle to let the marriage take place, but Rinaldo, desperately trying to keep the Este family from financial ruin, was not interested in this crownless exile, with no money and few prospects, and turned James down. In her bitterness, Mary wrote to Rinaldo, "I pray God pardon you the wrong you have done to my son, the King, and for the grief you have caused me." James would eventually marry a Polish princess, but by that time his mother was dead.

Although the new French king continued to support her, Mary was almost reduced to penury by the increasing demands of the growing horde of Jacobite refugees and the decreasing disbursements from Louis XV. None of the regal equipment that Louis XIV had supplied so generously 30 years before had been replaced over the years, so her effects were threadbare and she had few clothes and fewer luxuries. Only her religion sustained her.

In May of 1718 she caught a cold, the cold turned to pneumonia and she died within a week, at the age of 59. She was buried in her favorite place, the Salesian Convent of Chaillot, where the heart of her husband James II was also interred.

INTERLUDE II
(1688–1727)

Mary II, in a painting after William Wissing

WILLIAM AND MARY, ANNE, GEORGE I

ANOTHER GAP COMES IN THE RANKS OF QUEEN consorts during the reigns of two queens regnant, Mary and Anne, the Protestant daughters of Catholic James II, and of England's first Hanoverian king, George I, who was married, but whose wife, Sophia Dorothea of Zelle, never set foot in England for reasons that will be duly apparent.

Mary, the elder of James's surviving daughters by his first marriage to Anne Hyde, married her first cousin, William of Orange, in 1677 and with great reluctance. The marriage proved childless; after two miscarriages in 1678 and 1679 she was never pregnant again. William was both a neglectful and an unfaithful husband, taking as mistress in 1679 Elizabeth Villiers, Countess of

Anne, in a painting from the studio of J. Closterman

Orkney; but he was also—like his great-grandfather, James I—bisexual, with a distinct preference, particularly in his later years, for handsome young men.

Their return to England by invitation in 1688 as joint rulers did little to improve Mary's life. Hoping to reforge her ties with her sister and heir, Mary found that Anne was completely under the domination of the strong-minded Sarah Churchill, later Duchess of Marlborough, and the sisters quarreled endlessly. Her sufferings were short-lived, however, for in December of 1694 she contracted smallpox and died at the age of 32.

William III did not remarry, so when he died in 1702 the crown passed to Anne. In 1701, however, the important Act of Succession was passed whereby all Catholic royals were barred from the throne and all future royal Catholic marriages prohibited, thus greatly altering the provenance of all future queen consorts. It also decreed that if Anne died without an heir the throne would pass to the Protestant George of Hanover, great-grandson of James I through his mother, the Electress Sophia and her mother, Elizabeth of the Palatine.

Queen Anne certainly tried hard to produce that heir. After marrying the dim-witted Prince George of Denmark in 1683, she went through 18 pregnancies, all of which ended in miscarriages, still births, or infant deaths—only one son managed to make it to his 12th birthday before dying. Modern medical opinion is that she suffered from a bacterial infection of the womb called Listeria which can now be cured within a week with antibiotics but which then was untreatable and fatal to infants; this would account for the high death toll. It also seems that Anne, like cousin William, was bisexual. Although fond of her amiable husband George, who died in 1708, she doted and depended on her female favorites—first, Sarah Churchill, Duchess of Marlborough, and later, after 1708, Sarah's cousin, Abigail Masham.

Apart from her failure to produce a Stuart heir, Anne's most important contribution to future history was her abolition of Scotland as a separate kingdom by the Act of Union of 1707, which joined it to England as the United Kingdom. The Scots bitterly resented the move and henceforward would back all subsequent "Jacobite" attempts to regain the throne for the Stuarts: James III's abortive rebellion in 1715 and again his son Charles Edward's rebellion in 1745. The Scots paid a horrendous cost in both men and misery, but the rebellion led to the great enlargement of English colonies in the New World, particularly in Canada, to which large numbers of Scots emigrated after 1745. Anne died on August 1, 1714, attended to the last by Lady Abigail Masham, and the crown passed from the house of Stuart to the house of Hanover, where, despite two name changes over the years, it remains.

The English were to pay a high price for their insistence on a Protestant ruler, and rapidly were to conceive a deep dislike for the German Hanoverians. George I was 54 when he ascended the English throne in 1714: a gross, coarse man of small intellect but huge sexual appetite. He was totally uninterested in his new country, save as a source of revenue, and spent the bulk of his time in Hanover. He never even bothered to learn English. In 1682 he had married his beautiful cousin Sophia Dorothea of Zelle, and the marriage had produced two children—George, his heir, born in 1683, and a daughter, Sophia Dorothea (future mother of Frederick the Great of Prussia). George was consistently unfaithful to Sophia, who retaliated in kind by taking the Swedish Count Philip von Konigsmarck as her lover. George found out, had von Konigsmarck murdered—according to one account in front of Sophia—divorced her in 1694, and kept her in prison in the grim castle of Ahlden for the rest of her life.

While Sophia languished in prison, George went off to claim his new kingdom, accompanied by his two ugly and rapacious mistresses—one tall and skinny, the other very fat—who were immediately dubbed by the unenthusiastic English "The Maypole and the Elephant." He created them the Duchess of Kendall and the Countess of Darlington respectively, and was later to add an Englishwoman, Anne Brett, to his harem. The English aristocracy were so disgusted and dismayed by this state of affairs that court life virtually ceased to exist.

As time wore on George may have begun to feel a lack, for in the 1720s he offered to liberate and reinstate Sophia as his queen. She refused, purportedly with the words, "If what I am accused of is true, I am unworthy of his bed; and if it is false, *he* is unworthy of mine." She died in prison on November 13, 1726. George left her unburied for six months, but, worried by an earlier prophecy that he would not survive her a year, decided to return to Hanover to see her safely buried. He never arrived. Just before he reached Osnabruck, where he had been born, he suffered a massive stroke. He was rushed to the castle, where he died June 11, 1727 at the age of 67 in the same room in which he had been born. The prophecy was fulfilled.

George's constant neglect of England and English affairs had had one enormously favorable effect. It had permitted the unimpeded development of England's Parliamentary might, particularly that vested in its prime minister, at the expense of royal power and royal prerogative. And this balance of power the next queen consort of England would help enormously to make permanent.

THE HANOVERS

Caroline of Anspach, in a painting from the studio of C. Jervas

CAROLINE OF ANSPACH
(1683–1737)

m. George II   1705

Children: *Frederick, William, Ernest, Sophia, Caroline, Amelia, Louise, Mary*

No QUEEN CONSORT SINCE THE TIME of Catherine of Aragon had more of an impact on the future history of England than Caroline, the first of its many German queens; and it was an impact that was to be beneficial to the people of England, if not to the crown.

The blonde, beautiful and very intelligent Princess Caroline of Anspach (or Ansbach) married George Augustus, heir to the Elector of Hanover, in 1705. She had two things working for her from the very start: Her promiscuous husband fell in love with her, and, in spite of his countless infidelities, stayed in love with her. Also, being far more intelligent than he was, she very soon learned to manipulate him for her own ends. After their arrival in England, their subjects made up a couplet that runs "You may strut, dapper George, but 'twill be in vain, / We know 'tis Queen Caroline, not you, that reign."

From the start, she had to battle with her husband's endless promiscuities—those she could and did handle—and with the fanatical father–son enmity that existed between George I and George II, which was a far more difficult problem. She produced a family of three boys and five girls. Her father-in-law so detested son George that he ordained the children be removed from their parents and raised under *his* supervision, similarly indoctrinating their eldest son Frederick with a hatred for his father. This was particularly hard on Caroline, who was very fond of her daughters.

After George I's accession to the English throne in 1714 and the removal of the new royal family from Hanover to England, family tensions increased. Since George had no consort, the only English court possible was the household of the new Prince and Princess of Wales. Competition for places in this mini-court was considerable, even though thrifty Caroline paid her ladies-in-waiting half what Queen Anne had paid. The new ladies soon found, however, that their influence was negligible, owing partly to the bad relations between the king and his son. The princess, besides, knew her own mind and did not favor the politically minded among her entourage. The ladies-in-waiting, whose influence had played such an important part in court affairs since the time of Elizabeth and had reached its apogee in the reign of Queen Anne, would never again have clout in the affairs of England.

At first George I was delighted to let the Prince and Princess of Wales do all the royal entertaining and leave him free to devote his time to his beloved Hanover. Then, typically, he became jealous of their mounting influence and popularity, and in 1717 actually banished them from court. Caroline did not take this passively, and for the next three years she made their London home the center for opposition to George I; during this time she initiated what was to be a significant friendship and partnership with the politician Sir Robert Walpole.

It was Walpole who brought about an outward reconciliation between father and son in 1720, becoming George I's prime minister, and—to Prince George's disgust—seeming to desert the Wales's court. Caroline knew better, and bided her time. With her lively intelligence she had soon realized that England would be a far greater, richer and more stable inheritance for her children than Hanover, which still obsessed her father-in-law and, to a lesser extent, her husband. She particularly agreed with Walpole, the head of the Whig party, and his aims to keep England out of the endless European wars and to focus instead on developing her burgeoning, and potentially great, commercial and physical empire in the New World and Asia.

Her first great political coup came on the death of George I, with her husband poised to get rid of "traitorous" Walpole. She convinced her husband to change his mind. Walpole continued as Prime Minister, and thus began the powerful partnership between him and the queen that was to continue until her death. They would meet and agree on all important business; then she would work on influencing the king. Her method was simple but effective. George II was a conceited man, so, to quote the court chronicler Hervey, "She always at first gave in to all his notions, though never so extravagant, and made him imagine any change she wrought in them to be an afterthought of his own." The method worked like a charm.

Knowing that George could not be deterred from having his extramarital affairs, she was almost as clever in manipulating those to her advantage. His eye fell early upon Henrietta Howard, unhappy wife of Charles Howard, the penurious heir to the Earl of Suffolk. Henrietta was only too thankful for the change from her unsatisfactory husband, and when Caroline saw that she was no real threat, actually befriended her, keeping her out of her Howard husband's clutches and, when George finally tired of her, persuading her to remain at court as a counterbalance to his other affairs. Finally, even Henrietta had had enough, and in 1734 she begged to be allowed to leave court. This request led to a revealing comment by George: Caroline again begged her to stay, but the king protested, "What the devil do you mean by trying to make an old, dull, deaf, peevish beast stay and plague me when I had so good an opportunity of getting rid of her?" She had been a faithful mistress for 20 years.

Caroline had more problems at long distance when, on a visit to Hanover, George became enamored of Amelia von Walmoden (niece of one of George I's mistresses). He wrote Caroline that "he hoped she would love her as he did and for his sake" when he brought her to England. Caroline was not amused, communicating her displeasure in no uncertain terms. However, when she realized that George was staying on in Hanover just to be with her, she became alarmed at his long absence from his kingly duties in England and so sent a reluctant consent. George was delighted, and returned home, but without Walmoden—he needed his wife more than his mistress, although the affair continued whenever he returned to Hanover. Since the widowed Henrietta

Howard *did* retire from court, to marry again and live happily ever after, on his return he replaced her with Lady Deloraine.

In many ways, although Caroline did Anglicize herself she remained Germanic. At their coronation in 1727, she loaded herself with jewels, many either rented or borrowed, so that she actually clanked and jingled throughout the ceremony. "The more, the better" continued in her ideas of dress and adornment, although she kept tight reins on court expenses and worked her servants hard. In childbearing she insisted on having a German midwife attend her. Once after Caroline had been in labor several days, her ladies became alarmed and wished to send for an English doctor. The midwife issued an ultimatum, and George sent the ladies away. Caroline was in labor for five days and, not surprising, was delivered of a dead son. She also startled the English aristocracy, who had very little direct contact with their own offspring, by spanking the royal children hard and in public if they misbehaved.

Caroline appeared to be very fond of her daughters and was most upset when the eldest, the Princess Royal, insisted on marrying the hunchbacked and ugly Prince of Orange in 1734—but she treated him well when she saw that he was the husband her daughter really wanted. She was also close to the Princesses Caroline and Amelia, who were at her bedside when she died. She had no such closeness with her sons, and she joined her husband in his detestation of their eldest son and heir Frederick, who took after his gross grandfather. "Our first born," Caroline said, "is the greatest ass, the greatest liar, the greatest canaille and the greatest beast in the whole world, and we heartily wish he was out of it." She extended her dislike to his wife, Princess Augusta of Saxe-Gotha, a self-effacing young woman (who was to become a domineering older one with her son George III), and who also had to bear with a promiscuous husband. Caroline had little to do with her younger son, the coarse, cruel and equally promiscuous William, Duke of Cumberland, who would so richly earn the title "Butcher" Cumberland during the 1745 Jacobite rebellion. But she hated Frederick to the end. George kept him away from her deathbed and when he told her so, she said, thankfully, "At least I shall have one comfort in having my eyes eternally closed. I shall never see that monster again." In later years Prince Frederick would take two middle-aged mistresses, both with many children, and even the cynical court believed that in so doing he was seeking from them the motherly love that he had never had.

Not that Caroline was basically a "motherly" type—her interests were intellectual. Not only politics fascinated her, but also, and very deeply, philosophy and religion. She read widely, but husband George so detested seeing her with a book that she had to retire to a special little enclosure in the palace to do her reading, and also there to entertain her intellectual friends, like the philosopher Leibniz and two prominent Anglican divines, Clarke and Bishop Berkeley. She was very interested in ecclesiastical matters and did her best to amend the somewhat decadent and depressed state of the Georgian Anglican church, though with rather limited success.

While her intellectual faculties remained acute, Caroline began to decline physically after she passed her 50th birthday in 1733. She suffered from painful rheumatism and soon became aware that something much more was wrong with her. For a long time she kept her condition a secret, but by 1737 there was no disguising the fact that she was fatally ill. Whether she had cancer or a degenerative heart condition is difficult to tell, but by November of that year she was bedridden and clearly dying. Her distraught husband slept in a cot at the foot of her bed, her two unmarried daughters Amelia and Caroline taking turns to watch over her. Her mind remained clear, and as she felt the end approaching she begged George "to marry again when I am gone." Tears streaming down his cheeks, he sobbed, "No, never!—I shall have mistresses." "Ah," said Caroline drily, "marriage has never stopped that." She died on Sunday, November 20, at the age of 54.

George was to survive her for 23 years, but never even considered marrying again. He had, as promised, countless mistresses, including Amelia van Walmoden, whom he at last brought over from Hanover and created Countess of Yarmouth, but none had any influence over him in any but the domestic sphere. He mourned Caroline until he died.

If her death was a blow to George, it was an even greater one to Robert Walpole—"the greatest blow I ever received," he wrote. He thought of retiring and probably should have, for he had been greatly dependent on her support and wise handling of the king. He was driven from power in 1740, having been forced finally into a European war. But the cabinet system of government that had come to full flower during his long ministry had also taken firm root, and "the Whig Supremacy" would continue until the end of George II's reign, spawning such greats as William Pitt, Earl of Chatham, and later, William Pitt the Younger.

Caroline's hated Frederick never came to the throne, dying in 1751 before his father. Frederick's son George III succeeded to the throne and would undo some of the good the Whigs had achieved. But the foundations that Caroline had helped to cement held firm.

Charlotte of Mecklenberg-Strelitz, in a painting from the studio of A. Ramsay

CHARLOTTE OF MECKLENBERG-STRELITZ (1744–1818)

m. George III   1761

Children: GEORGE, *Frederick*, WILLIAM, *Edward, Ernest, Augustus, Adolphus, Mary, Sophia, Octavius, Alfred, Elizabeth, Amelia*

To THE ENGLISH SHE WAS ALWAYS A FIGURE OF RIDICULE. When the young king, George III, announced on July 8, 1761 that he had chosen her to be his consort and Queen of England, there was no reaction at all from his subjects save, perhaps, surprise. No one had heard of Charlotte or, for that matter, of Mecklenberg-Strelitz. So obscure were they both that one wit of the time wrote, "Lord Harcourt, the British Ambassador, is to be at her father's court, *if* he can find it!"

If they were surprised, Charlotte was even more so. Only 17, she had not yet been accorded adult status in the tiny and penurious north German principality over which her father ruled. She had never been allowed to attend an adult dinner party, but had lived almost in seclusion with her sisters in the palace nursery, only being allowed to "dress up" on Sundays to go to the long, tedious Protestant services of the area and then for their weekly treat, a carriage ride. She knew nothing of the proposed marriage until her brother came to take her from the nursery and told her to behave herself because she was going to meet the British ambassador, who had come to make her Queen of England. She was led into the drawing-room and laid on the couch. The ambassador put his foot on her to "claim" her for George. She was then sent back to the nursery while the adults talked over the business details.

How had George come to make this unlikely choice? The English upper classes knew well that his real love was the beautiful Lady Sarah Lennox, for whom he had been languishing for a couple of years, though neither his mother nor Lord Bute, his Prime Minister (of whom he stood in great awe), approved of her. He had almost worked up enough nerve to ask Sarah to be his wife and queen, but in the end stern duty and parental disapproval won out and he resigned himself to marriage with someone of his own rank. Dispiritedly, he had asked for a list of all eligible German Protestant princesses "to save a great deal of trouble, as it must sooner or later come to pass." By the end of 1761 he told the relieved Bute that of the select list the one he favored most was Charlotte, even though "she was not in every particular as I could wish, and yet I am resolved to fix there."

His choice may have been based on her being a musician and a linguist, two of his own talents; it was certainly not based on her looks. In an age that favored large, buxom women, she was small and thin, with sallow skin and a huge mouth. She was quite a contrast to the lovely and stately Sarah, who was so graceful and always dressed in the height of fashion.

Nonetheless, the die was cast, and a week after she had been "footed" by the British ambassador, Charlotte and her ladies were rushed to the coast and shipped out of Cuxhaven on the royal yacht, bound for Harwich. They had a terrible, stormy trip, but while all her ladies got very sick and took to their bunks, Charlotte did not. She enjoyed the trip, and spent some of it learning to play "God Save the King" on her guitar.

We get a second glimpse of the sterner mettle under her very unprepossessing exterior after she landed. Some English ladies, who had been sent from court to escort her to London, were quietly horrified by her ugly appearance and awful clothes. Knowing George liked his women pretty and well turned out, they tried to suggest how she should dress and fix her hair; but she would have none of it. "Let the king dress himself," she said, "I shall dress as I please." When George met his future wife she was arrayed in a shapeless blue satin quilted jacket, her hair going every which way and topped by a queer blue cap, and the whole ensemble dripping with ill-assorted jewelry.

Horace Walpole, that lively chronicler of the period, has left a memorable account of her at the wedding and coronation, which occurred the same day. She was completely swamped in an enormous mantle of ermine-lined purple velvet, which was fastened to her shoulders by a great bunch of pearls, and which was so heavy that it dragged all her other clothes off her shoulders. "The spectators knew as much of her upper half as the King would himself," says Walpole—probably more, as it turns out, for George spent the entire ceremony gazing at his lost love, Lady Sarah Lennox, the improbable chief bridesmaid.

But Charlotte, far from being embarrassed by the day's events, is reported to have entertained the crowd at the reception in St. James's Palace that followed by singing and playing on the harpsichord, then chattering brightly to her new husband all through the banquet until the early hours of the morning.

Unlike his Hanoverian forebears, George III went to his wedding couch a virgin. Charlotte, at least for a while, must have satisfied his strong needs. By the age of 40 she had borne him 15 children, 12 of whom lived to adulthood and nine of whom were boys. For the first time in centuries England had so many potential heirs to the throne that it almost ran out of titles to give them. The first heir, George, arrived promptly the year after the marriage, and from then on the children appeared as regularly as clockwork until the youngest, Amelia, was born in 1782.

While the people of England still laughed at her and lampooned her for her looks and dress, Charlotte and George settled down to a highly satisfactory domestic life together. They got along remarkably well; they both loved music and would often settle for a cozy evening at home, with George playing the flute and she accompanying him on the harpsichord. They often held musicales at the court, gave fêtes (with music) when they were in the country, and liked horse races. George loved walking and hunting, and that was fine with Charlotte so long as she did not have to go along too; and since she was pregnant most of the time she didn't have to. There was another aspect of their life that other people, particularly their children as they grew up, found very trying. George was frugal, and Charlotte, who had been brought up in a penurious household, went right along with his wishes on domestic matters. They skimped on food, on heating, on clothing, and on their children's allowances. This the royal sons found particularly hard to bear, and their courtiers were wont to think of an extended tour of duty at court as a prison sentence. Even as lively a person as the novelist Fanny Burney, who was persuaded to go to court as a mistress of the queen's robes and spent a miserable five years at it until her health broke under the strain, found the short rations and unbelievable dreariness too much to bear. From the pages of her journal we see a clear picture of the middle-aged George and Charlotte—kindly, considerate and undemanding people for their station in life, but terribly dull.

But George was also a king, and this was the source of all the troubles that tore apart their quiet domestic bliss and led to so much anguish for both of them. The snag was that they shared something else: They were both dreadfully ill-educated. For Charlotte this did not matter; she had her music, her languages and her family, and that was enough. For George it was catastrophic. On matters of state he had plenty of ideas, but because he was so ignorant, he had no idea that they were almost invariably the wrong ones. His two Hanoverian predecessors had been German-born and their main interests had lain in their former homeland of Hanover. The running of England they left to their ministers, so long as they provided their monarchs with enough money for their various pet projects. But George was English-born, even if he wasn't English-bred, and he wanted to rule in England. His English ministers thought otherwise, and an ongoing battle was waged, with George usually at the humiliating and losing end of it. In January of 1765, after one such particularly traumatic battle, his first breakdown occurred. We have almost a blow-by-blow account of this illness from the diary of the prime minister of the time, Lord Grenville,

At first it seemed just a feverish cold, and this is what the royal physician diagnosed, but it soon became clear it was much worse than that. Though heavy security was clamped down on the news, the king had become first rambling and then manic. During the breakdown all the repressions of his life started to surface. He talked continually of his lost loves, particularly of Lady Sarah Lennox, who had married long since. He started to make passes of a markedly sexual nature at the ladies of the court. Charlotte, pregnant at the time with the future William IV, had more sense than all the doctors treating him and realized he was having a mental, not a physical, breakdown. Although she did not understand it, she tried to keep his officers of state away from him, to give him a little ease from all the tensions he had been under and to help him regain his stability. Only after this situation had dragged on for a couple of months did anyone start listening to her. When they did he improved markedly, and by April was officially "better." But far from being the end of his illness, this was only the beginning.

Reams have been written on George III's madness and its origins, and the debate is still going on. Certainly no previous record exists of such mental illness in his family, and after the first outbreak he had many years of outward-appearing stability, even under heavy stresses. In 1772 George's mother, Augusta, died after a prolonged and painful illness. She had been the dominant figure of his early years, since his father had died young. She had fought with her father-in-law George II over her son's upbringing, had thwarted some early marriage plans, and must bear a large part of the blame for his lack of proper education and training for his future role. Nonetheless, even after his marriage and emancipation from her apron strings, George had remained a devoted son, and in her last illness he and Charlotte had visited her every day. In addition came the bad news that his favorite sister, Caroline, had been imprisoned in Denmark, and her lover, the Danish prime minister, executed, after they had been found in compromising circumstances by her husband, the king of Denmark. Yet neither of these traumatic events unsettled him to the point of madness.

It was again the pressure of political events that tipped the scale. During the long mismanaged agony of the war with the American colonies, George grew more and more distraught. His woes were compounded by his older sons, now growing up, who were causing all kinds of trouble with their extravagances and dissipated ways. The Prince of Wales, in particular, was always quarreling with him, and he had the additional grief of losing two of the younger sons, Octavius, his favorite, and Alfred, the youngest, in two successive years, at the ages of four and two respectively. A brief respite came after this in 1787, when the Prince of Wales patched up a peace of sorts with him, swore to behave, get rid of his mistresses and marry and settle down. His marriage to Princess Caroline of Brunswick was then arranged and celebrated—and turned out to be a disaster from the start. Then came more trouble with his ministers and with Parliament. In June of 1788 George cracked again.

Charlotte had tried to keep him away from stress by staying at Windsor Castle, which he loved, and away from the strains of his capital. But this time his illness was much worse. In addition to the constant babbling and agitation, George was now assaulting the ladies-in-waiting, and fantasizing about raping the leading beauty of the time, Lady Elizabeth Pembroke.

The situation must have been particularly difficult for Charlotte. In the Rabelaisian courts of his forebears such behavior would scarcely have lifted an eyebrow, but in their 27 years of married life she and George had sanitized the atmosphere and habits of the court, and had imposed on it the rigid puritanical standard of conduct they themselves maintained. They had tried to gather people of like mind around them; now these same ladies were the last ones to overlook a king exposing his genitals to them in corridors and assaulting them sexually if the opportunity arose. No wonder Charlotte was often seen weeping and red-eyed at this period, although she still did a masterly job of keeping the bad news from leaking beyond the court. In one of his more lucid moments George gave her the best compliment she was ever to receive. "The Queen," he said, "is my physician, and no man can have a better. She is my friend."

But the malady got worse and in November entered a violent phase. He attacked some of his pages, and when the Prince of Wales came to visit, he attempted to strangle him. This frightened his fat heir, and instead of keeping his father's attack secret he spread word of it everywhere. There was malice in the prince's action, because he saw this as a heaven-sent opportunity to set his father aside and have himself declared regent, and in this his brothers aided and abetted him.

The king's condition was so bad that Charlotte was no longer safe herself. She moved out of the royal bedroom into one at some remove, where she was guarded by two gentleman-courtiers. Even so, one horrendous night the king managed to slip past them, and Charlotte was awakened to the terrifying sight of her bedcurtains being torn open and her husband standing there glaring down at her as if he would kill her. She lay in terror for half an hour while he stared silently at her, but finally the fit passed and he went away. Even the royal princesses, who had always been favored by their father over his unruly sons, were no longer safe with him. In desperation they all decided to move him to Kew Palace, away from the court entirely and under a new set of doctors, where he was kept completely segregated and under restraint a great deal of the time.

What with coping with George, wrangling with his doctors and trying to head off her son's plans to become regent, by the end of December poor Charlotte was completely exhausted herself. Parliament was beginning to go along with son George's ideas, and in February of 1789 the Regency Bill was close to passage. When her sons visited their father, Charlotte made it plain that she loathed what they were doing to him, and as a countermeasure to their tale-spreading started to take George out in public again with his daughters. The ploy worked, and the Regency Bill was killed. He was, however, far from cured. In her journal, Fanny Burney recorded a terrifying encounter with him as he chased her around Kew Gardens before being recaptured by his guardians.

There then began a peculiar half-life for them all as the king seesawed between madness and lucidity, with Charlotte having to keep up a brave public front. The country, after an initial burst of sympathy, soon settled back into its old pattern of dislike and ridicule, and in 1801 Charlotte was involved in yet another terrifying incident when the royal coach was surrounded and stoned by a crowd of rioters. George was fully cognizant, at this stage at least, of his need for her: During the Napoleonic War, when the threat of French invasion of England was at its height, he drew up elaborate and quite sensible plans to evacuate and save her and his daughters.

She managed to maintain this precarious existence until 1810, but in that year Amelia, their youngest daughter and George's favorite child, died at the age of 28, and again his mind toppled. In addition, he went blind. There was no blocking her feckless son's ambitions then, and in 1811 he officially became regent. She and George were pushed into the background.

In one sense it must have been a great relief to her, and in her last years she tried to reinstate something of her old life—entertaining, going to the races, and acting with a degree of dignity that provided a marked contrast to the behavior of her son's silly and scandal-ridden court. In 1817 she presided over the wedding of her youngest surviving daughter, Elizabeth, and after that it seems as if Charlotte just gave up. She had done what she could, as well as she could for as long as she could, and she was worn out. She passed peacefully away the next November, and the king was so far gone by this time that he never even realized that his wife of over 50 years was dead: He survived her by two years.

Oddly enough, the fertile Charlotte had produced a remarkably infertile family. Or perhaps one should say it produced few *legitimate* offspring, for her unsatisfactory sons, reacting against the rigid morality of their parents, had bastards almost by the dozen. But neither of her married daughters produced children who lived. Before her death she had seen only one legitimate grand-child born, the only daughter of feckless George and Caroline of Brunswick; the child had been named Charlotte after her. Before Charlotte's own death this unfortunate grandchild died in 1817 in a bungled childbed delivery that precipitated the rush of her sons into late matrimony and belated attempts to provide the throne with legitimate heirs. They bore a meager and feeble crop, but there was one that would have pleased Charlotte's sorely tried heart. The result was not a king but a queen on the throne of England; Victoria, daughter of Charlotte's fourth son, Edward of Kent.

Charlotte had no hand or say in the great events of George III's reign—the American Revolution that was to turn the world in a new direction; the Napoleonic Wars; the beginnings of the reform movement in England itself. Her influence was in the domestic sphere, where she had troubles enough to break stronger and cleverer women. For enduring as she did, history has to give her credit.

Caroline of Brunswick, by T. Lawrence

CAROLINE OF BRUNSWICK
(1768–1821)

m. George IV   1795

Child: *Charlotte*

NO GREATER CONTRAST TO HER TWO predecessors could have been found than Karoline Amalie Elisabeth of Brunswick, who seemed born to be her own worst enemy. But to understand her fate it is vital to understand the hopeless situation into which she was plunged and the character of her husband, who was one of England's most unpopular kings—not without reason.

George was the eldest of seven lusty sons the tiny Charlotte had borne to George III. Despite their Puritanical upbringing they all kept mistresses and produced bastards from a very early age. In all of this, George had led the way—like his Hanover forebears—and from the age of 16 was on extremely bad terms with his father.

Alarmed by his sons' escapades and aware of the disastrous marriages that his own two brothers, the Dukes of Cumberland and Gloucester, had made to "commoners," George III enacted in 1772 the "Royal Marriage Act," which, in effect, was an enlargement on the vetoes imposed by the 1701 Act of Succession and ordained that any marriage made by a member of the royal family would be valid only if the king's permission had been obtained.

This, in the case of son George, was to lead to a truly absurd situation. George, in spite of flagrant infidelities, fell genuinely in love with a woman who was, from the royal viewpoint, the most unsuitable he could have chosen. She was a twice-widowed middle-class commoner—and she was Catholic. Her name was Maria Fitzherbert and she was what the English in any age would have termed "a thoroughly nice and virtuous woman," who lived quietly as an affluent widow in the tiny Sussex seaside town of Brightheimstone (now Brighton). She, unlike the series of women who preceded her, resisted the Prince of Wales' amorous advances, although he tried everything—including a faked suicide attempt—to make her change her mind. The only way to get Maria was to marry her and, finally, that is what he did. In December of 1785 they were secretly married in the little Catholic church near her home in Brighton. They proceeded to live together as man and wife for the next 10 years, and it did not worry Maria, secure in having done the right thing by her conscience and her faith, that she was regarded by the world as just another mistress. Much as George loved her, he was no more faithful to her than George II had been to his Caroline, and in 1794 he began a hot affair with Frances Villiers, Countess of Jersey. Maria had tolerated his infidelities up to this point, but this was one step too far, as Frances was a thoroughly hateful woman. Maria and George separated.

In a way George was relieved, since he was in full lust after the countess and also beset by mounting money problems. Although married in the eyes of God and the Catholic Church, his conscience was buffered by the twin Acts of Succession and Royal Marriage, under which he was still single. With Maria out of his life he could indulge himself with the accommodating Frances while looking around for an "approved" royal wife to provide the necessary heir to the throne and, he hoped, to augment his income.

Looking over the roster of acceptable Protestant princesses, his choice fell upon his first cousin, Caroline of Brunswick, the daughter of its Duke and of George III's younger sister Augusta, who was still unmarried at the age of 28.

Caroline was, and always had been, completely slovenly in her habits—a fact well known to all her relatives, who did nothing to enlighten George. She was unclean in her personal hygiene and habits, a messy dresser and a messier eater, with little intelligence and less common sense. In social situations she tended toward overexcitement to the point of acting strangely, making outrageous statements and telling tall tales—all of which would contribute to the scandals of her later life. Nonetheless the marriage was duly approved and Caroline shipped off to England.

A bevy of ladies-in-waiting and courtiers were sent out to greet the bride-to-be, who was to be lodged at Greenwich Palace prior to the wedding. Among them was the malicious Countess of Jersey, more than usually bent on spite. Under the pretext of befriending her, she made up Caroline's naturally florid face until she looked like a clown, persuaded her to change her dress for one that was totally unsuitable and showed her flabby figure, and so arranged the proceedings that when the fastidious George first saw Caroline he almost fainted with horror—she looked awful, she smelled awful, and, in her own nervousness, she acted like a neurotic fool.

But it was too late to call off the marriage, which took place April 8, 1795. To make sure the wedding night would go badly, the Countess of Jersey slipped laxatives into Caroline's food at the feast, while the horrified groom got quietly and thoroughly drunk. The wedding night itself certainly was a disaster, with George throwing up in the empty grate and then passing out for the rest of the night, while Caroline sat on the commode. That night, according to Caroline's own later testimony, was the beginning and end of their marital relations. On January 7, 1796, exactly nine months later, their only child and heir to the throne, Princess Charlotte, was born.

It soon dawned on the deserted and neglected Caroline who was sharing her husband's bed and company, and she started to wage a vehement campaign to remove the Countess of Jersey from her household and her home. When her strategy had no effect on George, she committed what to him was the unforgivable act of complaining to her uncle the king and his prudish queen. After several months, and with the knowledge that a child was on the way, they too put pressure on their son, and the countess was forced to leave the household. But George simply moved the countess and her complaisant husband to a new residence, next-door to his, and spent all his days and nights there. To infuriate him further, the vast income he had expected after the marriage was not forthcoming from the niggardly Parliament, and this, too, he held against his wife.

Although Caroline appeared to win the day after the birth of her daughter and the disappearance of the countess from underfoot, any hope the royal family may have had for the reconciliation of the couple gradually died: George could not stand to be near her. So in August of 1797 a formal separation was agreed upon, Caroline and her household moving to a rented mansion in Blackheath, although apartments were still kept for her in Carlton House, George's home, just for appearance's sake.

In Blackheath Caroline proceeded to lay the foundations for the scandalous reputation that was to dog her thereafter. She gave endless parties and flirted with local "gentlemen," scandalizing her ladies. When her ever-penurious husband demanded she cut down on expenses, she agreed with amazing alacrity by replacing the aforesaid ladies with more accommodating successors. She saw practically nothing of her daughter, for even the royals agreed she was a bad influence on the child, filling her head with endless plaints against her father.

In 1798 George finally tired of the spiteful Countess of Jersey, but did not give a thought to returning to Caroline. Instead he paid court to his other wife, Maria Fitzherbert, whom he besought to come back to him, and, after checking with the Pope, Maria did return to him in the spring of 1800. This time they lived amiably together for another nine years, until a new infatuation of George's with the middle-aged Marchioness of Hertford was once again too much for Maria, and in 1809 she and George came to a final, but amicable, parting.

All this time Caroline had been compounding her own follies. In 1801 she had become overly friendly with another lady of dubious character, Lady Charlotte Douglas, "a showy, bold woman" whom she promptly engaged as one of her ladies and who soon became a repository for her confidences and tall tales. One of these fabrications was that she was expecting a child, and when Lady Douglas came back from a trip abroad in 1803, sure enough there was a small infant in the household. The bosom friends then fell out, and in 1804 Lady Douglas was banished from Caroline's household. The next year Lady Douglas got her revenge by revealing the story about the child, which, if true, would have been high treason on Caroline's part. Of course it was not true, but as a result the so-called "Delicate Investigation" was launched, revealing that the child was actually the baby of a poor dock laborer and his wife whom Caroline, for some bizarre reason, had adopted. But the investigation also revealed she had been flirting and worse, and for a time she was barred from the king's court.

Realizing she had overstepped the bounds, she tried to mend fences with her offended uncle, and succeeded to the extent that she was given apartments in Kensington Palace (where a closer eye could be kept on her). She still, however, continued to delight in shocking her ladies with outrageous tales and behavior.

England had all the while been engaged in the grim Napoleonic Wars with France, and George III had been sinking deeper into madness. Caroline's husband George, whose hands were itching for power (and the money that went with it), had tried again and again to be made his father's regent, and in 1811 finally succeeded. As soon as he was so appointed by Parliament, he tried to get rid of Caroline once and for all. She was banished from court and he reopened "the Delicate Investigation" with an eye to divorce. But he had overestimated his power, and the chivalrous Parliament rose to the defense of the distressed Caroline, who was exonerated. The unpopular George became more unpopular than ever with the common people, who demonstrated their support of the "injured" Princess of Wales.

By 1814, however, her own antics had made her position in England problematic and, with the apparent end of the war with France, she decided to go traveling. To give but one instance of her astonishing behavior: On a rare visit to her teenage daughter at Windsor Castle, she contrived to lock her in a bedroom all night with one of the bastard sons of the Duke of York. Luckily, the young man had enough sense not to lay hands on the heir to the throne, so the young princess emerged unscathed from her compromising night.

George was only too thankful to see his wife out of England and so underwrote her travels around the Continent. Once away from England she threw off all restraint, shedding her English ladies-in-waiting one by one and replacing them with more lowly-born foreigners who condoned her adventures. For several years she settled in Italy, where she almost certainly had an affair with her courier, Bartolemeo Pergami, whose sister "Countess" Oldi became her constant and closest companion. She did not return to England for the marriage of her daughter Charlotte to Prince Leopold of Saxe-Coburg in 1816, nor for her funeral the next year after Charlotte's tragic death in childbirth— one of the most horrifying cases of medical malpractice in history and one which was to have monumental repercussions on the history of England. Caroline seemed quite content with her wandering life.

Then in January of 1820 the blind and mad George III died, and husband George finally became king after a regency of nine years. Caroline decided to return and become Queen of England. George IV tried to bribe her to stay away, but she was determined to receive what she considered her due and in June she returned, accompanied by the Countess Oldi.

George had kept an eye on her doings all these years and was convinced he had enough grounds to divorce her for adultery and deprive her of her queenship. The bill was introduced to Parliament in July and the hearing lasted from August 17th to November 10th in the House of Lords; Caroline diligently attended. She was helped by a brilliant defense counsel, Henry Brougham, and George's case was greatly hindered since she had had no English ladies with her, so that most of his "evidence" was secondhand and therefore inadmissible. The bill of divorcement was abandoned.

Caroline thought she had won, but in reality she had lost, for George had no intention of seeing her crowned and consecrated Queen of England. On July 19, 1821 she turned up at Westminster Abbey for the ceremony and sought admittance. She was thrown out, while inside her husband made eyes and winked throughout the ceremony at his latest mistress, Lady Conygham. Caroline was so upset that she immediately became ill, and just 19 days later died of "inflammation of the bowels." At the last she was attended only by the Countess Oldi and one of her former ladies-in-waiting, Lady Anne Hamilton. She instructed them to bury her in Brunswick and directed that her coffin be inscribed "Caroline, the injured Queen of England." As one wit remarked, "It is observed she says 'injured' not 'innocent.' "

George was to outlive her by nine years. He never remarried, although with daughter Charlotte and her baby both dead there was no longer a direct heir to the throne. Instead, his elderly brothers, reluctantly abandoning their mistresses and bastards, went into an undignified scramble to marry legally and beget heirs—with meager results. When George died in 1830 he requested that he be buried with a miniature of his wife around his neck—his wife, Maria Fitzherbert.

Adelaide of Saxe-Meiningen, by W. Beechey

ADELAIDE OF SAXE-MEININGEN
(1792–1849)

m. William IV   1818

No surviving issue

THE MOST PHILANTHROPIC OF ENGLISH QUEENS—and indeed of British royalty in general—Adelaide must have been in an extremely charitable mood when she agreed to marry William, the 53-year-old Duke of Clarence, in 1818. His offer of marriage had already been turned down by at least a dozen European Protestant princesses, and he was known to be syphilitic, coarse-mouthed, a noted womanizer and the father of 10 acknowledged bastards.

The third son of George III, after George, Prince of Wales, and Frederick, Duke of York, no one had thought that William would ever be king, and so at the age of 13 he had been shipped off to the Royal Navy, where he had served during the American Revolution, had become friends with Horatio Nelson, and had lived the typical rough sailor's life, with many girls in many ports. By the age of 24, as he wrote to brother George, he had already had three bad doses of "the pox." All this womanizing infuriated his father the king, who forcibly retired him from the navy and insisted he settle down.

William settled down all right, but not in the way George III had hoped. He fell in love with an Irish actress playing comic roles in London, named Dorothy Jordan, who was almost as coarse-mouthed as he was and who had already produced three children by assorted fathers. She and William lived happily together for the next 20 years, and in that time she bore him 10 children, five boys and five girls, the "Fitzclarences," and the huge family of 15 lived at Bushy House near Hampton Court. They were so strapped for money that she had to keep on acting to make ends meet, leading to a popular contemporary jingle: "As Jordan's high and mighty squire / her playhouse profits deign to skim, / some folks audaciously enquire, / If *he* keeps her, or *she* keeps him?"

This arrangement came to an end in 1811 when, partly to please his anxious mother Charlotte, but mostly to try to improve his own financial position with a rich wife, William parted from Dorothy forever, although he supported her and their family. Years later, they met by chance on the street and both of them burst into tears.

William hunted for his rich bride in vain, and then in 1817, with the death of the heir to the throne, Princess Charlotte, and her child in childbirth, his situation altered and it became imperative for him to marry and produce heirs. His next-older brother Frederick, Duke of York, had already married his cousin Frederika of Prussia in 1790, but she was barren; Frederick had produced numerous bastards from even more numerous liaisons than William.

William's hunt for any wife—rich or not—was proving hopeless until Adelaide said an unexpected yes; perhaps because at 26 she was already considered too old to be eligible for marriage. Also, Saxe-Meiningen was as obscure a principality as Charlotte's Mecklenburg-Strelitz had been, and England offered a more opulent life than she had at home, so she was prepared to turn a blind eye to her elderly suitor's reputation. From her portraits she appears to have been a very pretty woman.

Arriving in England, she found she would even have to share her wedding, for William's next-younger brother, Edward, Duke of Kent (who had just given up his mistress of 24 years, Julie St. Laurent) was going to marry the widowed Victoria of Saxe-Coburg, Princess of Leinengen. The joint ceremony took place at Kew Palace on July 11, 1818—in both German and English for the sake of the brides—and the race to produce heirs was on.

Adelaide did her best. In March of 1819 she gave birth to a sickly little girl who did not survive infancy. To add to her sorrows, the Kents had a strong baby daughter on May 24th of that year, and she was named Victoria after her mother. The next year Adelaide had another baby girl, who also died in infancy. Two years later she produced twin sons—stillborn. After that came several miscarriages but no more living children, and Adelaide would write sadly to her sister-in-law the Duchess of Kent, "My children are dead but your child lives, and she is mine too." The Duchess of Kent, who was not noted for her charitable nature, had other ideas, particularly after the following January when the Duke of Kent unexpectedly died at the age of 53 and she was again left a widow.

Although theirs was a marriage of state that had failed in its main purpose, this May and September couple settled down and became extremely fond of each other. Adelaide did a remarkable job of changing the aging William: She cut down his drinking and swearing, smoothed some of his rough social edges—and there were no more mistresses. She was still in the midst of her fruitless childbearings when George III died in 1820 and George IV was crowned, with all the attendant scandal of his divorce proceedings against Caroline, the coronation fiasco, and Caroline's subsequent death. So Adelaide distanced herself from the scandalous doings as far as possible. George IV's raunchy court was not to her taste either, and she tried to keep at a distance from it.

In the meantime George's younger brothers had been having a certain amount of success in the heir-producing line. In addition to little Victoria there was George, also born in 1819 to the obnoxious Earnest, Duke of Cumberland, and his sinister bride (rumored to have murdered her first two husbands). William's youngest brother Adolphus, Duke of Cambridge, likewise had a son George in 1819, followed by two daughters, Augusta, born in 1822, and finally Mary Adelaide, born in 1833, the future mother of Mary of Teck, destined to be George V's queen. In short, the Hanoverian succession, if belatedly, had been secured.

Then in 1827 the situation altered again, when Frederick, Duke of York, died at the age of 65 and Adelaide's husband William became heir-presumptive to the throne. George IV's lifelong overindulgences in drinking and womanizing were fast catching up with him—three years later, in 1830, he too died. He had been no more popular as king than he had been as regent or as Prince of Wales, so the national feeling was more one of relief than of mourning as they turned to their new king, "Sailor Billy," and his decorous Adelaide.

An incident at their coronation underlined a continuing battle that was to cause Adelaide much pain. She had become very fond of the little Princess Victoria, now heir-presumptive to the throne; but the Duchess of Kent demanded that the 11-year-old Victoria should have her own special procession at the Abbey. William IV, who could not stand his sister-in-law, saw this demand as a slight to Adelaide. "Certainly not," said he. "There is no reason why the Queen should not still have a healthy family." He decreed that his niece attend merely as Princess Victoria of Kent. "Very well," replied the Duchess, "then she will not go at all"—and she didn't. The Duchess would always use every excuse to keep Victoria firmly in her own claustrophobic grip and away from court, to the great sadness of the warm-hearted Adelaide.

As queen, Adelaide proceeded to clean up the court just as she had cleaned up William. Banished were the "shady ladies" and the roistering elements, gone the extremely revealing gowns. Adelaide insisted on high necklines and restrained behavior, even though William loved entertaining, the more informally the better. She even barred some ladies, like the Duchess of St. Albans, whose only fault was having once been an actress. By contrast, all 10 of William's bastards were at court with their father—another weapon in the Duchess of Kent's arsenal. Adelaide worried about the little princess, so firmly in the clutches of her domineering mother and an equally formidable German governess, the Baroness Lehzen, and tried constantly to lighten Victoria's load, but with limited success.

Although William was not a born ruler, never having been trained for the task, he was vastly more popular with the common people than George IV had ever been. Being more of a "man of the people" himself, he enjoyed going out among them, and so the popularity of the royal family once more began to rise, having reached a nadir during George IV's last reclusive years. Adelaide helped restore the family's reputation by her own unending charities. She regularly gave away one third of her income to worthy causes, and was the first and only queen to employ a full-time almoner to investigate applications for royal charity. This she was to continue to her dying day.

Not that things were always serene. She came in for her share of unpopularity when her husband dragged his feet over the vitally important

Reform Bill of 1832. The bill was not so much a blow to the crown as it was to the landed aristocracy, for its aim was to enlarge the franchise to include on voter rolls *all* property owners (though not working-class "renters") and it recognized the growing role of the commercial and industrial middle classes in English government. The public, knowing she had influence on her husband, thought Adelaide was behind William's opposition to it. In reality it is doubtful whether she was even aware of the issue; her influence on William was restricted to the personal and domestic sphere. She also had to face her own share of scurrilous gossip when, in 1835 at the age of 43, she was rumored to be again pregnant—not by the king but by a courtier, Lord Howe! The rumor was as false as the pregnancy.

By 1835 William IV was starting to fail in health, and the same year Adelaide was very alarmed when the Princess Victoria came down with a severe attack of typhoid fever. The 16-year-old Victoria recovered, and in her recovery showed some of the mettle of her developing strong personality. Her mother and her "advisor" Sir John Conroy (who some said was the Duchess's lover) tried to make her sign a document while she lay ill, nominating him as her private secretary when she became queen. Since it was clear that they wished to dominate her and her actions, the teenager stoutly refused, and the result was estrangement—the first step towards throwing off her mother's domination, although the Duchess and Conroy kept up the pressure constantly during the next two years. Even as William lay dying on June 20, 1837 they were so persistent that Victoria had to shut herself away in her room at Kensington Palace and refuse to speak to either of them.

William died that day, with Adelaide by his side, and she mourned him genuinely. After attending "Vicky's" coronation at the Abbey on June 28, 1838 as Dowager Queen, Adelaide retired to a quiet life of charity and watched with approval as the young queen became more worthy a ruler than her own husband had ever been. She attended all the important court events from then on: Vicky's wedding on February 10, 1840 to her first cousin Albert of Saxe-Coburg-Gotha (her mother's nephew), and the christenings of their first six children, born between 1840 and 1848—two boys and four girls. The aging Adelaide was quietly delighted that Vicky, with all the passion of the Hanovers, was madly in love with her husband, who in 1843 managed to get rid of the Baroness Lehzen. The exit of this domineering governess led not only to a reconciliation between the queen and her mother, but also between Adelaide and her sister-in-law.

For such a genuinely charitable and generous woman, Adelaide had one mean little quirk—she had a fetish about plain ordinary pins. She kept them in orderly rows in endless pincushions, and if one of her ladies borrowed a pin, it had to be replaced exactly where it had come from; if a pin were dropped on the floor, *hours*, if necessary, would be spent looking for it until it was found and replaced in its proper row. The origin of this extraordinary fetish is wide open for speculation: Had Adelaide been punished as a small child by some dragon of a German governess for losing a pin? Was that why she developed this mild neuroticism about pins? Another of history's small mysteries that is insoluble.

In 1849, when the queen was expecting her seventh child, Adelaide started to fail, and she died quietly at the age of 67. She was buried beside her husband of 19 years at Windsor, after a widowhood of twelve years. Vicky had been fond of the Dowager Queen, and her death sparked the idea of building a mausoleum to house the remains of the current devoted royal couple. It was built at Frogmore in Windsor Park, and, 13 years later, would house the prince consort; not for another 39 years would Vicky be laid by his side.

William and Adelaide were not a dynamic couple but they performed a great service to the royal family. Royal houses were being toppled all over Europe by the wave of republicanism that had been sweeping the Continent since the French Revolution, and in England George IV had left the reputation of the British monarchy at its lowest point. But William and Adelaide had restored faith in the crown. It has been written of William, "He inherited a monarchy in tatters, he bequeathed to his heir the securest throne in Europe"—a fair statement, and a fitting memorial to them both.

INTERLUDE III
(1837–1901)

Victoria, by Lady Abercromby after H. von Angeli

VICTORIA

THE 19TH-CENTURY GAP IN QUEEN CONSORTS is filled by the longest reign in England's history, that of the Queen Regnant Victoria, who came to the throne at the age of 18 and died at the age of 81.

Victoria's reign is a paradox. On the one hand, she became monarch of the greatest and most far-flung empire the world has ever seen: queen not only of the United Kingdom but of Canada, the subcontinent of Australia, New Zealand, large chunks of Africa, "Empress" of India and sundry smaller possessions on every continent—a process of acquisition that had been going on since the time of Elizabeth I. On the other hand, by the end of her long reign, all the actual governing power of the monarch had vanished, and the monarchy had become what it remains today—a symbolic superstructure of state that condones the action of its government but has no say in its operations. Since the role of the monarch has changed, so has the role of the queen consorts who followed Victoria; it has become purely social and domestic.

The attrition of royal power had been continuing for centuries, and had been greatly accelerated since the succession of the Hanoverian dynasty, first by George I's neglect of his new kingdom, then by Queen Caroline's active support of the growing power of the prime minister and his cabinet, which was accepted by husband George II. Then George III made a concerted attempt to recapture some of the lost royal prerogative, but his long madness thwarted this effort. Subsequently, and by the very nature and character of the sons who succeeded him, the irresponsible George IV and the incapable William IV, no lost power was regained. Both kings were forced to accept measures that were totally against their wishes—in George's case the Catholic Emancipation Bill, and in William's the Reform Bill of 1832—because they no longer had the power to override the wishes of Parliament.

When young Victoria came to the throne it looked as if this process might be halted or even reversed. Although now the question was one of partnership between queen and prime minister, she was heeded and did have influence, at least for the first 25 years of her reign. But in 1861 Victoria's world fell apart with the death of her beloved husband, Prince Albert, of typhoid fever. She was 42. Her mourning for him was carried to extremes, as she entirely withdrew from the public gaze, filled the royal palaces with busts, statues and morbid memorabilia of her beloved, and draped herself in black for the remaining 40 years of her reign.

If this self-imposed seclusion had only been of short or even reasonable duration there might have been no lasting damage, but by the early 1870s there was a serious movement in England to abolish the monarchy entirely and set up a republic. At no time since the English Civil War had the monarchy been in greater danger.

That the change never took place was really no thanks to her. It stemmed from the near-fatal illness of the Prince of Wales, Albert Edward, whose cliff-hanging fight against typhoid, the same illness that had killed his father, appeared to shock the people of England out of their ugly mood. It also shocked Victoria enough to bring her, reluctantly, out of seclusion and into the public gaze once more, and to prompt her to take a more active part in royal affairs. Her public appearances increased during the '80s and '90s, due partly to the influence of her Scottish manservant John Brown, who had managed to cheer her up somewhat, even if he couldn't replace Albert. And by sheer longevity, with her Golden Jubilee of 1887 and then her Diamond Jubilee of 1897, she had once more become "Our beloved Queen" to the English.

In this period, however, all royal governing power vanished and was replaced by party politics and party leaders. It is significant that three more reform bills (of 1866, 1867 and 1884) were passed during her long withdrawal and neglect, cumulatively extending the right to vote to all adult males of whatever condition in the realm. (It would take a World War to extend the right to women.) Her statues dominated the scene in every capital of the Empire from New Delhi to Ottawa, but she had nothing to say about what went on in her empire.

Where she did have a profound, if indirect, influence was on the future of European history; that arose from her own fecundity. By her beloved Albert she had nine children; five girls and four boys, all of whom lived. Of the girls, with the exception of her eldest and favorite daughter Victoria, who married Frederick III, King of Prussia and Emperor of Germany, none made outstanding marriages. But they were equally fertile, and their children married into all the remaining royal families of Europe, thereby making Victoria literally "the Grandmother of Europe." To list them in order of birth: Daughter Victoria's son "Willy" became Kaiser William II of Germany; daughter Sophia married King Constantine of Greece; Edward, Prince of Wales's daughter Maud married King Haakon of Norway; Alice's daughter, the ill-fated Alexandra, married her cousin, the equally ill-fated Tsar Nicholas II of Russia; Alfred, Duke of Edinburgh's daughter Marie married Ferdinand, King of Rumania; Arthur, Duke of Connaught's daughter Margaret married Crown Prince Gustave of Sweden; and Beatrice's daughter Ena married Alfonso, King of Spain. In the political arena Victoria's influence had the ultimate ironic outcome in World War I, when grandson Willy, the German Kaiser, was pitted against grandson King George V of England and Victoria's granddaughter Alexandra of Russia's husband Tsar Nicholas II.

To some of their descendants Victoria and Albert had also passed an unfortunate genetic trait—hemophilia, a disease that is recessive in the female but dominant in the male. It is debatable whether the disease was already present in Albert of Saxe-Coburg's family or whether its appearance resulted from the union of first cousins; but in any case it was to affect the sole male offspring of Tsar Nicholas and Alexandra of Russia and to spread through most of the male offspring of King Alfonso and Queen Ena of Spain—with fatal results.

It is a moot point whether the monarchy would have retained some autonomy if Victoria had only handed over the reins of power to her eldest son, Albert Edward, Prince of Wales (later Edward VII) during her long seclusion.

But here another recurring Hanoverian theme comes into play: the bad blood that existed between ruler and heir. "I don't trust Bertie," said Queen Victoria, and that was that. He was doomed to a seemingly endless wait for the throne and was deliberately kept from any involvement in matters of state. By the time the 59-year-old Edward VII came to the throne in 1901 it was too late—the monarchy had become a symbol and nothing more.

Alexandra of Denmark, in a replica of the painting by L. Fildes

ALEXANDRA OF DENMARK (1844–1925)

m. Edward VII   1863

Children: Albert Victor, GEORGE, Louisa, Victoria, Maud

ENGLAND HAS HAD ITS QUOTA OF BEAUTIFUL QUEENS, but none more noted for her looks than England's second Danish queen, Alexandra. She was considered breathtaking, and with the fine bone structure that ensured that the beauty would last (albeit with considerable help) into old age. Unfortunately for her, neither her intelligence nor her personality matched her appearance.

Born to Prince Christian of Denmark, heir to the throne of his childless brother, King Frederick, and his wife, Louisa of Hesse, a descendant of George II, Alexandra was one of five children brought up in what for royalty was near-penury. They lived in a ramshackle palace provided by Louisa's miserly father, the Landgrave of Hesse, and, not being able to afford governesses and tutors, the prince and princess taught the children themselves. The girls had to make their own clothes and "Alix" had to share a bedroom with her sister Dagmar. In spite of this relatively deprived childhood the family did extraordinarily well in later years, Dagmar becoming Empress of Russia as the wife of Alexander III, Frederick eventually succeeding his father as King of Denmark, and the eldest son, George, becoming King of Greece.

When the possibility of marriage to England's Prince of Wales was first mooted when Alix was 17, the family was thrilled—her parents because powerful England would be a great ally for tiny Denmark against the growing power of Prussia, which was hungrily eying Denmark's province of Schleswig-Holstein, and Alix by the prospect of the brilliant and opulent life she would at last lead. She knew enough of royal marriages not to expect too much, and so was pleasantly surprised, when the young prince turned up to do his courting, to find him nice-looking, although already on the plump side, and extremely affable and easygoing. He, understandably, was swept off his feet by her beauty.

She was marrying a man who, with all his many faults, was rather to be pitied, for neither of his parents cared for him and he had grown up in the shadow of their eldest and favorite child, the intelligent "Vicky," who always outshone him. When he was only six, Lady Beauville, a lady-in-waiting, would write, "The Prince of Wales is weaker and more timid [than Vicky], and the Queen says he is a stupid boy, but the hereditary and unfailing antipathy of our Sovereigns to their Heirs Apparent seems thus early to be taking root and the Queen does not much like the child." He was very sensitive to this situation, as is apparent from the exchange he had with the Empress Eugenie in Paris when he was 14. He had had such a good time at the court of Napoleon III that he wanted to stay on after his parents returned home. Eugenie tactfully said they would not want to be parted from him. "Not do without us! Don't fancy that. They don't want us, and there are six more of us at home," he snorted.

Although the serious-minded and highly moral Prince Albert equally doted on Vicky, he was more attentive and concerned about his son, but unhappily without any real understanding of Bertie's abilities and character. Ambitious for his son, he mapped out an educational program for him that would have daunted an Einstein and that was completely beyond his capabilities; not surprisingly, the program failed miserably and was a constant source of worry to the prince consort. Bertie, unlike his father, was preeminently a social person; he loved people and was very good with them. Also, like the good

Hanoverian he was, he would overtop in promiscuity even his great-uncles, and in his teens had already managed several escapades, to the further worry of his abstemious father. His parents had been on a wife hunt for him from the time he was 18, and it was Albert's uncle, King Leopold of Belgium, who had first suggested the then-14-year-old Alexandra, although the English royal couple had made it clear they would prefer a "solid" German wife for him.

Disaster struck when Prince Albert died in 1861, and Alexandra's family panicked, fearing that the wedding would be called off. Luckily, Prince Albert had already sanctioned the marriage, and the grief-stricken Victoria would carry out any wish of her late beloved's, even though she privately blamed Bertie for having hastened his father's death by all the worry he had caused, and did not really approve of the marriage. She also took pains to make very clear to Alix that England would not involve itself in the Danish–Prussian dispute—after all, Prussia was Vicky's.

The wedding took place on March 10, 1863—not in the Abbey, as expected, but in St. George's Chapel, Windsor. The mourning Victoria would not show herself in public and even insisted on sitting up in the gallery, gazing miserably at the bust of Albert throughout the ceremony. There was much criticism of this rather shabby treatment of the 22-year-old Prince of Wales and his beautiful 19-year-old bride, but the young couple did not care; he was free at last and she had all the wealth and luxury she had hitherto lacked. Neither could foresee the incredibly long apprenticeship they would have to serve until the crown was theirs: it would be almost 40 long and often painful years.

With plenty of money, a castle in Scotland, the Palace of Sandringham and the elegant Marlborough House in London at their disposal, the young couple settled down to enjoy themselves in an almost constant round of social pleasure. Since the queen was firmly out of the way in seclusion at Windsor, the Wales's "court" was the only one available, and all the aristocracy flocked to this young, gay circle. Prince Albert had never liked the English aristocracy, and so only its more sober members had ever graced Victoria's dull court; now all this was changed. But the aristocracy was also very different from that which had flocked to the courts of yore: The old aristocracy had held real political power and ambitions; all that was left to them now were their riches and the high social positions—and the "idle rich" life devoted to pleasure.

It is from this period that there came a great split in English society that still exists in attenuated form to the present day: two vitally different cultural norms of behavior. The soberly monogamous union of Victoria and Albert and its attendant large family became the standard for all the middle classes that had grown so enormously in both size and political clout in the past hundred years. The pattern of the Wales's circle, whereby men (and women too if they were discreet enough) could have countless affairs and devote themselves entirely to social pleasure rather than to family life and social responsibility, became the norm for the aristocracy.

Into this hectic round Alexandra plunged with delight, insofar as she was able, for between the years of 1864 and 1869 she produced five children, two boys and three girls; and an unrecognized tragedy would attend the birth of their eldest child, Albert Victor or "Eddy." Alexandra was seven months pregnant by January of 1864 and, like most northern Europeans, loved winter sports, so, against all advice, she went to enjoy ice skating on the frozen pond at Frogmore after having attended a hectic children's party for young royals. As a result, she went into premature labor and was delivered of a three-and-three-quarter-pound baby boy, promptly wrapped in cotton wool, who, amazingly, managed to survive. Unfortunately, the premature child obviously suffered from oxygen deprivation to the brain, and in later years Eddy would be considered "incapable of learning," "incapable of concentration," and "vacant," and this, linked with typical Hanoverian sexual weaknesses, would render him a highly unsuitable prospective king of England. No such grave complications attended the births of the other four—George, born the following year in 1865; Louisa, in 1867; Victoria, in 1868; and Maud, in 1869; and after each birth Alix was back in the social swing after only a few weeks.

She was, however, soon to find thorns in her luxurious bed of roses. At about the time of Eddy's birth Denmark had become embroiled in a war over Schleswig-Holstein with a militant Prussia, which was busily gobbling up all its surrounding principalities by armed might and founding a "united" Germany. Denmark lost the war and the territory, but that was not the worst of it. When a European tour was proposed for the Prince and Princess of Wales Queen Victoria made it very clear that she did not want them to visit Denmark, where Alix's father had now become King Christian IX, because it might upset the Prussians (and darling Vicky), but she insisted they visit Prussia. This upset Alix terribly, and they did visit her family, but only stayed a short while, principally because Bertie found them boring. She felt an added slight when Queen Victoria's daughter, 19-year-old Helena, was married to Prince Christian of Schleswig-Holstein, who had sided with the Prussians against Denmark, and she refused to go to the wedding. Bertie, who had also initially refused on her account, eventually gave in to his mother and went to the wedding.

These were state matters, so, on a domestic level, they could in due time be set aside; but she was soon to experience painful disillusionment right at home. After the birth of Louise, Alix became very ill with terrible leg pains and a very high fever. The illness was diagnosed as rheumatic fever but may well have been polio, judging by its aftereffects. The Prince of Wales showed himself totally unconcerned and uncaring, and went on with all his usual amusements as she lay day after day in excruciating pain. The tide did turn, but it took her weeks to recover, during which the prince was carrying on with other women. She was left permanently lame in one leg, and a slight hereditary deafness she had inherited from her mother had been greatly aggravated so that she would become progressively very deaf indeed.

She could bring herself to ignore Bertie's affairs, but his insensitive neglect of her when she had really needed him was something she could never forget. Marital tension increased when, on a trip for a "cure" at the spa of Weisbaden for her leg, the prince insisted she meet with Denmark's enemy, the King of Prussia. Alix was not without spirit, so she refused. Bertie, caught between his mother's and sister Vicky's anger and his wife's intransigence, decided against her and, white with fury, she was forced into the meeting. Even then Victoria was not satisfied, and instructed her prime minister "to express to the Prince and Princess of Wales the *importance* of not letting any private feeling interfere with their public duties." The long, hard apprenticeship had begun, but it did little for the marriage.

Alix soon found herself turning to her children, and found through them the emotional satisfaction she otherwise lacked. She never tried to beat her husband at his own promiscuous game. Even then, her attachment to her children did not prevent her from "keeping up with Bertie" on his endless social rounds and his many European visits, although she was shocked into a greater sense of responsibility when, on a trip to Copenhagen in 1871, she gave premature birth on April 6th to another son who died in a few days. She blamed herself bitterly for the child's death—and so did Queen Victoria.

It was a time when the reputation of the royal family was at its lowest ebb and there was much talk of establishing a republic in England. The prince had gone one step too far in his affairs—he had been named in a divorce suit by Sir Charles Mordaunt as having been one of a crowd of men who had committed adultery with his wife Harriet, and Bertie had even had to appear in open court. Alix stood staunchly by him, but both were booed and hissed in the streets, and, with the queen still stubbornly in seclusion, there was more and more talk along the lines of "Who needs them?"

Then, having caused most of the trouble, Bertie proceeded, albeit inadvertently, to assuage it—by almost dying. The 30-year-old prince contracted typhoid while staying at a house party at Londesborough Lodge, and fell ill shortly after returning to Sandringham in November of 1871 (two other members of the same party were to die of it). For weeks he hovered between life and death, and it was not until mid-December that the tide turned and not until the following February that he had fully recovered. The nation had been shocked, as had Queen Victoria, who agreed to appear at the public procession to a thanksgiving service in St. Paul's Cathedral on February 27, 1872. There the same people who had booed and hissed the prince and princess just six months before greeted them with wild acclaim. The queen had emerged from her seclusion, her heir was saved, and the republican movement was dead.

Another by-product of this illness was to draw Alix closer to her redoubtable mother-in-law, who hitherto had thoroughly disapproved of her and everything she did. Victoria began to appreciate her, and, well aware of what Alix had to put up with from irresponsible Bertie, became increasingly supportive; so that from being her least favorite "in-law" Alix became her most favored.

Knowing she could not change him, Alix did a remarkably fine job handling the prince's endless promiscuities. So long as he kept to mistresses of the lower orders—and fortunately he was extremely partial to actresses—Alix did not mind, and in fact became friendly with some of them, like Lily Langtry, "the Jersey Lily." But when it came to public involvement, or long-term affairs with more aristocratic mistresses, then she balked. In the Aylesford divorce case of 1876, in which the prince was named for adultery, Lord Randolph Churchill had to do some hard talking to induce the princess to meet the prince on his return from an overseas trip; and when he became infatuated with Frances, Lady Brooke, called "Daisy," in 1891, Alix was beside herself with rage.

It looked for a while as if he had finally overstepped the bounds and that this time Alexandra would not forgive him. Here again fate stepped in in a rather grisly form with the sudden death of Eddy, Duke of Clarence, a few weeks before his own scheduled wedding with Princess Mary of Teck, and this reunited his parents in mutual grief, for, despite his shortcomings, they had been extremely fond of their eldest son. Eddy's death at the age of 28 was a blessing for England, for he would have made a disastrous king. Not only was he dim-witted but he was a notorious bisexual, promiscuous with men and women alike, syphilitic and irresponsible. Their heir became the steady and sober George, Duke of York, who was quickly married off to his deceased brother's fiancée Mary of Teck.

The mistress of Bertie's sunset years was far more to Alix's taste—a middle-class, very pleasant and tactful woman, Mrs. Alice Keppel, who came into his life after Daisy had faded out in the mid-90s and who remained devoted to him until the end. Alix even summoned her to the dying king's bedside, and she was with him when he died. Alexandra also gained some rights of her own when Bertie went off on his overseas bashes (current mistress often in tow), and she would go off to visit her sister Dagmar, now Empress of Russia, or her family in Denmark, and have a delightful time herself.

But one facet of her character took a far more deadly turn over the years. Ill-educated and with no intellectual strength or inner resources to fall back on, and with little or no emotional satisfaction from her unheeding husband, she became hungrily possessive of her children. Every time either Eddy or George would leave her—a frequent happening in the case of George, who was in the Royal Navy—there would be hysterical scenes, and they had to be in constant touch with "Motherdear" [sic]. As for the girls, she wanted to keep them with her always and never let them go, even though her love for them was evidently not as deep as for her sons. She drove away their suitors on the flimsiest of excuses and kept them all as virtual bond-slaves at her beck and call. The eldest, Louise, managed to escape with the connivance of Queen Victoria, by marrying a commoner, a rich Scotsman, whom the Queen obligingly created Duke of Fife. The second daughter, Victoria, never did escape, and lingered on an embittered, hypochondriacal "old maid," a virtual servant to her mother until the latter's death, only surviving her by 10 years. The youngest, Maud, did not escape until her late twenties, by which time she too was embittered and a dedicated grumbler. Finally she was married off to her first cousin, Prince Charles Christian of Denmark, who was then in the Danish Navy; but that didn't suit her because he was always away. But in 1905, by invitation of the Norwegians, he became their king as Haakon VII of Norway, and so she ended up a queen. By that time, however, she was so set in her pattern of bitterness that she continued it until her death in 1938.

If the girls had a hard time with their mother, her only daughter-in-law, Mary of Teck, had a worse one. Although Alix had been resigned to Mary's marrying Eddy (whom no one else in their right mind would have), she bitterly opposed the idea of her marrying "darling Georgie," and made the lives of the young couple as difficult as she could. The determined Mary would need years to wean her enthralled husband away from his mother's apron strings.

Although George was now his father's heir and was a sober, serious-minded man totally unlike Bertie, Queen Victoria continued her pattern and was no more inclined to let her grandson in on matters of state or give him training than she had his unsatisfactory father. And so the years dragged on, with both men hanging idly in limbo, sparking the bitter remark from Bertie, "I don't mind praying to the eternal Father, but I must be the only man in the country afflicted by an eternal mother." It was not until June of 1901 that the waiting ended with the death of the 82-year-old queen. The Victorian age was over and the uniquely flavored Edwardian era began, as the 60-year-old Bertie ascended the throne as Edward VII and Alix became queen at last.

Even then it looked as if the long-awaited prize might be snatched from them when, two days before the coronation, Edward was stricken with acute appendicitis. An immediate operation was necessary—no light thing in 1901, especially in view of Edward's enormous girth, which had earned him Alix's nickname of Tum-tum. The surgery was successful, and the postponed coronation took place in August, seven weeks after the original date. Alix was still astonishingly beautiful, and Edward, even though his failings were well known, was regarded with affection, so the new reign was greeted by the people of England with enthusiasm.

Alix adjusted to her queenly duties, although in many ways she was unsuited for them. From childhood she had always been a chronic latecomer— an unforgivable fault in royalty. By now she was almost stone deaf, and indeed had had to use an ear trumpet during the coronation—another grievous handicap. Also, she was not much mindful of formal protocol and would gaily wear her Garter Star in the wrong place "if it didn't fit in with the rest of my jewels," thus irritating her husband to distraction.

The very first thing she did on becoming queen was to redecorate the royal palaces, particularly Buckingham (home of the monarch since George IV's time), Windsor, and Balmoral, which, she wrote triumphantly, she had rid of Victoria's "tartanitis." Nearly all the morbid memorabilia of "beloved Albert" that infested all of them was also discreetly removed. And, once the period of mourning for Victoria was over, the court resumed its gay, slightly rakish flavor as "the Marlborough House set" became "the Buckingham Palace set."

The powerless queen of a powerless king had to set new rules of royal behavior, and for this Alix evidently looked back to the example set by William IV's Queen Adelaide. She became heavily involved in causes—hospitals, the poor, prisons, and the veterans of England's many foreign wars. From Victoria's daughter Princess Helena, who had started it, she took over the Military Nursing Service, which became The Queen Alexandra Imperial Nursing Service. Her compassion was real, as is illustrated by her visits to the "Elephant

Man," John Merrick, at whose grotesque appearance frailer ladies had been known to swoon. Alix became truly interested in this unfortunate man, and her visits to him became a high point in his brief life. So, in spite of her handicaps, she became very well loved.

While she was involved in her causes, Edward VII was busy doing the only thing he knew how to do—international diplomacy. Although he was completely ignorant of England's domestic policies, because Victoria had kept him that way, his many journeys and many connections in Europe had given him some expertise in the international field, and he was increasingly concerned about the aims of nephew "Willy," the German Kaiser, who, having gobbled up all the German principalities, was now aching to acquire some of Europe's smaller independent countries. Edward loathed Willy, and vice-versa—as did Alix—and having always preferred France and the French, he set about making an alliance with the French and with his Russian cousins against Germany. In this he succeeded with the "Entente Cordiale" of 1904.

But all the years of overindulgence in food, wine and women were catching up with Edward and, stressed by a serious constitutional crisis wherein the House of Lords was locked in battle with the House of Commons, in late April of 1910 he fell ill. Alix was away on a Mediterranean cruise but was told to hurry home. She got back on May 5th and Edward died the next day. As a final compassionate gesture, Alix had summoned his long-time mistress Alice Keppel to his bedside, and it was she who was with him when he died. His funeral has been described as the "swan song of European royalty," for in it marched nine kings and five heirs apparent, and it was attended by seven queens and countless minor royalties representing more than 70 different countries. Within a decade most of them would be either dead or in exile. With Edward went a lot of the fun and excitement in English life—and in Alix's.

She must have known what would come next, for although "darling Georgie" would not turn his back on his "Motherdear," there was no love lost between her and the new Queen Mary. She was shoved quietly but firmly on the sidelines. There was no place for her at the rigidly punctual and stiff court of George V and Mary, and so she lived quietly at Sandringham with daughter Victoria, still attending to her charities and seeing her royal grandchildren, of whom she was very fond, particularly George's shy and sensitive second son "Bertie" (the future George VI). She had always been appalled by their mother's indifference to them, but her bad relationship with Mary had not helped her own cause.

From the sidelines she watched as Europe plunged into the horrors of World War I, with her son ranged with Edward's allies France and Russia against the combined might of Germany and the Austrian Empire of the Hapsburgs. On a visit to the western front in 1915 King George was badly injured when his horse slipped in the mud and rolled on him—injuries from which he never fully recovered. Grandson Bertie fought in the naval Battle of Jutland; grandson David, the Prince of Wales, served in a ludicrously protected fashion for a short period on the western front. She watched with horror as Russia collapsed into revolution and her darling sister Dagmar's son and his whole family were exterminated at Ekaterinburg, soon followed by countless others of her relatives and dear friends in the ensuing Bolshevik bloodbath. But after four blood-soaked years, England and her allies stood triumphant, Kaiser Wilhelm was in exile, and Germany was in shambles.

She lived to see some gaiety return to life in the Roaring Twenties and, in 1923, to see the wedding of "darling Bertie," the Duke of York, to the wife of his choice, Lady Elizabeth Bowes-Lyon. But by now, although still beautiful, she was incredibly frail and she knew it would not be long. "Think of me as I used to be, now I am breaking up," she wrote to a friend. In November of 1925 she had a fatal heart attack. The king and queen were by her side at the end; her grandsons David and Bertie arrived just a few minutes too late. She was buried in Windsor beside Edward VII, to whom, with all his failings, she had been faithful and for whom she had done the best she could. A sad little anecdote reveals her true feelings. At Edward's Lying-in-State she remarked to a friend, "In spite of all the others, he loved me best." Well, maybe.

THE WINDSORS

Mary of Teck, in a photograph by B. Park

MARY OF TECK
(1867–1953)

m. George V   1893

Children: *EDWARD, ALBERT (GEORGE), Mary, Henry, George, John*

LIKE HER PREDECESSOR, ALEXANDRA, MARY OF TECK was of royal blood and had a highly insecure and penurious childhood. There all resemblance ends, for Mary was blessed with a fantastic memory and great intellectual curiosity. She lacked beauty, charm and gaiety, but what she had in their place was an unswerving determination and a pragmatic materialism that never altered throughout her long life.

It is significant that she was born in the same room in Kensington Palace that had seen the birth of Queen Victoria 49 years earlier—for if ever a woman was to take another as a role model it was Mary, who would owe much to Victoria and would try to be as much like her as possible. Not that the two women were essentially alike, for underneath the grimly proper exterior "the Widow of Windsor" was a passionate woman, capable of great loves and great hates that would often cloud her judgment and sap her will; Mary was not.

Her parents were an odd couple who can best be described as "royal scroungers." Her father, Prince Franz, Duke of Teck, was the son of his father's morganatic marriage* to a Hungarian countess and thus had no claim to the throne of Wurtemburg; nor had he any money except his military pay and sporadic handouts from the Austrian emperor. This did not stop him from being a playboy or having expensive tastes; he was a weak, foppish man. When he met Princess Mary Adelaide, the youngest child of Prince Adolphus (George III's youngest son), born in 1833 (when her father was almost sixty), Franz thought his troubles were over. They were married in 1865, she hugely fat and at the "advanced" age of 32 and he at 28. Sad disillusionment was to follow, because she was as penniless as he and even more extravagant. What she did have was good connections, especially her first cousin Queen Victoria, whom she was constantly and unmercifully asking for funds. The queen was not the only one; Mary Adelaide also sought handouts from her older brother, the charming, raffish George, Duke of Cambridge; and from her older sister, the autocratic Augusta, Grand-Duchess of Mecklenberg-Strelitz, who was the family matriarch.

Queen Victoria could not allow her cousin to live in poverty, so she provided the south wing of Kensington Palace for their home—hence the prestigious birthplace of Mary of Teck (always called May by the royals because of her birth month and to distinguish her from her mother). She was followed by three brothers, Adolphus in 1868, Francis in 1870 and Alexander in 1874. In spite of Victoria's generosity, May's entire youth was spent in an atmosphere of financial crises and domestic worries, and in 1883 when she was 16 the debts of her extravagant parents had reached such monumental proportions that their possessions were about to be seized and they had to flee to exile in Florence. They remained in Italy for two years, and while the Duke of Teck sat around complaining and

---

*A morganatic marriage is a marriage between a person of royal (or noble) blood and one of inferior rank that is not officially recognized as a "royal" marriage, hence the children of the marriage are not considered viable heirs to the titles or property of the parent of higher rank.

Mary Adelaide wrote begging letters, May made the best of it by studying languages and art history.

Mary Adelaide was then once again bailed out by the queen, who paid off their debts, recalled them, and gave them the White Lodge in Windsor Park as their home. It was from there in 1886 that May made her society debut, which was a disaster. She had little in the way of beauty or charm to offer, was stiff and dour, not to mention penniless, and her family was the laughingstock of society. So in that lively marriage market not one man took any interest in her. She retreated to White Lodge, where she continued her studies, acted as her mother's secretary and did what she could to bring order to the chaotic household. Her future looked extremely bleak.

Then, in November of 1891, she received a summons to Balmoral from the queen. The hunt for a wife for Eddy, Duke of Clarence, was on, and she was being considered as a possible candidate. May knew through her well-informed, gossipy mother all about Eddy—his homosexual escapades, his impossible love for the Catholic Princess Helene of France, his involvement with other, less suitable, women, his refusals by sundry other suggested brides, his dim-wittedness, and her own memories of being bullied by him at royal children's parties. None of that mattered. This was her one big chance and she was determined to succeed.

At Balmoral she did not put a foot wrong. Queen Victoria was impressed by her intelligence, her practicality and her fluency in languages, and by the time she left was firmly on her side. This left the next step—Eddy's parents, the Prince and Princess of Wales—and in December May was summoned to a house party where Eddy proposed and was accepted immediately. May was in in a big way, for she would be marrying a man only two steps away from the crown of England.

Her reception by the Waleses was markedly less enthusiastic—Bertie because this solemn, rather plain young woman would not be to his taste, and Alix because she hated to part with any of her children, particularly to this rather intimidating younger woman. But they were so desperate to see Eddy settled without further scandal that they went along with the plan. The queen's approval of the match was followed by another lengthy stay at Windsor, where May spent far more time with the queen than with her fiancé. By the end of the visit Victoria was calling her "My darling grand-daughter," but even May's courage was beginning to fade on close acquaintance with Eddy, and her ambitious mother had to prop up her flagging resolve. Victoria must have sensed this and, fearing she might change her mind, set a very early wedding date of February 27, 1892.

Then disaster struck, for in early January Eddy fell ill and within a week was dead; in his delirium he called out for Princess Helene. May was at his deathbed along with the rest of the Waleses, including his brother George, recently recovered himself from a severe case of typhoid. While the Wales family was truly grief-stricken, May was stunned, as her one great hope seemed to be over. She had only one thing still going for her: The Waleses in their grief appeared to have accepted her as one of the family and began including her in their activities, thereby putting her much in the company of Prince George. Although serious and sober-minded, he was in his own words "a very ordinary fellow," ill-educated, very attached to "Motherdear" but primarily a "man's man" after his long years in the Navy, and only just recovering from a long-term love affair with Julia Stonor, a Catholic commoner who had married a French marquis the previous year. He had never paid the slightest attention to May. This did not daunt her; urged on by her desperate mother—again in debt up to her ears and frantic for a wealthy marriage—May began to assiduously cultivate George, and with some success.

Then the Waleses decided to go to the south of France to recover from their grief, and May was not invited. Her mother immediately decided that the Teck family would go there also and settle nearby (financed by brother George, Duke of Cambridge). The maneuver only partially succeeded, for the Waleses could not stand the senior Tecks and Alix was horrified by May's easy transfer of her affections from "dearest dead Eddy" to "darling Georgie." The summer passed with nothing settled, and the Tecks withdrew briefly to Germany. But a more powerful hand was at work behind the scenes: Queen Victoria had made up her mind that George should marry "darling May." "The Prince of Wales must *not* prevent the marriage," she wrote to her private secretary. "Something dreadful will happen if he does not marry." And to take the domestic heat off her chosen granddaughter-in-law she took over the Teck's financial affairs, installed a controller in White Lodge to manage their budget, and once again paid off their debts. Mary Adelaide was furious at these restrictions but there was nothing she could do about them.

Alix took George with her on a trip to see her brother, the King of Greece, hoping no doubt to break his budding interest in May. Her husband, being more of a realist and knowing his mother had made up her royal mind, decided at least to extract something for his son and requested he be made Duke of York—a title Queen Victoria had omitted to give any of her sons because she had loathed her uncle, the rascally Frederick Duke of York. She grudgingly agreed, and

George was recalled from Athens. On May 2, 1893 he proposed to May, and was accepted with the speed of light. The wedding date was set for July 6th.

Alix remained in Athens, but accepted the inevitable with good grace, although she did not return to England (still in mourning garb for Eddy) until a few days before the wedding. But the battle lines were being drawn, for Mary was no longer her "darling May."

The young couple had very little in common, for George, like William IV, was a typical rather rough-and-ready sailor boy who would always love the sea, who doted on hunting, shooting and fishing—all of which May loathed— and whose sole intellectual interest was his vast stamp collection. He also had a very wry sense of humor, and nearly gave the serious May a heart attack when he announced during their short engagement: "Sorry, May, we can't get married after all. I hear I have got a wife and three children." The comment came in the wake of a rumor that he had married an American and sired three children by her while stationed in Malta (years later the perpetrators were sued and imprisoned for libel). What was important, however, was that they understood and would indeed complement each other extremely well and with no great discord, while pursuing their own interests. Queen Victoria attended the wedding—a far more brilliant affair than the Waleses had had—and as May sailed triumphantly down the aisle, with her ecstatic family watching, she knew full well to whom she owed her triumph. From now on, as impressed upon her by her benefactor, "Duty to the Crown" would be her watchword.

The living quarters assigned to the young couple were far from ideal from her point of view. Their main home was York Cottage, just a hundred yards from Sandringham and right under the noses of the Wales household, and in London they were assigned a dark and dreary wing of St. James's Palace: Alix was not about to make life too easy for her daughter-in-law. May settled down to the long process of "educating" George, of weaning him away from his mother, and of bearing him his heirs. This she did in no uncertain style—five boys and one girl. In order of their appearance came David (Edward VIII), born in 1894; Bertie (George VI), born in 1895; Mary, born in 1897; Henry, born in 1900; George, in 1902; and John, in 1905.

Unfortunately for her children, she was sadly lacking in maternal fondness; small infants and their needs disgusted her and she was only too willing to hand over their care to others. Therein lay misery for her older children, because the nanny she engaged to oversee the nursery bullied, terrified and neglected the children. As David would record in his memoirs, when she would take the children for their daily visit with their parents, she would twist their arms savagely before going in until they were crying and sobbing throughout the whole 30-minute ordeal. Mary just thought they were being naughty, and it took years before the situation was discovered and rectified. By that time they were emotionally scarred—David by a masochistic equation between pain and female attention; the more sensitive Bertie by health problems, an incurable stammer, shyness, and a deep-rooted insecurity that made him a "non-achiever" throughout his youth; Mary by an equally deep-rooted superstitious fetishism that would almost amount to mania; and Henry by a speech impediment.

Even when they were older May found it difficult to relate to them fondly or with any warmth. She appeared to be at her happiest when she was away on "royal duties" with George, particularly on overseas trips. On these she could satisfy her intellectual curiosity and interests and play her regal role far away from the presence of her mother-in-law and George's sisters, whom she found tiresome, unintelligent and frivolous, and who had a tendency to laugh at her for her solemnity and her intellectual pursuits. On these trips her children would write her letters twice a week (by order of their father) and in return she would send them picture postcards or letters telling all that she had seen and done, but with nary a personal word for them or interest in their own small world. At home she "taught" them, but did not involve herself with them.

But it is in her treatment of her youngest son John that Mary's character and failings become most apparent. John was born with respiratory problems after a very difficult labor, and in 1909, by the time he was four, he was evidently retarded and epileptic. His mother rarely would visit him, but Alix (now Queen) would spend hours with the handicapped child when she was at Sandringham. As soon as she became queen in 1910, May ordered the removal of John from the family home to a farm two miles from Sandringham; he was to live there in exile, apart from the family, in the care of his nurse, Lala Bill, who mercifully was devoted to him. Now that they were the royal family May thought his presence and increasing epileptic fits were an undesirable "image." This attitude greatly upset his next-older brother George, who was nine and had always loved him, and indeed all the rest of the children. George would doggedly trudge the two miles to see John every single day. May herself never mentioned him or wrote of him, nor was he even allowed to attend their coronation. After another epileptic fit brought about a heart attack, the boy died in his sleep in January of 1919. "I cannot say how grateful we feel to God for having taken him in such a peaceful way," wrote May. Only the Dowager Queen Alexandra lingered long and sorrowing at his grave after a quiet family funeral at Sandringham.

May not only had in-law trouble, but after her marriage found her own family an increasing problem. Victoria had obligingly created May's oldest brother Adolphus Marquis of Cambridge, her middle brother Francis Earl of Athlone, and her youngest brother Alexander would eventually become Duke of Teck; she was also of course looking after May's parents financially, and May considered that she had done quite enough for her family by her marriage. But Mary Adelaide was a warm, if demanding, mother and was keenly interested in her grandchildren, so she was always eager to visit York Cottage. May tried to discourage her as much as possible because, among other things, George was irritated by his mother-in-law. She was not saddled with this particular problem for very long, though, as in 1897 Mary Adelaide's obesity caught up with her and she died after an emergency operation. Possibly a fall down a long staircase at York Cottage had accelerated this process in the 297-pound princess. She was followed to the grave by her feckless husband three years later. If May did not mourn her mother greatly, the people of the East End of London did, for Mary Adelaide had been an enormously generous and charitable woman and had done her best for them. True to type to the very end, she died 70,000 pounds in debt, in spite of all Victoria's precautions. The person May did mourn long and sincerely was Queen Victoria, when the old queen died in 1901, even though this meant she was now Princess of Wales and would undoubtedly one day be queen.

Apart from her vast respect and admiration for Queen Victoria, May was just as impressed by her Aunt Augusta, the autocratic Duchess of Mecklenberg-Strelitz, who ruled her family with an iron hand and to whom May would always turn for advice. She thought of men in general as a weak lot, though interestingly enough she would never have any interest in women's emancipation—doubtless because the very thought would have horrified Victoria. Throughout her life she would make some good female friends to whom she could unbend, but never any male friends. She eventually achieved a domestic dominance over her husband and, in later years, was not above poking him sharply with her omnipresent umbrella should he be too long-winded or should he let drop a sailorly curse in public. In her own daughter Mary, of whom she had expected much, she was sadly disappointed, for Mary was plain, a little "peculiar," and singularly lacking in personality, even though she was her father's favorite child. May was relieved when Viscount Lascelles (later Earl of Harewood), though 15 years Mary's senior and a rather unpleasant man, showed some interest in her. He was very rich, so her mother encouraged the marriage, which took place in 1921.

One of the few good things that can be said of May's relationships with her sons is that she did encourage them to marry the women of their choice, provided that they were suitable, and it could be argued that she achieved a far closer relationship with her daughters-in-law—Elizabeth Bowes-Lyon, Bertie's wife; Alice Montagu-Douglas-Scott, wife of Henry, Duke of Gloucester; and the beautiful Princess Marina of Greece, the chosen wife of George, Duke of Kent—than she ever had with her own sons. Likewise, she was much closer to her female grandchildren. Although she was never close to Mary's, Henry's, or George's sons, she was deeply attached to Bertie's daughters, Elizabeth and Margaret Rose—particularly "Lilibet," who became Queen Elizabeth II, and who resembled her in looks and to a certain extent in personality.

On the death of Queen Victoria at least her living conditions improved, for when Edward VII and Alexandra moved into Buckingham Palace the new Prince and Princess of Wales inherited Marlborough House. There they continued to live very quietly since they did not fit easily into any of the Society sets in London. They did not enjoy the royal set at court and, while May may have gazed hungrily at the intellectual set, this was not to George's taste, so they stayed home between royal engagements, beset by domestic worries such as David's growing rebellion and Bertie's poor academic showing at both Osborne and Dartmouth Naval Academies.

All this changed with the death of Edward VII in 1910 and the accession of George as George V and Mary as his queen. As soon as the coronation was over she set about "cleaning house." Alexandra was shunted back to Marlborough House and everything became punctual and shipshape at the Buckingham Palace court. All raffish elements were quietly expunged and only the more sober members of society welcomed. With the outbreak of World War I the family was faced with another crisis: If George was to fight "Cousin Willy" they had to rid themselves of their own heavily Germanic image. Although the Hanover bloodline continued, together with its hereditary problems, Victoria in good wifely style had adopted Albert's name, so they were now officially the House of Saxe-Coburg-Gotha. If Englishmen were now to be asked to shed their blood by the hundreds of thousands, they would do it more readily for an English name. Since Saxe-Coburg-Gotha could hardly be Anglicized the name was somewhat arbitrarily changed to the House of Windsor, as it still remains. Anglicizing of German names that remained closer to the originals went on in the junior branches of the royal family, so that the Battenbergs (descendants of Victoria's daughter Alice through *her* daughter Victoria) became Mountbattens.

The war showed Queen Mary at her best, for she was a good organizer and she plunged into an unceasing and exhausting round of relief work on the home front. Although she won great admiration and respect, she did not become loved, because she was simply incapable of dropping her stiff royal image. People all preferred the "dizzy" Queen Alexandra, who did much less but was much more charming.

After the war and with all the family back home more or less intact, the queen thought their lives would settle down, but instead they were faced with mounting crises both at home and abroad. Abroad, the first cracks in the mighty British Empire were appearing: The older dominions of Canada and Australia were agitating for autonomy from England, and India was starting its fervent march to independence. The Roaring Twenties, when the survivors of the heavily decimated ranks of the aristocracy whooped it up, and into which her eldest and youngest sons jumped with abandon, were not at all to her Victorian taste. In the flapper era of shorts skirts and bobbed hair she grimly clung to her long skirts, long hair and the high-crowned hats that would remain part of her appearance to the end; she was equally faithful to her strict Victorian values. David, Prince of Wales, in true Hanoverian style, was trying to be as unlike his parents as possible and was harking back to Edward VII's mores and morals, causing both his parents great worry and eliciting from his gruff father the famous remark, "You dress like a cad, you act like a cad, you *are* a cad." Despite his parents' disapproval of him, the people of England adored him: He was their Prince Charming.

To Mary, who over the years had become fonder of him than of any of her other children, his dissipations, his drinking, his mistresses and, above all, his irresponsibility when it came to his princely duties, were all sore burdens. And in all these things his youngest brother George, Duke of Kent, the handsomest and most intelligent of her children, was not far behind.

In 1935 it was Mary who decided to celebrate their Silver Jubilee as monarchs. Hitherto, the few sovereigns who had lived that long had only celebrated Golden and, in the case of Victoria, Diamond Jubilees, but George was becoming very frail and she knew he would never live to see a Golden Jubilee. The occasion was celebrated with all due pomp and circumstance, and would be perpetuated as a custom when her granddaughter Elizabeth II celebrated her first 25 years as queen. It was to be their royal swan song, for on January 20, 1936 George V died at the age of 70. The still unmarried David ascended the throne at the age of 42 as Edward VIII, and then began one of the most traumatic periods of Mary's life.

After a succession of other mistresses, for the past five years David had been passionately in love with Wallis Warfield Simpson, an American who in October of 1936 had been granted her second divorce. It became plain that David intended to marry her. Mary threw the whole weight of her family authority against the marriage. Only one divorced woman (the formidable Eleanor of Aquitaine) had ever been an English queen, but she had been of the blood royal and the event had occurred centuries ago. This proposed queen was a twice-divorced commoner, and an American to boot, fit perhaps to be a mistress but not to be a queen of England. The people and Parliament of England agreed with Mary and, rather than give up Mrs. Simpson, Edward VIII abdicated on December 11, 1936. After his abdication speech David returned to the Royal Lodge, Windsor, where Queen Mary and all the remaining family awaited him. They were all very upset or, as in the case of the new King George VI, stunned. His mother showed no emotion, but called for her coat to return to London with her daughter, the Princess Royal. "Goodbye, David, God be with you," she said, then turned to her second son Bertie, curtsied deeply, said "God Save the King!" and left without a backward glance. David had failed in his royal duty.

In his sad wanderings in exile after marrying the woman for whom he had given up his throne, David, now Duke of Windsor, found that his mother never once budged from her unrelenting stance. She would not receive his wife, she would not receive him if he brought his wife to England, they were not even allowed to live in England, and, on his rare visits to her, he was treated coldly and she never bothered to note the visits in her diary. When the 78-year-old Duke died in 1972, his valet at the bedside recorded that his last words were, "Mama, Mama, Mama, Mama!" Even had she still been around it is doubtful whether his mother would have responded.

She turned all her service and devotion to the new royal family, which presented the same stable image she and George always had. Her daughter-in-law was too gracious and warm-hearted a person to shunt her aside as *she* had Alexandra, and she was included in everything that went on in the royal circle—weddings, christenings, celebrations of all kinds. Mary, like her Aunt Augusta before her, had become the family matriarch.

She lived to 85, the second longest life span of any queen consort, and in those long years of widowhood saw much joy and some sorrow. She saw the wedding of her favorite grandchild Elizabeth to her cousin Prince Philip Mountbatten of Greece, and the birth of her first two great-grandchildren, Charles and Anne. She suffered the untimely deaths of two of her sons, George,

Duke of Kent, in a plane crash during World War II at the age of 40, and George VI in 1952 of lung cancer, and lived to see the subsequent crowning of her granddaughter as Elizabeth II. She remained stalwart and clear-minded until the end.

One aspect of her character was apparent from the moment she became Duchess of York, and that was her passion for material possessions. Not since Henry III's Eleanor of Provence had there been such an acquisitive queen. Mary loved "things." The cascades of jewels and expensive clothes were understandable in light of her penurious youth, but her passion went far beyond that. She collected constantly—antique furniture, paintings and *objets d'art* of all descriptions. Her penchant became particularly marked after she became queen, and her technique was simple and unvarying. She would appraise any home she visited carefully, and if something struck her fancy would openly admire it. If it was not immediately pressed upon her by her hostess, she would proceed to stage two. With her "thank you" note she would pointedly include a reference to the object of her choice: "that *darling* vase," "that *beautiful* chair." If that did not work, she would then proceed to stage three: Her equerry would be sent around with a discreet offer to buy the object, and would persist until victory and the object were gained. However, most of her hosts were not courageous enough to hold out beyond stage two, and with extreme celerity a royal van would roll up to collect her spoils. Her magpie ways became so well-known that prospective hosts took to hiding away their more precious possessions when she visited. The collection over the years grew to enormous proportions and, typically, when she died she left the whole lot to her granddaughter, the queen, and not a single individual item was left to her remaining friends. When the collection was appraised it was found that Queen Mary had not been quite as much of an expert as everyone had supposed, and many of her purchases from dealers were fakes. No matter; she had got what she wanted and that was all that mattered to her.

When she died in March of 1953 the last vestiges of Victorianism died with her. As she wrote to her son David shortly after his abdication, "All my life I have put my country before everything else and I simply cannot change now": admirable, perhaps, but definitely not lovable.

Elizabeth Bowes-Lyon, by Sir Gerald Kelly

ELIZABETH BOWES-LYON
(1900–)

m. George VI   1923

Children: *ELIZABETH, Margaret Rose*

AFTER SO MANY SAD TALES IT IS GOOD to be able to end the list of queen consorts on a happy note, for England's second Scottish queen is a worthy successor to the first, Henry I's long-remembered "Good Queen Mold." Not only is Elizabeth the longest-lived of all queen consorts and, as of this writing, still going strong at the age of 91, but also one of the most charming, with a genuine warmth that has affected everyone it has touched. If a popularity poll of all the royals were to be taken in the British Isles today, the Queen Mum, as she has affectionately been called for decades, would win by a landslide. And yet this role was not of her seeking, for seldom has there been a more reluctant royal bride.

Born into a large, united and affectionate family, she had almost a storybook childhood, with horses and pets of all kinds and loving homes in comfortable and protected circumstances. She was the youngest daughter and second-to-youngest child of the 14th Earl of Strathmore and Glamis—one of Scotland's oldest earldoms—and his wife, Cecilia, who was a Cavendish-Bentinck and, on the maternal side, descended from the Duke of Wellington's brother, the Marquess Wellesley. They presented the very model of a solid Victorian family, having had 10 children; many of them were already grown by the time Elizabeth was born, and her parents were already well into middle age. Her father had a positive horror of the royal court, particularly that of Edward VII, and would keep as far away as possible, so the family lived the typical comfortably affluent life of the landed gentry, dividing their time between the family seat, Macbeth's Glamis Castle in Scotland, and a beautiful 18th-century mansion in Hertfordshire at St. Paul's Walden Bury.

Like all her generation, Elizabeth saw her teen years shadowed and changed by World War I. Her older married brother Fergus was killed in 1915, another brother Michael wounded and imprisoned by the Germans. Glamis was turned into a convalescent home for war wounded, and when her mother collapsed from sheer exhaustion in 1916 it was Elizabeth who took over as hostess and organizer of the vast castle-hospital. She was supported by the help and devotion of her youngest brother, David, to whom she would remain very close until his death in 1961.

The war over, her father, who was a very reasonable man, took a house in Bruton Street in London's posh Mayfair, so that Elizabeth could make her delayed society debut and so that she and David could have some fun. Her debut was a wild success; she was pretty and irresistably charming, and there were many suitors—among them Albert, Duke of York—"Bertie"—who fell madly in love with her. But Elizabeth was unimpressed by this shy, stammering and obviously insecure young man.

They had met as children but had lately been reintroduced through Mary, the Princess Royal. Mary shared with Elizabeth a great interest in the Girl Guides, and they became such good friends through these activities that Elizabeth was a bridesmaid at her wedding to Viscount Lascelles in 1921. By this time Bertie had proposed and had been turned down. According to some authorities this happened five times; others say three; but her continued rejections over a period of two years sent him into deep depression and despair, and his mother Queen Mary, having looked Elizabeth over and liked what she saw, tried to take a hand. Her parents would not pressure her, but they, particularly her mother, liked Bertie, and he was invited to Glamis. There his perseverence finally paid off, for in January of 1923 she finally said yes, and the ecstatic Bertie wired his parents "All right! Bertie."

Later apologists have conjectured that her reluctance was caused by her intimidation at the prospect of royal duties and responsibilities. But she liked duties and responsibilities and had already been very good at shouldering them; what she probably did not want was the responsibility of Bertie.

She, however, like everyone else, had underestimated him. Bertie and his older brother David had been like the tortoise and the hare: No matter that he had finished last in his class at Osborne and at Dartmouth, where the more intelligent David had breezed through; Bertie refused to give up, serving in the Navy in World War I, transferring to the Royal Naval Air Service in 1917, and qualifying—again with great effort—as a pilot, and then transferring into the peacetime Royal Air Force in 1919. That year his father decreed that he should attend Cambridge for a year, along with his younger brother Henry, Duke of Gloucester. David had already been to Magdalen College, Oxford, where he had concentrated on amusing himself. At Trinity College in Cambridge Bertie studied seriously while the dull, phlegmatic Henry did nothing. Bertie had clearly inherited Queen Mary's intellectual curiosity and, above all, her perseverence. When he knew what he wanted he energetically pursued it—and he wanted Elizabeth.

At least his royal parents had enough sense to give their immediate consent to the marriage, even though in "royal" terms Elizabeth was considered a commoner and therefore not a commensurate match for a royal prince. Bertie was only second in line to the throne, though; had he been Prince of Wales, the story would have had a different ending. What Bertie had always needed was someone to love him and to give him confidence in his own abilities; this he was to find in the woman he loved.

They were married on April 26, 1923 in Westminster Abbey, and once in the royal circle Elizabeth charmed everyone just as much as she had charmed her besotted husband. George V adored her and would forgive her any lapses in protocol, such as being late to meals, that usually brought down his roaring wrath.

They were given, rather to their dismay, White Lodge in Richmond Park for their residence. This may have been fine for the large Teck family in Queen Mary's youth, but the young couple rattled around in it like peas in a drum, and it was far enough out of London to be inconvenient for their many royal engagements in town; so they "borrowed" Chesterfield House near Buckingham Palace from the Princess Royal and moved there. Once settled, Elizabeth applied herself to the awesome task of making over her husband.

Happy probably for the first time in his life, Bertie bloomed, as long as she was by his side. His short, explosive temper, often sparked by frustration at his inadequacies, lessened; his public confidence increased; and they even found a speech therapist who helped him modify, though never entirely obliterate, his stammer. (Why the royal family had not sought such professional help for him up to then is an interesting question.) On their frequent flag-waving trips abroad—to France, Ireland, East Africa—Elizabeth captured all hearts and he basked in the reflected glow. Whether she was as completely happy as he was at this stage in the marriage is a moot point; in many early portraits she looks somewhat less than thrilled. However, all that changed with the birth of their first child, the future Queen Elizabeth II, in April of 1926. From then on Elizabeth was committed to the marriage and her family, although being dispatched on a "round the world" tour with the king just a few months after the birth of the baby sparked one of her rare public outbursts of anger. "We are not supposed to be human!" she cried, at the thought of being separated from her daughter. Their trip to Australia and New Zealand and points between was as smashing a success as the other trips. On their return they abandoned White Lodge and moved into a town house at 145 Piccadilly, right in the heart of London—their home until their succession. In 1930 their family was completed when Princess Margaret Rose was borne (by Caesarean section, like her sister) at Glamis Castle—the first English "royal" to be born in Scotland since Charles I. Elizabeth wrought a small miracle with her husband during those peaceful, private years between 1926 and 1936, so that a close friend could write of her: "That was her measure of greatness as a woman. She drew him out and made him a man so strong that she could lean on him."

Just as well, as it turned out, for in 1936, the "Year of the Three Kings," their peaceful idyll was to be shattered. George V died and his son David succeeded him as King Edward VIII. He also clearly intended to marry his mistress, Mrs. Simpson, as soon as her second divorce was final in October. In her solid opposition to this idea, Elizabeth was at one with her mother-in-law Queen Mary, although not for the same reasons. It was certainly not because she wanted to be queen, knowing how much her husband dreaded the very idea of being king; she simply did not like Mrs. Simpson and everything she stood for. From Elizabeth's point of view, she brought out the bad in her brother-in-law, of whom she was none too fond, anyway, partly because of what she perceived as his shallowness, but also because he had shown much latent cruelty in his shabby treatment of his ex-mistresses since the advent of Mrs. Simpson. Like Queen Mary, Elizabeth would never budge from this stand, and the only time she would meet the Duchess of Windsor would be at the Duke's funeral in 1972—a meeting short and anything but sweet.

It was doubly unfortunate that at the time of Edward's subsequent abdication Elizabeth was laid low by a severe bout of influenza. So traumatized was her husband, without her by his side, that Bertie, now George VI, suffered a short nervous collapse. To add to their stresses it was decided to go ahead with his coronation on the date originally scheduled for Edward, in May of 1937, instead of waiting the customary year between kings. George felt totally inadequate to the task ahead: He had never so much as seen a state paper, never been trained as David had been to assume the role of king. Elizabeth had to prop him up in those months, and was helped by George's cousin, Lord Louis Mountbatten, who would always be a tower of strength to the royal family and who pointed out to George that his father had been similarly untrained but had made a good job of it. As it turned out, Louis Mountbatten was right; tortoise George persevered and plodded on and made a very good king.

Less than three years after their accession, England was plunged into the Second World War. During the next six grim years the royal family demonstrated that it still had an important role to play in the affairs of England. This time England itself was under heavy attack, and London was a particular target for the Germans. King George, whose personal courage no one had ever questioned, refused to leave the city. Elizabeth stayed with him, having delivered one of her most-quoted remarks: "The children won't leave without me, I won't leave without the King, and the King will never leave." The alarmed Parliament wanted at least the royal princesses, the heirs to the throne, to be sent out of harm's way to Canada; but the royal pair stood firm, and the only concession they would make was to send the girls to Windsor during the worst of it. They, themselves, were very nearly killed when Buckingham Palace suffered a series of direct hits. "I'm glad we have been bombed, now I feel I can look the East End in the face," Elizabeth said stoutly, and learned how to fire a gun in the face of the threatened German invasion. They went constantly into the bombed areas, not only in London but in all the other devastated cities, and the sight of them and the tireless work they did to succor the homeless did more to stiffen the morale and will of the people than all the wartime propaganda. When Princess Elizabeth reached the age of conscription, she dutifully joined the humble Army Transport Service, *not* the prestigious Women's Royal Naval Service. And when the king went off to tour the various fighting fronts, as his father had done in World War I, the queen carried on alone, putting a brave face on private worries.

With the end of the war in 1945 the monarchy was faced with a kingdom in economic shambles, its populace exhausted, and an empire in full process of dissolution. India became independent in 1948, opening the floodgates for the further secessions that would continue throughout the reign of Elizabeth II until all that remained was a handful of small islands. The "empire on which the sun never sets," that had taken centuries to build, would dissolve within a generation.

But in royal circles all was not gloom. In 1947 George and Elizabeth were invited to tour South Africa, which was already straining at the bit of empire. They went by sea, and included in the naval complement was Lieutenant Philip Mountbatten. Princess Elizabeth was now of marriageable age and, like her mother, had had her youth overshadowed by war; it was time for her to have some fun. No one was surprised that at the end of the tour her engagement to her cousin Philip was announced. It was far more of a state marriage than her parents' love match had been, but Philip was of royal blood and eminently suitable, and the young royals were fond enough of each other. On their return they were married in Westminster Abbey in November of 1947, and a year later Prince Charles was born. He was to be a source of unending delight and comfort to his grandmother.

Then storm clouds gathered anew. Like George V, George VI had never been very robust, and the war years had been a great strain on him. At the beginning of the 1950s he suffered from a variety of ailments—thrombosis, arteriosclerosis in his legs—and then in 1952 he had an operation for lung cancer, which was thought to have been successful. It wasn't, and on January 22, 1952, while his daughter was away touring East Africa with her husband, George VI died in his sleep. England had another queen regnant in the 25-year-old Elizabeth II.

The loss of her husband after almost 30 years of a close and loving marriage was a tremendous blow to Elizabeth. Much has been written about the great love affair of the Duke and Duchess of Windsor, little about the love idyll of George and Elizabeth. Not only were they interdependent; they were also intensely compatible, loving country life, gardening, everything to do with horses, youth movements and organizations, and their family.

For a while it looked as if Elizabeth would go the way of Queen Victoria and submerge herself in grief, but three things saved her. First, friends led her to the Castle of Mey, just a few miles from Scotland's northernmost tip, John O'Groats; she bought the place and it became her refuge, and indeed the future refuge for other royals in need of sanctuary. Second was her intense devotion to her grandchildren, particularly Prince Charles. And third was the help of a psychic, for which there was a royal precedent, and for exactly the same reason. Queen Victoria had emerged from her own deep despair after "communicating" with Albert through seances. Elizabeth was to seek the same succor and apparently she found it, for within a couple of years she was back with the same smiling, charming image she has maintained ever since. Since the Dowager Queen Mary was still alive, a unique situation of two dowager queens was created, a pattern that had never happened before in England's history. Elizabeth solved the confusion by decreeing that her title should be "Elizabeth, the Queen Mother"—and so the "Queen Mum" came into being.

The Queen Mother has always remained close to her daughters. In their rearing and education she looked back to her own happy childhood and followed the same pattern, ignoring the changes in the world that had percolated even into the rarified royal circle. At a time when the minor royals had started to attend public schools and even university, the princesses were educated entirely at home with governesses and tutors, with no thought of either one attending a university. Their main interests were "country things": dogs, horses, and, as one critic sniffed, "the doings of the 'tweedy' set." All fine for a country gentlewoman, but a bit limiting for a queen.

The Queen Mother also is a traditionalist as to moral behavior, with a tendency to bury her head in the sand when faced with an unpleasant issue. One example is her handling of "the Townsend affair" and of Princess Margaret, who has always been more of a handful than her stolid, dutiful sister. Margaret fell deeply in love with Group Captain Peter Townsend, who had been an equerry of her father's since 1944; but Townsend was a married man with two children. In 1952 he divorced his wife on the grounds of adultery and the whole country thought the lovers would be married. Not so; the royal family could not countenance the marriage of a royal princess to a divorced man. When they became engaged they were told to wait a year; when that year was up they were told to wait another; and by the autumn of 1955, as Margaret would later say, both of them were so "thoroughly drained and demoralized" that they ended the engagement and Townsend married someone else. The Queen Mother had been dead against the match. But four years later the volatile Margaret married Anthony Armstrong-Jones, a society photographer, resulting in a catastrophic marriage that was to end in divorce in 1978.

More recently the Queen Mother played an important role in bringing about the marriage of her "darling Charles" to Lady Diana Spencer; again the traditional idea of having a virgin bride was obviously uppermost in her mind—and mature virgins are hard to come by in the modern world. Hence, although Charles had been linked with a number of women and was extremely attached to at least two of them, none of these was considered suitable for the Prince of Wales. Charles had entered his thirties with no sign of a royal bride, even though it was high time for him to marry. So the Queen Mother became a matchmaker. Diana was a granddaughter of Lady Fermoy, a lady-in-waiting and close friend of the Queen Mother. Born in 1961, she was only 19, a nursery school teacher—and "pure." Charles had always listened to his grandmother and she saw to it that the two were much thrown together. The plan worked, for in February of 1981 they became engaged and in July they were married with much romantic fanfare in St. Paul's Cathedral. Cynics at the time eyed this "great romance" askance, and, as it turned out, with reason. The 33-year-old groom had inherited the serious-minded, slightly waspish character of his father, Prince Philip. Diana is beautiful, a devoted "mum" but, in her own words, "as thick as a plank." She has no intellectual interests and primarily likes to have a good time with friends her own age. Although Diana has matured rapidly and her embracing many worthy causes has endeared her to the British public, it has not had the same effect on her husband. After the initial flush, they discovered they had nothing in common, and it is not surprising that the couple is already estranged.

In the public sphere the Queen Mother has not been entirely free of criticism, although to nowhere near the same extent as her son-in-law or Prince Charles. For instance, in one of her many public posts the Queen Mother is chief patron of the Royal Society for Mentally Handicapped Children and Adults, which exists specifically to prevent people from abandoning their retarded family members in institutions. Some enterprising journalist found out that two of her Bowes-Lyon retarded nieces had been "forgotten" in an institution in 1941 and had been listed in Burke's Peerage as having died that year—although one was still alive in 1988. The old cry of "royal hypocrisy" went up, even though the Queen Mother probably never knew about it.

The maladjustments of modern life have already crept into the heart of the royal family. Not only has Margaret divorced, but Princess Anne has divorced her "commoner" husband Mark Phillips and remarried; the Prince and Princess of Wales have separated and seem to be heading in the same direction; and Andrew, Duke of York, was allowed to marry not only a "commoner" but one who openly lived with another man before their marriage. And this marriage has itself already failed; the two have separated and are on the brink of divorce, with much attendant publicity. Prince Edward, Queen Elizabeth's youngest son, has refused to follow family tradition in joining one of the Armed Forces and is widely thought to be gay. None of these developments can sit too well with the traditionally minded Queen Mother.

Much has been made of Queen Mary's "devotion to duty," but no queen, either as queen or Queen Mother, has done more in the line of duty than the Queen Mum or with such unwavering charm. For that she will be long remembered by her subjects—just like "Good Queen Mold."

APPENDIX I

THE ROYAL ORDER OF SUCCESSION IN ENGLAND

THIS NOTE IS APPENDED TO CLARIFY SOME POINTS about the royal succession in England that may have puzzled some American readers—as, for instance, why Victoria should have inherited the throne while several of her paternal royal uncles were still alive and kicking.

Unlike many European countries where the ancient Salic Law, under which no female could inherit the throne, prevailed, England never subscribed to this idea and, technically, a woman not only could but from the 16th century on sometimes did reign as monarch. Nevertheless, the basic rule of inheritance was and remains male primogeniture; only if the king has no male heirs can a woman inherit. An illustration is the succession of Henry VIII's children. His youngest child but only son Edward inherited the throne after Henry's death, and when Edward died without issue he was succeeded in turn by his oldest sister Mary, and then, she also having died without issue, by his sister Elizabeth.

Normally the crown passes to the king's eldest son, then to *his* son or, occasionally, grandson, as in the case of Edward III's crown passing to grandson Richard II, only surviving son of Edward, the Black Prince, to the exclusion of Edward III's younger sons; or in the case of George II's crown passing to his grandson George III, son of Frederick Prince of Wales; George succeeded to the exclusion of his uncles.

Should the eldest son die without issue the succession passes to the next son and his heirs, and so on down the line. If all male heirs fail, then a woman may inherit, or, more likely, that woman's son, as in the case of Stephen, son of William the Conqueror's daughter Adela; Stephen usurped the throne from Henry I's daughter, the Empress Matilda; and as in the case of James VI of Scotland, who became James I of England through his mother's right of inheritance.

In the case of Victoria, her succession was due to a multiple failure of heirs of either sex by her older royal uncles. George IV's only daughter died; his next brother, Frederick, Duke of York, had no legitimate issue and died before him; his next brother, William, Duke of Clarence, inherited the throne as William IV, but had no living legitimate issue; and so the succession devolved upon George III's fourth son, Edward, Duke of Kent, who predeceased William IV but who had fathered Victoria.

This pattern is also demonstrated in the present House of Windsor. When Edward VIII abdicated without legitimate issue, the throne automatically passed to his next brother as George VI, and George VI's eldest child Elizabeth then became heir apparent and, on her father's death, Queen Elizabeth II. But if she had had a brother, he would have inherited, even though she was George VI's eldest child.

The present order of succession is, first, Charles, Prince of Wales; second, his elder son, Prince William; third, his second son, Prince Henry. In the unlikely event that all of them should die before Queen Elizabeth, the succession would go to Andrew, Duke of York, and then to his two daughters, Beatrice and Eugenie, in order of birth. Even though Princess Anne is Andrew's older sister, she would not inherit unless *all* her brothers and their heirs had died.

APPENDIX II

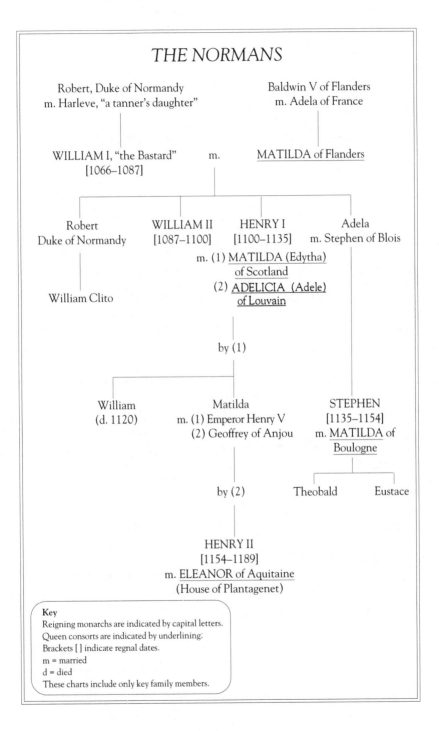

THE NORMANS

Robert, Duke of Normandy
m. Harleve, "a tanner's daughter"

Baldwin V of Flanders
m. Adela of France

WILLIAM I, "the Bastard"   m.   MATILDA of Flanders
[1066–1087]

Robert Duke of Normandy	WILLIAM II [1087–1100]	HENRY I [1100–1135]	Adela m. Stephen of Blois

m. (1) MATILDA (Edytha)
of Scotland
(2) ADELICIA (Adele)
of Louvain

William Clito

by (1)

William (d. 1120)	Matilda m. (1) Emperor Henry V (2) Geoffrey of Anjou	STEPHEN [1135–1154] m. MATILDA of Boulogne

by (2)   Theobald   Eustace

HENRY II
[1154–1189]
m. ELEANOR of Aquitaine
(House of Plantagenet)

Key
Reigning monarchs are indicated by capital letters.
Queen consorts are indicated by underlining.
Brackets [ ] indicate regnal dates.
m = married
d = died
These charts include only key family members.

THE PLANTAGENETS

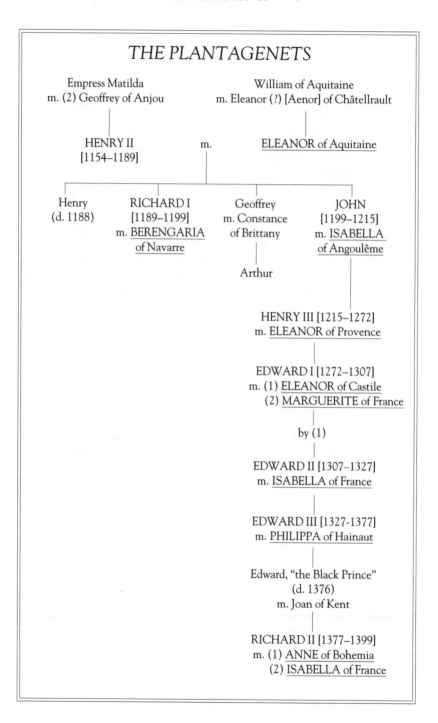

Empress Matilda
m. (2) Geoffrey of Anjou

William of Aquitaine
m. Eleanor (?) [Aenor] of Châtellrault

HENRY II
[1154–1189]

m.

ELEANOR of Aquitaine

Henry
(d. 1188)

RICHARD I
[1189–1199]
m. BERENGARIA
of Navarre

Geoffrey
m. Constance
of Brittany

JOHN
[1199–1215]
m. ISABELLA
of Angoulême

Arthur

HENRY III [1215–1272]
m. ELEANOR of Provence

EDWARD I [1272–1307]
m. (1) ELEANOR of Castile
(2) MARGUERITE of France

by (1)

EDWARD II [1307–1327]
m. ISABELLA of France

EDWARD III [1327-1377]
m. PHILIPPA of Hainaut

Edward, "the Black Prince"
(d. 1376)
m. Joan of Kent

RICHARD II [1377–1399]
m. (1) ANNE of Bohemia
(2) ISABELLA of France

THE PLANTAGENETS 2
HOUSES OF LANCASTER & YORK

EDWARD III   m.   PHILIPPA of Hainaut
[1327–1377]

Edward "the Black Prince"   John of Gaunt (4)   Edmund   Lionel (3)
(d. 1376)   m. (1) Blanche of   Duke of York (5)   m. Elizabeth
m. Joan of Kent   Lancaster   m. Isabella of Castile   de Burgh

by (1)

RICHARD II   HENRY IV   Richard, Earl of Cambridge
[1377-1399]   [1399–1413]   m. Anne Mortimer
m. (1) ANNE   m. (1) Mary de Bohun   (great granddaughter)
of Bohemia   (2) JOAN of Navarre
(2) ISABELLA
of France   by (1)

HENRY V   Richard, Duke of York
[1413–1422]   (d. 1460)
m. KATHERINE of France   m. Cicely Neville

HENRY VI
[1422–1461]
m. MARGARET of Anjou   EDWARD IV   RICHARD III
    [1461–1483]   [1483–1485]
Edward, Prince of Wales   m. ELIZABETH   m. ANNE
m. ANNE NEVILLE   WOODVILLE   NEVILLE

ELIZABETH of York   EDWARD V   Edward
m. HENRY VII   [1483]
[1485–1509]
(House of Tudor)

Key
Reigning monarchs are indicated by capital letters.
Queen consorts are indicated by underlining.
Brackets [ ] indicate regnal dates.
m = married
d = died
These charts include only key family members.

THE TUDORS

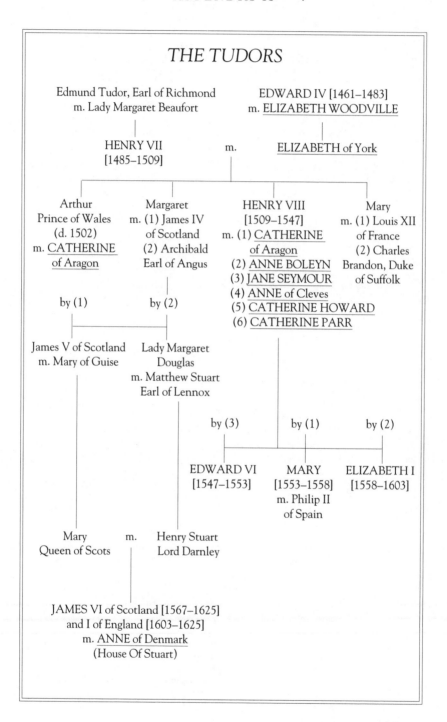

Edmund Tudor, Earl of Richmond
m. Lady Margaret Beaufort

EDWARD IV [1461–1483]
m. ELIZABETH WOODVILLE

HENRY VII
[1485–1509]

m.

ELIZABETH of York

Arthur
Prince of Wales
(d. 1502)
m. CATHERINE
of Aragon

Margaret
m. (1) James IV
of Scotland
(2) Archibald
Earl of Angus

HENRY VIII
[1509–1547]
m. (1) CATHERINE
of Aragon
(2) ANNE BOLEYN
(3) JANE SEYMOUR
(4) ANNE of Cleves
(5) CATHERINE HOWARD
(6) CATHERINE PARR

Mary
m. (1) Louis XII
of France
(2) Charles
Brandon, Duke
of Suffolk

by (1)

by (2)

James V of Scotland
m. Mary of Guise

Lady Margaret
Douglas
m. Matthew Stuart
Earl of Lennox

by (3)

by (1)

by (2)

EDWARD VI
[1547–1553]

MARY
[1553–1558]
m. Philip II
of Spain

ELIZABETH I
[1558–1603]

Mary
Queen of Scots

m.

Henry Stuart
Lord Darnley

JAMES VI of Scotland [1567–1625]
and I of England [1603–1625]
m. ANNE of Denmark
(House Of Stuart)

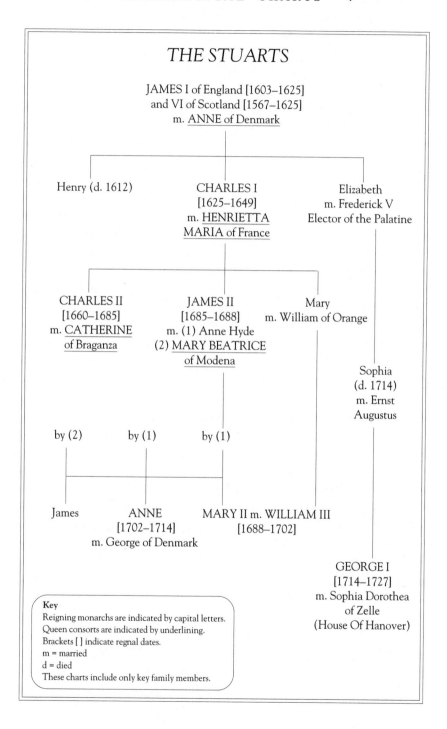

THE STUARTS

JAMES I of England [1603–1625]
and VI of Scotland [1567–1625]
m. ANNE of Denmark

Henry (d. 1612)

CHARLES I
[1625–1649]
m. HENRIETTA
MARIA of France

Elizabeth
m. Frederick V
Elector of the Palatine

CHARLES II
[1660–1685]
m. CATHERINE
of Braganza

JAMES II
[1685–1688]
m. (1) Anne Hyde
(2) MARY BEATRICE
of Modena

Mary
m. William of Orange

Sophia
(d. 1714)
m. Ernst
Augustus

by (2)   by (1)   by (1)

James

ANNE
[1702–1714]
m. George of Denmark

MARY II m. WILLIAM III
[1688–1702]

GEORGE I
[1714–1727]
m. Sophia Dorothea
of Zelle
(House Of Hanover)

Key
Reigning monarchs are indicated by capital letters.
Queen consorts are indicated by underlining.
Brackets [ ] indicate regnal dates.
m = married
d = died
These charts include only key family members.

THE HANOVERIANS

JAMES I of England [1603–1625]
m. ANNE of Denmark

|

Elizabeth
m. FrederickV, Elector of Palatine

|

Sophia (d. 1714)
m. Ernst Augustus, Elector of Hanover

|

GEORGE I [1714–1727]
m. Sophia Dorothea of Zelle

|

GEORGE II [1727–1760]
m. CAROLINE of Anspach

|

Frederick, Prince of Wales (d. 1751)
m. Augusta of Saxe-Gotha

|

GEORGE III [1760–1820]
m. CHARLOTTE of Mecklenberg-Strelitz

|

GEORGE IV [1820–30] m. CAROLINE of Brunswick	WILLIAM IV (3) [1830–37] m. ADELAIDE of Saxe-Meiningen	Edward (4) Duke of Kent m. Victoria of Saxe-Coburg
Charlotte (d. 1817) m. Leopold of Saxe-Coburg-Gotha		VICTORIA [1837–1901] m. Prince Albert of Saxe-Coburg-Gotha (House of Saxe-Coburg- Gotha & Windsor)

THE HANOVERIANS 2
HOUSES OF SAXE-COBURG-GOTHA & WINDSOR

Edward, Duke of Kent
m. Victoria of Saxe-Coburg

Ernest, Duke of Saxe-Coburg-Gotha
m. Princess Louise

VICTORIA
[1837–1901]

m.

Prince Albert
of Saxe-Coburg-Gotha

Victoria
m. Kaiser Frederick III
of Germany

EDWARD VII
[1901–1910]
m. ALEXANDRA of Denmark

7 others

Kaiser William II

Albert Victor
(Eddy) (d. 1892)

GEORGE V
[1910–1936]
m. MARY of Teck

3 others

EDWARD VIII [1936]
m. Wallis Simpson

ALBERT (GEORGE VI)
[1936–52]
m. ELIZABETH BOWES-LYON

4 others

ELIZABETH II [1952–]
m. Prince Philip of Greece

Margaret Rose

Charles, Prince of Wales
m. Lady Diana Spencer

Anne

Andrew, Duke of York
m. Sarah Ferguson

Edward

William

Henry

Beatrice

Eugenie

Key
Reigning monarchs are indicated by capital letters.
Queen consorts are indicated by underlining.
Brackets [ ] indicate regnal dates.
m = married
d = died
These charts include only key family members.

SELECTED BIBLIOGRAPHY

Hundreds of books and original sources on England's queens were consulted in compiling this volume, but in the interests of brevity and practicality the books listed here for ongoing study are ones that are most readily available in libraries and bookstores. Listings are arranged chronologically.

GENERAL

For the political and social background in which the queens' lives were set the best source is the 12-volume *Oxford History of England,* edited by Sir George Clark and issued by Oxford University Press, Oxford, England, comprising the following:

Poole, Austin L., *From Domesday to Magna Carta 1087–1216,* 1955.
Powicke, Sir Maurice, *The Thirteenth Century, 1216–1307,* 1962.
McKisack, May, *The Fourteenth Century, 1307–1399,* 1959.
Jacob, E.F., *The Fifteenth Century, 1399–1485,* 1961.
Mackie, J.D., *The Earlier Tudors, 1485–1588,* 1952.
Davies, Godfrey, *The Early Stuarts, 1603–1660,* 1959.
Clark, Sir George, *The Later Stuarts, 1660–1714,* 1956.
Williams, Basil and C.H. Stuart, *The Whig Supremacy, 1714–1760,* 1962
Watson, J. Steven, *The Reign of George III, 1760–1815,* 1960.
Woodward, Sir Llewellyn, *The Age of Reform, 1815–1870,* 1962.
Ensor, Sir Robert, *England, 1870–1914,* 1936.
Taylor, A. J. P., *English History, 1914–1945,* 1965.

Also recommended is the highly concentrated one-volume *The Oxford History of Britain* by Kenneth O. Morgan, published by Oxford University Press, Oxford, England, 1988.

For biographies of the queens and their husbands, the best reference work to consult is the latest edition of the *Encyclopaedia Brittannica* which, under individual entries, provides the latest and soundest biographies in print.

For specific periods the following books are recommended. Titles are listed by subject.

THE NORMANS AND PLANTAGENETS

Howarth, David. *1066, The Year of the Conquest*. New York: Dorset Press, 1978.

Linklater, Eric. *The Conquest of England*. New York: Dorset Press, 1990.

Costain, Thomas B. *The Conquerors*. New York: Doubleday, 1949.

Fraser, Antonia. *The Warrior Queens*. New York: Vintage Books, 1990.

Given-Wilson, Chris and Alice Curteis. *The Royal Bastards of Medieval England*. New York: Routledge & Kegan Paul, 1984.

Hallam, Elizabeth, ed. *The Plantagenet Encyclopedia*. New York: Grove Weidenfeld, 1990.

Costain, Thomas B. *The Conquering Family*. New York: Eagle Popular Library, 1960.

———. *The Magnificent Century*. New York: Eagle Popular Library, 1951.

———. *The Three Edwards*. New York: Eagle Popular Library, 1952.

———. *The Last Plantagenets*. New York: Eagle Popular Library, 1962.

Castries, Duc de. *The Lives of the Kings and Queens of France*. New York: Knopf, 1979.

THE TUDORS

Morris, Christopher. *The Tudors*. London: Collins, Fontana, 1967.

Somerset, Anne. *Ladies-in-Waiting*. New York: Knopf, 1984.

Starkey, David. *The Reign of Henry VIII*. New York: George Philip, 1985.

Williams, Neville. *Henry VIII and His Court*. New York: Macmillan, 1971.

Ashdown, Dulcie M. *Royal Paramours*. New York: Dorset Press, 1986.

Hoffman, Ann, ed. *Lives of the Tudor Age 1485–1603*. New York: Barnes & Noble, 1977.

THE STUARTS

Ross, Stewart. *Monarchs of Scotland*. New York: Facts On File, 1990.

Riddell, Edwin, ed. *Lives of the Stuart Age, 1603–1714*. New York: Barnes & Noble, 1976.

Kenyon, J. P. *The Civil Wars of England*. New York: Knopf, 1988.

Randall, David. *Royal Follies*. New York: Sterling, 1987.

Aronson, Theo. *Kings Over the Water*. London: Cassell, 1988.

Mitford, Nancy. *The Sun King*. London: Hamish Hamilton, 1966.

THE HANOVERS

Cleeve, Roger, ed. *Lives of the Georgian Age, 1714–1837*. New York: Barnes & Noble, 1976.

Longford, Elizabeth. *Encyclopedia of Royal Anecdotes*. Oxford: Oxford University Press, 1989.

Longford, Lord. *A History of the House of Lords*. London: Collins, 1988.

Longford, Elizabeth. *Queen Victoria*. New York: Harper & Row, 1964.

Rhodes, Robert. *Prince Albert*. New York: Knopf, 1984.

Hibbert, Christopher. *The Royal Victorians*. New York: Lippincott, 1976.

Cowles, Virginia. *Gay Monarch*. New York: Harpers, 1956.

THE WINDSORS (George V onward)

Longford, Elizabeth. *The House of Windsor*. London: Crown, 1984.

Edwards, Anne. *Matriarch*. New York: William Morrow, 1984.

Marie-Louisa, Princess. *My Memories of Six Reigns*. London, Evans Bros., 1957.

Warwick, Christopher. *King George VI & Queen Elizabeth*. London: Beaufort Books, 1985.

Morrow, Ann. *The Queen Mother*. London: Stein & Day, 1984.

Lacy, Robert. *Majesty*. London: Harcourt Brace Jovanovich, 1977.

INDEX

Boldface headings are reserved for the queen consorts. **Boldface** locators indicate chapter location. *Italic* locators indicate illustrations. The letter "g" with locators indicates genealogical chart.

A